The Explanation of
Social Behaviour

The Explanation of
Social Behaviour

R. HARRÉ and P. F. SECORD

OXFORD · BASIL BLACKWELL

ISBN 0 631 17140 1

First published in paperback 1976
Reprinted 1979

Printed in Great Britain by offset lithography by
Billing & Sons Ltd, Guildford, London and Worcester

Preface

Our aim in this book is to provide a systematic and unified theoretical account of the new ways of thinking about people, and the new methods of studying their behaviour, which are becoming increasingly dominant in the human sciences. Our argument involves two major shifts in perspective. We develop the naturalistic conception of a human being as a rule-following agent, in contradistinction to all other models of man. We show how this idea is connected to recent developments in philosophy as well as to sophisticated exploitations of ideas derived from the application of system theory to animal and human behaviour. We establish that all these lines of thought converge on the model that people have of themselves, and that is embedded in much of the logic of ordinary language.

The idea that a human being *must* be regarded in his social behaviour as a rule-following agent has been the basis of much contemporary criticism of social science, and has indeed been used by such writers as P. Winch (*The Idea of a Social Science*, Routledge and Kegan Paul, London, 1958) to attack the very conception of a scientific study of human social behaviour. We believe that this conclusion is mistaken, and that it derives from a misleading conception of the nature of science, developed in the schools of positivist philosophy. The second shift in perspective in this book is the sketching out of the main features of the realist, non-positivistic conception of science. It emerges that from this point of view the idea of men as conscious social actors, capable of controlling their performances and commenting intelligently upon them, is more scientific than the traditional conception of the human 'automaton'.

The theory and its associated methodology turns out to be very complex, as one might expect, given the complexity and difficulty of the phenomena under study. We are well aware that even in this length of book we have been able only to develop a very general conceptual scheme, and that there is tremendous scope for the filling in of detail. If we have really provided here the basis for a science, then that is exactly what one should expect. We have attempted to cope with the complexity of our theory both by a progressive elaboration of the basic themes, approaching them from various points of view, and by the use of analytical introductions to each chapter, giving a fairly detailed preview of the way ahead. We have not attempted to give a complete bibliography, nor to refer to every work which bears upon our theme. Rather, we have chosen certain books and papers which we regard as especially archetypal, and have so organized our references to form a manageable reading programme for each chapter.

Our debt to others is enormous. To all those who have helped us, and there are very many, by encouragement in this enterprise, by showing us how to develop our originally rudimentary ideas, and by all manner of criticism at every stage of the project we wish to express our most grateful thanks.

The authors are indebted to the National Science Foundation which provided a grant in support of interdisciplinary work in philosophy at the University of Nevada, and which made it possible for the first author to come there as a visiting professor. The second author is also indebted to the National Institute of Mental Health which awarded him a special research fellowship for study and work on this manuscript at Oxford University in England.

R. HARRÉ
P. F. SECORD

Contents

CHAPTER ONE

An Outline of the Theory

'They wanted to find out my reactions before they told me. But people don't have reactions. They just try to do what is expected'.

Nicholas Moseley, *Impossible Object*,
Hodder and Stoughton, London, 1968,
p. 161.

We are concerned to discuss the possibility of a scientific study of those psychological states, conditions and powers which are to be attributed to individual people when they are engaged in social activity. We will develop our methodology out of a general theory of social action and its genesis. The need for a comprehensive theoretical treatment of social psychology and for a reformed methodology we feel to be pressing, and to be evident from the increasing dissatisfaction with the state of social psychology, even within the citadels of the profession. The underlying reason for this state we believe to be a continued adherence to a positivist methodology, long after the theoretical justification for it, in naïve behaviourism, has been repudiated. At present there is scarcely any coherent body of theory. In such a vacuum it is still possible to carry on empirical studies which make sense only if people are conceived of in the mechanical tradition as passive entities whose behaviour is the product of 'impressed forces', and whose own contribution to social action is the latent product of earlier impressed experience. A methodology of experiment survives in which the typical investigation is recommended to be the manipulation of 'variables', and the typical result a correlation in the manner of Boyle's Law.

In the last ten years or so, a number of psychologists, linguists and philosophers have tried to 'ride herd' on the great mass of behavioural scientists doing research within this antiquated framework, to bring them out of the deserts of methodological positivism and into the pursuit of real science. In the course of these attempts a great many valuable insights have been gained. We are very well aware that practically everything we want to say has been said in recent times by others, and no doubt often said better. But we are not aware of any general theoretical study of social psychology and its methodology in the light of which the various things which have been said can be shown to hang together in a coherent point of view. We hope that this is what we can offer. We are encouraged to think we are on the track of an adequate unitary theory by the fact that, on several occasions, one or other of us has drawn a conclusion from some feature of our view of social science which we have later found to be held independently by others on independent and sound grounds.

In our view, an adequate social psychology can be developed only as a co-operative enterprise between psychologists, philosophers and sociologists. No one of these groups seems able to be successful alone. Psychologists have often been concerned with too narrow a conception of social action, and have been severely handicapped by conceptual naïvete. Philosophers have not lacked conceptual sophistication but have too often been ignorant of social and psychological facts, while sociologists, despite great breadth of conception, have been unable to develop adequate theories of individual social action, and have suffered, with psychologists, from conceptual naïvete. We hope that in this study some of these difficulties can be ameliorated by collaboration.

In order to avoid some misunderstandings in advance, it may be helpful to try to identify some sources of incomprehension between behavioural scientists and philosophers. When a behavioural scientist reads philosophical writings, he often feels that the philosopher is being dogmatic and arbitrary, that he is legislating truth instead of leaving it to empirical investigation to discover. When a philosopher reads psychology, he often thinks that the conceptual basis of the study is naïve and ill-secured, and developed in a haphazard manner without adequate critical thought, so that the empirical work is vitiated because it is ultimately confused, overlooking distinctions that seem to him obvious. A philosopher is often put in mind of the analogy to alchemy, where an enormous amount of empirical and experimental work was done, some of which was later incorporated into real chemistry, but most of which was vitiated because of an inadequate conceptual basis.

The behavioural scientist's failure to comprehend the philosopher arises from a misunderstanding of what the philosopher is trying to accomplish. In work on the philosophy of mind, for example, philosophers write about motivation, emotion, desire, thinking and other topics, that nominally, at least, seem to the behavioural scientist to be those in which he is interested. But before he has read far he finds the discussion strange. This sense of strangeness arises from a failure to appreciate that the philosopher is not stating *empirical* generalizations, but is analysing the *conceptual* properties, of words that deal with mind. So, in analysing the concept of motivation, for instance, the philosopher is interested in describing the ways in which the concept is ordinarily used, and in identifying the *logical* properties of these various uses. In the course of his investigations, the philosopher examines the relation of this concept to other related concepts, such as 'drive', 'desire', 'emotion', 'habit' and 'need'. He points out the logical restrictions inherent in certain uses. He discusses a range of cases, where some clearly represent a particular category of use, and others represent a borderline area. He has a particular interest in borderline cases, because it is in a thorough discussion of these that the clarification of meanings, the delimitation of uses, and the logical implications of these important concepts is brought out.

But the behavioural scientist is accustomed to dealing with material that consists largely of empirical generalizations, along with a modicum of theory. So it is very easy for him to assume that a philosopher is making empirical assertions in his discussion of psychological concepts. For example, in discussing the concept of motivation, the philosopher, R. S. Peters, makes the following statement[1]: 'The paradigm case of human action is when something is done in order to bring about an end. So the usual way of explaining an action is to describe it as an action of a certain sort by indicating the end which Jones had in mind. . . If we ask why Jones walked across the road, the obvious answer will be something like "to buy tobacco"'.

R. Brown, an anthropologist who is quite sophisticated in his knowledge of philosophy, nevertheless makes the mistake of assuming that the first sentence of the quotation is an empirical generalization.[2] He complains that there are other sorts of human actions, such as unintentional actions, habitual actions and expressive actions. But Peters had no intention of making the generalization that all human action is to an end. Indeed, he talks about other forms of action in his book. His assertion here is to be taken as having the following meaning: 'I am going to select as a paradigm for discussion that case of human action in which something is done for an end. It follows *logically* that such actions are usually described by indicating the end that the actor had in mind'. Notice that nothing empirical is being stated. Logical consistency determines the relation between the first sentence and the second. Of course, a full discussion will include those borderline cases which limit the application of the concept in this particular signification. The behavioural scientist reading the philosophy of mind must bear always in mind the fact that the philosopher is engaged in conceptual analysis, in which logical and not empirical matters are at issue. While this is perhaps the most important source of misunderstanding, it is not the only one, but we will leave the text to resolve whatever else remains at issue.

Philosophers' irritation with much of behavioural science has its source partly in the apprehension of genuine failings, but partly in misunderstanding. It is difficult for philosophers to grasp or sympathize with the elementary character of much experimental investigation in social psychology. But it reflects a deliberate simplification in the hope of rendering the situation reasonably comprehensible. In that context, psychologists are using terms with extremely restricted meanings, deliberately referring only to the phenomena in question. The fact that many of these terms are used generally with much wider connotations does not make the psychologists' discoveries false or trivial. Nor does the recent fashion of deliberately restricting the phenomena to be studied to those exterior to the people involved mean that the relations discovered between those conditions and subsequent forms of behaviour are mythical. It may be that psychologists have over-estimated the status and generality of these discoveries, but the discoveries remain.

We begin our discussion by noting that much of experimental psychology and other empirical approaches in behavioural science are based upon three assumptions: (a) that only a mechanistic model of man will satisfy the requirements for making a science, (b) that the most scientific conception of cause is one which focuses on external stimulation and which excludes from consideration any treatment of the mode of connection between cause and effect, and (c) that a methodology based on logical positivism is the best possible approach to a behavioural science. All three are mistaken, and the deleterious effects of such views on the form that experimentation and theory still take in social science are discussed in some detail in Chapters Two and Three. One of the most important consequences of these views is that they encourage unwarranted assumptions about the degree to which people are alike, so person parameters are allowed to vary at random in experimental studies, a mistake that vitiates much of the experimental work and makes generalizations to the life situation dubious. We observe that a radically different view of the nature of human behaviour and the means for studying it empirically can be found in the work of Kant, as further developed by contemporary philosophers of science and of mind.

Having looked at these features of the behavioural sciences, we turn in Chapter Four to the method of the advanced sciences, to see whether some guidance for new strategies might be found. Scientists try to explain non-random patterns in nature. To do this, they extend their observational techniques, and develop various means of checking the authenticity of generalizations. Their methods involve both exploration of naturally occurring phenomena, and experimentation, in which phenomena are generated artificially. While the former is extensive in the advanced sciences, particularly in their most formative periods, it is apparently downgraded in the behavioural sciences, unjustifiably so. The ultimate task of the scientist is seen to be causal explanation—the rational explanation of non-random patterns, through the discovery of the mechanisms that generate such patterns. There is no simple route to discovering such mechanisms. Some may be simply inspected; others are only quasi-accessible. But in the first instance, our ideas of most generative mechanisms come from a disciplined use of the imagination. The use of analogy through the key concept of model is important here, for it is analogies which control the imagination so that models are plausible analogues of the unknown, causal mechanisms which produce the known non-random patterns of phenomena.

While early physics was based on a metaphysics of substances and qualities, modern physics is increasingly based on power and potentiality conceptions. Such concepts as agency, potentiality, spontaneity, and power are important in this context. The concepts of powers and potentialities can be applied to humans, as we demonstrate later. The ascription of a power to a thing or substance hinges upon enabling conditions, which are satisfied by the existence of certain intrinsic states, for instance, the poisonousness of a substance is related to its chemical composition. Intrinsic enabling conditions are marked off from all other circumstances surrounding the possession and exercise of powers because of their connection with criteria of identity of the individuals who have the power—thus, powers are related to the essential natures of things or people.

In Chapter Five, we present an *anthropomorphic* model of man advocating the treating of people for *scientific purposes* as if they were human beings. This model is rooted in contemporary ideas about the nature of a person, ideas that stem from the way that concept functions in the grammar of our language and in the system of our commonest thoughts. The visible identity of a person is his biological organism. Through his stable bodily qualities and his powers and capacities, he is recognized as the same person at different times and places. Considering man as a language user, we undertake a logical analysis to identify those features that individuals must have for them to be language users. The most unique feature of a potential language user is the capacity to monitor the control of one's own actions. In the anthropomorphic model, the person is not only an agent, but a watcher, commentator, and critic as well.

It is a mistake, we believe, to think of a biological individual as *necessarily* associated with a single or unitary social self. A normal human biological individual is potentially associated with a whole set of possible unitary social selves. A social individual is made up of a fairly consistent set of inner and outer responses to his fellows and to the social situation, and is backed up by accounts for his actions in terms of a unified set of rules and plans and a coherent system of meanings. Such an entity, which consciously self-monitors its performance and is capable of anticipatory commentary, is bound to put that power to use in generating its own performances and in interacting with other things of its own and different kinds. In this process, the use of rules and plans in the control of actions is common.

Acceptance of the anthropomorphic model of man leads to the introduction of personal reports as a crucial element in psychological study. We try to justify this by arguing for the *open souls doctrine*, a stand taken in our attempt to bring into behavioural science the phenomenal experience of individuals. The things that people say about themselves and other people should be taken seriously as reports of data relevant to phenomena that *really exist* and which are *relevant* to the explanation of behaviour. This contrasts with the mistaken view that the statements themselves are the phenomena. It is essential to take self reports seriously in arriving at adequate explanations of behaviour. Traditional arguments against taking self reports seriously overlook the fact that at least some statements are not a *sign* of a state of mind, but themselves constitute that state of mind (e.g., to complain is to be discontented). It is through reports of feelings, plans, intentions, beliefs, reasons and so on that the meanings of social behaviour and the rules underlying social acts can be discovered.

Further logical analysis pertaining to the nature of a person takes up the spectrum of typical attributes of people that range from the corporeal to the mental. This analysis raises the question of what it is to be a person. The outcome is crucial, for explanations of the behaviour of people and of things are seen to take different forms. Strawson's argument that mental predicates typical of a person can be applied only to entities that are conscious is rejected. We prefer to think of a series of gradually stronger necessary conditions culminating in full self-consciousness and self-awareness, for calling a thing a person, rather than a total discontinuity between persons and non-persons. In this view, sufficiently advanced robots might be considered people for some purposes; even a talking chimpanzee might be similarly regarded.

One condition for being a person suggested by Hampshire is that the individual be aware (in a weak sense) of what he is doing, that is, be capable of saying what he was up to. We regard this criterion as central to any conception of a person. It leaves room for deception and for self-correction in ascribing mental attributes, and it does not require full attention and awareness in the second order of monitoring. A necessary condition for having the concept of oneself as a person is that other individuals should be able to recognize one as a person. Unless we can see that other individuals see us as a person, we cannot see ourselves as such. So it must be possible for one person to know that another person is aware of what he is doing.

Attributes ranging along the spectrum from the physical to the mental are ordered in terms of two criteria. The first is concerned with the overt behaviour, the second, with monitoring of behaviour. Those attributes that satisfy both criteria are person attributes in the fullest sense. Only the actor himself can give an authoritative report on the monitoring of his own behaviour. We need *not* worry about the unreliability of the actor's reports. The fact that he is the ultimate *authority* does not entail that only he has access to his thoughts and feelings. Other people frequently have some access to the feelings of another, and, if they speak the same language, to his thoughts as well. A special case must be made for the observer's discrepant report, if we wish to deny the actor's report.

Chapter Seven outlines preliminary arguments for a new methodology, based upon the anthropomorphic model of man and a non-positivist conception of science.

Regularities in human behaviour may be explained according to several different schemata. Two extremes are: (1) the person acting as an agent directing his own behaviour, and (2) the person as an object responding to the push and pull of forces exerted by the environment. The former emphasizes self-direction; the latter, environmental contingencies. Most contemporary social psychologists fall somewhere in between the extremes of environmental contingency accounts and the admission of full self-monitoring or self-direction as the main generating process of social behaviour. Each of these several schemata are legitimate forms of explanation for certain selected behavioural phenomena. This book, however, will strongly emphasize self-directed and self-monitored behaviour, because it has been generally neglected in the behavioural sciences, because this is the prototype of behaviour in ordinary daily living, and because we believe it to be the main factor in the production of specifically *social* behaviour. Indeed, much behaviour that would quite naturally be explained in such terms is traditionally forced into less compatible forms of explanation in the belief that they are more scientific—the most typical predilection here being for environmental contingency explanations.

Much habitual behaviour, considered when fully established, falls between environmental contingency and self-direction explanations —it was initially learned through self-direction and self-monitoring, but these elements eventually drop out of awareness and it seems no longer correct to describe the behaviour as self-controlled. So it would be a mistake to view habitual behaviour as adequately explained by environmental contingencies.

If we follow the paradigm of non-positivist science, explaining behavioural phenomena involves identifying the generative 'mechanisms' that give rise to the behaviour. The discovery and identification of these 'mechanisms' we call *ethogeny*. We believe that the main process involved in them is self-direction according to the meaning ascribed to the situation. At the heart of the explanation of social behaviour is the identification of the meanings that underlie it. Part of the approach to discovering them involves the obtaining of *accounts*—the actor's own statements about why he performed the acts in question, what social meanings he gave to the actions of himself and others. These must be collected and analysed, often leading to the discovery of the rules that underlie the behaviour. The explanation is not complete, however, until differing accounts are negotiated and, further, put into the context of an *episode* structure, to be discussed shortly. Greater precision of meaning through such procedures is analogous to greater accuracy of measurement in the physical sciences. An important tool in obtaining these meanings is ordinary language, which is well adapted for explaining a pattern of

B

social interaction in terms of reasons and rules. Two cardinal principles in using the concepts of ordinary language as developed by
philosophers are:

1. The conceptual system embedded in ordinary language should
provide the basis for the concepts employed in a realistic psychology,
and should serve as a model for other logical connections, and new
concepts introduced by psychologists.

2. Given the existence of carefully checked description of social
behaviour, a detailed exploration of particular cases by the analysis
of accounts should next be undertaken. The justificatory context of
the accounts is dominant here, and leads to the discovery of how
behaviour is monitored by the actor, because in such a context he
must turn his attention most fully upon what he has done.

Chapters Eight and Nine develop a conceptual system for classifying human interaction in terms of episodes, and for analysing the
accounts given by people of their own behaviour. Social psychologists should turn more of their attention to life situations, but they
need a technique to do this. Ordinary language concepts are the
only concepts we have for describing *action*-meaningful behaviour.
The use of ordinary language allows for explanation of behaviour in
terms of the actor's point of view. Here, the ethogenic approach
merges with the phenomenological tradition. This extends beyond
ethology, because the latter does not and cannot deal with the
animal's non-existent point of view. Since animals have no language,
their point of view cannot be an empirical concept, and is, at best,
an explanatory metaphor.

Central to all analysis of social life is the concept of the episode.
Even the powers and liabilities that people have are often dependent
upon the structure and meaning of the episode in which an action
occurs. An episode is any sequence of happenings in which human
beings engage which has some principle of unity. Episodes have a
beginning and end that can usually be identified. The concept of
episode is discussed at some length in two later Chapters.

An important distinction in human actions is that between things
that are done *by* a person, including what he says, and things done
to a person. Psychological research tends to focus primarily on the
latter. Of course, many cases are intermediate, and cannot be readily

classified as one or the other. An action acquires its social meaning through being identified as a performance which, when completed, constitutes by convention an *act*. Acts are not to be identified either with the actions needed to perform them, nor with the movements involved in the action. There are many different ways in which the same act may be performed. All have the same meaning through their identity with respect to the act, of which they are the performance.

Considerable confusion has been generated in arguments over the relative merits of explanations of behaviour in terms of causes and in terms of reasons. The relations between these forms of explanation can be resolved through the following distinctions:

1. Both reasons which are logically related to what they explain, and causes, which are related through some physical mechanism, can appear in the explanation of happenings, whether these happenings are the actions of people, or the movements of animals.

2. Reasons are usually offered in human affairs in the course of providing a justification or excuse for some action. These are extraordinarily varied in form and content. Different commentators can use different explanations for the same action: one may use reasons, and the other, causes. Some episodes cannot be given an account by the actors, nor can they provide an explanation in terms of reasons. But if an explanation of a sequence of actions is referred to the act performed then an exclusively causal account is necessarily defective.

In the discussion so far, the unifying principle for a series of actions is the identification of them as the performance of a certain act. A different but logically similar unifying principle is found in the following of a plan or purpose, a special case of rule-following. Both principles involve actions that are meant or intended. In the description of such purposive actions there must be mention of the end or outcome.

In the next two Chapters, the structure of episodes is taken up. Formal episodes are characterized by reference to explicit rules—written, printed, or at least capable of being stated explicitly. In causal episodes, sequences of happenings are related by the operation of a causal mechanism (e.g., the development of an infectious disease because of invasion by germs). While *some* reasons are causes, some other reasons are definitely not. Since reasons bear logical relations to one another, we might expect in social life to find a 'deep structure' something like the deep structure Chomsky finds in language.

Most episodes cannot be clearly classified: they are *enigmatic*, having neither an explicit set of rules, nor produced by well-established causal mechanisms. Enigmatic episodes are explained by applying to them concepts used in the explanation of those paradigmatic episodes which themselves have *clear* explanations, be they formal or causal. The structure of episodes has two levels: overt and covert. The former consists of the act-action sequence, contained in the episode; the latter, of the permanent and transitory powers and states of readiness and the flux of emotions that underlie the episode.

Since formal episodes involve the conscious following of explicit rules, they may be used as the source of imagined forms that might underlie enigmatic episodes. We imagine a set of rules for enigmatic episodes. For example, by imagining that a face-saving episode is governed by a ritual, Goffman was able to identify the conventions which seem to operate in those episodes where a gaffe is covered up. Some of Berne's life games have a structure explicable as the following of ritualistic rules. Some can be understood by reference to rules of competitive game-playing.

Rules are propositions and they guide action, through the actor being aware of the rule and of what it prescribes. But identifying the rule still leaves open the question of why that rule was chosen or why he decided to follow it. So a further account of wants or needs is required, showing how they relate to a choice of rule. Rules are future-directed; they not only guide action, but also determine expectations concerning the actions of other persons. The propositional nature of rules fits them to appear in accounts of and commentaries on action. The question of the authority of a rule is a matter for empirical investigation. It is the self-monitored following of rules and plans that we believe to be the social scientific analogue of the working of generative causal mechanisms in the processes which produce the non-random patterns studied by natural scientists.

A complementary concept of considerable importance is that of role. A role is that part of the act-action structure produced by the subset of the rules followed by a *particular category of individual*. A person's role, then, is the set of actions he is expected to take within the act-action structure of a certain kind of episode. Role expectations may be clear, or they may be only dimly perceived.

The rules referred to by social actors in justification of their actions, and thus in explanation of them, can be systematically classified by reference to the kind of episode they generate. We offer a sketch of a taxonomy based upon the following distinctions: some episodes are made up of the genuine performance of the actions constituting the act-action structure of the episode, while in other episodes the very same actions may be only a mock or simulated performance. In this way there can be real marriages, and simulated marriages on the stage, real murders and simulated murders in a TV serial, real illnesses and the simulated illnesses of a skilled hypochondriac. Under each family, we distinguish a spectrum of episodes from the purely ceremonial where the actions constitute the act only because of the social meaning given them, as e.g. religious ceremonies, to those where the actions are bound into a structure by purely causal links. We reserve the term 'ritual' for the more ceremonial structures. Within this broad classification we distinguish between those episodes which involve co-operation between the participants and those which are more or less competitive. The 'game' concept is restricted by us to competitive episodes, though some writers have used it more widely.

A ritual may be associated with a liturgy, i.e. an explicitly formulated set of instructions for performing the actions required for the kind of episode we want to generate. For some enigmatic episodes, a liturgy can be imagined for the unknown and unformulated conventions and rules. Thus, one creates the liturgical model. This would constitute the basis for an explanation of the enigmatic episode by analogy with a type of formal episode, if certain criteria are met. Where we recognize some form of competition we can imagine it in the form of a game with an explicit set of rules. They can be supposed to determine what is and what is not in the game. Competition is possible in rule-governed episodes if the rules specify only a type of action, leaving room for skill and luck. The kind of outcome a competitive episode may have is an important dimension for the most fine-grained analysis. To think of the episode in this way is to apply to it the concepts of the agonistic, or game model.

The role-rule model developed by considering the episode structure and the roles and rules underlying it, has both a descriptive and an explanatory role. The former is related to the way in which the episode is described from the social point of view, and the latter as to how participation in it is accounted for from an individual point of view.

Our system is not yet complete. Chapter Ten introduces what has come to be called the dramaturgical standpoint. For a full comprehension of what is going on in an episode or a series of them, it is necessary to monitor the monitoring by which the actors control the *style*, as well as the actions, of the performance. The observer must step back not only from the performance, but also from the control of the performance, and become aware of his manner of control. Goffman's concept of role distance gives an inkling of what is meant here—when taking distance from his role, the person can control the style or manner of his performance and can subtly mock the role performance. This is only possible for someone who is observing and capable of controlling the manner of his first-order performance. The most generalized form of role distance is the dramaturgical standpoint. In taking this standpoint, we ask ourselves how we would perceive what we or other people are doing were we acting deliberately, and following a script in a play and the stylistic instructions of a director. This enables us to discover the appropriate role-rule model, and to produce a commentary consisting of the rules and including the social meanings of the actions performed.

The role perspective, as it has usually been used, does not provide a sufficiently complete explanation. Action is seen as resulting from the social prescriptions and the behaviour of other persons on the analogy with stage performances, but there has been no attempt to develop the analogy into a larger perspective beyond a simple structure of scripts, performers and so on. The dramaturgical viewpoint adds a further dimension of possible analysis, as well as this larger perspective in that it can be used to introduce the *content* of the performance. Act-action structures may be classified in the same manner as plots of plays are classified. A character in a play corresponds to a role in life, not to a person. The actions of the character are all meaningful with respect to the acts of which the plot consists; the role selects those actions which satisfy the rule-conventions for bringing about the acts of the act-action structure. The nearer a major character is to matching a real human being, the less he is of use as the basis for a concept to be used in a role analysis, but the more his actions are valuable in the identification of the act-action structures.

Two principles appear in the application of role-rule models, particularly to the problem of the understanding of style of performance:

1. THE CONSTITUTIVE PRINCIPLE. People exercise a higher order control, sometimes consciously and sometimes not, on their performances, and superimpose socially important stylistic elements on other activities. Generally, when fully understood, this may be seen in some larger coherent framework, as when a dramatic performance is put on to impress. Dramaturgical concepts are held to elucidate style, while liturgical and game concepts obtained from accounts provide coherence and meaning to the performance in allowing identification of the roles and rules.

2. THE EXPLANATORY PRINCIPLE. In order to understand what people do, one must see their activities in terms of deliberate followings of rules, suggested by one or more of the role-rule models, and modified by higher order dramaturgical principles. Thus, role and rule concepts must figure in the accounts given both by people and by social psychologists. This seems to be the essence of Goffman's method. He explicitly and subtly exploits role-rule models, developing a conceptual system for making an analysis of the act-action structure and style of episodes from the dramaturgical standpoint.

Chapter Eleven deals with the 'checking-out' of role-rule models. In social life, it is not what movements are made and utterances delivered that is important, but what the aims and intentions of the actors are in making them. By adopting the dramaturgical model, the social psychologist achieves distance from the performance of the actions, and puts himself in a position to give an account of the slice of life he is studying. Actual life situations often require more than a single model, sometimes a complex shifting from one to another. Somewhat different accounts may be given by actors and audience. Actors may be their own audience, and the scientist as social psychologist may be an actor as well. His account as an actor or member of the audience must square with his account of the role-rule model underlying the episode. Differences are resolved through negotiation involving all the parties.

The concept of role by itself is inadequate to deal with all forms of episodes. Only in the case of formal episodes and for enigmatic episodes having an act-action structure resembling a formal one is the concept of role useful. Role is a *normative* concept, focusing on what is proper for a person in a particular category to do. The term role has been applied by social psychologists to categories of persons for whom it is impossible to specify any definitive set of act-action structures corresponding to the role. Thus, the *female role* is unduly vague, for this reason, and might better be referred to as a style of life. The role of priest, on the other hand, is associated with definite and specifiable act-action structures.

In treating people like priests, actors, or players, we are departing from the mechanical model, which assumes that the attributes of such entities as people can be treated as parameters—some parameters held constant, others varied. At the heart of this inadequate model is the idea of logically independent properties. Most probably, the attributes of people are not logically independent, but are interactive, and the most important ones of all may not even exist in isolation. Yet the idea of experimental design relating independent variables to dependent ones requires the assumption of logically independent attributes.

By looking not only at correlations and statistics, but also scripts, liturgies, and sets of rules derived from the analysis of accounts, we are going beyond the descriptive level to construct explanations of the phenomena described. In some episodes, the application of the role-rule model is literal—these episodes *are* like ceremonies and games. It is the analogy between entities of the same kind, namely people enacting episodes in human life and actors in a play that justifies the role concept, an important point in traditional role theory. On the role-rule model, similarities in people's behaviour do not necessarily derive from similarities in the stimuli to which they are subjected, but from shared meanings and commonly accepted conventions and rules. The mechanistic model has no literal employment in human social life, except, perhaps, for explaining an occasional bizarre lapse from sequences governed by roles and rules. The mechanistic model is strongly deterministic; the role-rule model is not. Rules are not laws, they can be ignored or broken, if we admit that human beings are self-governing agents rather than objects controlled by external forces, aware of themselves only as helpless spectators of the flow of physical causality.

In our system, explanation by meanings and reasons seems to differ in two important ways from explanation of physical phenomena in terms of causal mechanisms: the person offers accounts which (a) are subject to *post-hoc* modification, and (b) may be changed if the person can be persuaded that his account is wrong. There is no possibility of an absolutely objective, neutral account by which these ambiguities may be resolved. Accounts can only be negotiated. Involved in this process are three persons: two who are primary interactants, and an observer. Each will offer a somewhat different account. The open-endedness of this method of verification is no more disturbing than is the impossibility in physical science of knowing for certain if one's theoretical explanations are correct, and the never-ceasing possibility that they may have to be revised.

Chapter Twelve deals with the concept of human powers. This Chapter brings into a single system, by means of the powers concept, the description and explanation of behaviour in the ordinary language of everyday life, the discoveries of psychologists expressed in psychological terms, and the knowledge of emotions and feelings including their basis in physiology. The word *power* is used in two ways: (a) to refer to very general capacities, such as the power of speech, and (b) to refer to short-term capacities or liabilities, states of readiness, such as the readiness to shed tears produced by a state of grief. Both uses of the power concept depend upon a person having differentiable 'inner' states, and upon the individual being an agent capable of controlling his performance, and being aware of the manner of that control. Complementary to these powers concepts are liabilities, where the person is a patient rather than an agent, as in the tendency to yield to a particular impulse. Much of human life is seen as the exercise and circumvention and blocking of the exercise of powers or the activation of liabilities.

Having a power or liability is being in such a state that one is likely to behave in a particular way. The ascription of powers may be characterized according to the following formula:

If $C_1, C_2, C_3 \ldots C_n$, then B in virtue of N.

C represents a set of conditions forming an open disjunction, B represents the ensuing behaviour, and N represents the nature and state of the individual, in virtue of which he is capable of doing B should any of the conditions $C_1 \ldots C_n$ obtain. The C and B elements taken together we call the D-component of the powers ascription. Both the D-component and the N-component *can* be expressed entirely in ordinary language terms. Sometimes, however, they relate readily to ordinary language or become a part thereof. Psychological terms may form a part of the C- or N-components, but can be a part of the B-component only if consonant with the logic of ordinary language. Physiological terms form a separate scientific vocabulary and may enter into the C-component or the N-component, but *not* the B-component. This is what distinguishes psychological from ordinary medicine. Thus, physiological conditions and N-states and processes pertaining to schizophrenia may be specified, but schizophrenic *behaviour* may only be described in ordinary language terms and certain related psychological terms.

The N-component pertains to *enabling conditions*, producing a state of readiness in the individual. *Circumstances*, residing in the environment, which make the behaviour possible, we comprehend in the C-component. Since these complex statements ascribe powers stimuli may often have to be described independently. Some intrinsic enabling conditions are relatively permanent and pertain to the possession of a power; others are transitory, producing a state of readiness. Intrinsic enabling conditions may include both physiological and psychic elements: a man's nature is a psycho-physiological mix,

Chapter Thirteen provides an interpretation of the concept *human nature* in terms of our system. The system allows the use of *type* terms, like *coward*, which are not merely summary terms for a form of overt behaviour, but are intended to have explanatory force. Such terms represent an unknown mix of psychic and physiological components, but they indicate the existence of a focus for empirical investigation. A man's nature may also include components represented by highly theoretical psychological terms, e.g., Freudian structure or dynamics. Each social self is seen as a cluster of powers and liabilities.

The three routes to the knowledge of an individual's nature are by way of ordinary language, physiology, and psychology. The identification of physiological entities depends upon the independent identification of psychological phenomena, and thus cannot be substituted for them. Ordinary language terms are useful only in some contexts; particularly those in which a man interacts socially with his fellows, but they do not adequately characterize a biological individual in all settings.

Finally, in Chapter Fourteen we append some detailed proposals for specific research programmes that stem from the adoption of the ethogenic point of view.

Thanks to the work of Kuhn it is now possible to express the aim of this book in a more general context. We are trying to bring a *paradigm-shift* into focus. This notion was introduced by Kuhn in an attempt to make clear the intellectual and social structure of scientific revolutions. By a paradigm he can be interpreted to mean that complex of metaphysics, general theory of action and methodology which forms a coherent background to the science of a particular time, and which is often given concrete expression in some admired archetype of scientific work, such as Newton's *Principia*. We believe that the present state of social psychology particularly, is explicable as a transition from one paradigm to another, from what we shall call 'The Old Paradigm', to that which we shall call 'The New'. It is our aim to articulate the New Paradigm.

We will sum up our general thesis in these Kuhnian terms. The Old Paradigm involves the conception of a theory as a deductive structure from which the empirically ascertained laws are to be derived by strict logical inference. It conceives of the function of theory as confined to the bringing of order into the empirically ascertained laws. This view of theories has the important consequence that provided the theory performs well logically one may be fairly casual about the verisimilitude of its terms. In the Old Paradigm a law has the form F(x,y) where x and y are dependent and independent variables, and it is assumed that all properties of the system in which this 'law' is observed to hold can be treated as parameters, that is maintained constant without materially affecting the relationship between those allowed to vary. This assumption is thought to be justified in its turn by the general principle that the aim of science is to discover correlations between changes in the properties of systems. In the farthest background lies Hume's theory of causality according to which such correlations *are* causal laws. The Old Paradigm has been very clearly articulated for psychology by C. L. Hull,[3] and is particularly well exemplified in social psychological contexts by the work of experimentalists such as R. B. Zajonc.[4]

In this paradigm it is clear that the meaning of theoretical concepts must be *fully defined* in terms of the operational concepts used to give empirical meaning to the variables correlated in the basic generalizations, since the Old Paradigm restricts a piece of science to such functions and their logical permutations in a deductive theory. The characteristic mathematics associated with the Old Paradigm will be an exploratory use of statistics, in the search for functional correlations between parameters, and at a higher level of abstraction, information theory. In that theory matrices of probabilities of inputs and outputs express the results of the search for correlations, while all the concepts used to describe the intermediary channels such as 'entropy' can be shown to be fully definable in terms the elements of the matrices.[5]

Lastly it is very important to realize that this paradigm was not derived by abstraction from real scientific work, but was an invention of philosophers. In modern times it has its origin in Berkeley's attempt to establish the existence of God and other spirits by denying that matter had causal powers and by insisting that science was really no more than a set of rules for anticipating sense experience.[6]

This idea was taken up by Hume[7] and developed by John Stuart Mill,[8] from whom it was adopted as a methodology by the infant social sciences. There is a measure of irony in the strict adherence by social scientists to a methodology which they hoped would give them scientific respectability, when that methodology derives from such an ancestry!

The New Paradigm derives from a double shift. The First Shift involves passing from a philosophers' conception of how science ought to be to the use of methods which are actually employed in the advanced sciences. The most important aspect of this paradigm shift for the social sciences is in the understanding of the role of theory. In the New Paradigm theory describes models of the real processes which generate behaviour, and so must be taken with the utmost seriousness. Testing for whether the states and processes hypothesized really exist becomes a central activity of scientific work.

The differing attitudes to theory are vividly illustrated in a series of papers in recent years, discussing the theory of cognitive dissonance. We shall often have occasion to refer to this theory, which can be considered within either of the paradigms. The hypothesis of cognitive dissonance as a state of a person which produces certain changes in attitude or behaviour is illustrated in such papers as that by Festinger and Carlsmith.[9] In the early papers it was unclear whether the theory was being enunciated in the Old Paradigm or the New. Attempts to criticize and test it under the New Paradigm have been made. The point of such investigations must necessarily be obscure to anyone working within the Old Paradigm. This is shown by the discussion of the theory and its critics by R. B. Zajonc, which remains firmly within the Old Paradigm, so that the very nature of the investigation eludes that author.[10] Festinger and Carlsmith try to move out of the Old Paradigm. Chapanis and Chapanis[11] offer a critique from the standpoint of the New Paradigm, while Zajonc, working from deep inside the Old Paradigm, treats the considerations advanced by those operating from within the New Paradigm as irrelevant.

The Second Shift concerns the nature of the entities that are being studied and their mode of action. Conceiving of human beings as people, and their mode of action as social beings to be self-monitored rule-following, means that very different models of the processes which generate social behaviour must be used. One important feature of such models will be that they must contain some form of 'feed back', by which the various orders of monitoring of performance can be achieved. The mathematics of the New Paradigm will then be Systems Theory, and statistics will be used as in the advanced sciences, not as an exploratory tool, but as part of the theory of error. The general form of such psychomathematics can be found in summary form in a paper of D. Macfarland.[12] The Second Shift takes us into what we have called the Anthropomorphic model of Man.

The form of the mathematics and the nature of the theories so expressed are closely connected. Information theory and statistical forms of the parametric method are the mathematics of the Old Paradigm, since it is concerned with correlational relations between 'behaviours' and their conditions, and in the spirit of the positivist conception of science is quite casual about their *connection*. We have already noticed that in information theory, concepts describing the channels themselves are logical functions of the concepts describing input and output, so that realistic hypotheses as to the neural mechanisms cannot be generated from within that theory. It follows from the considerations we have been advancing that Systems Theory, the mathematics of the New Paradigm, enables us to express

(a) the control of performance by monitoring, and so, given the relation between neurophysiology and performance,

(b) to generate realistic hypotheses as to the structure of the entity which is capable of the performances we have identified as essential to social life, and Chomsky has identified as essential to using language, that is as to the physiological basis of competences and powers.

The essential structure of the anthropomorphic model from a scientific point of view, can be viewed most easily in the rather narrow context of individual psychology.

In each human being there is a complex pattern of sequential physiological states, which for illustrative purposes can be supposed to be decomposable into linear sequences. Let such a sequence be

$$P_1 - P_2 - P_3 - - - - - - P_n.$$

Applying the realist scientific method to the understanding of this sequence leads to the postulation of physiological mechanisms $M_1 - M_n$ which produce the sequential pattern. Those elements of the pattern which are related through the operation of one or more of these mechanisms can be called 'cause and effect'.

We also know that in each human being there is also a complex pattern of sequential psychic states, such as emotions and thoughts of various kinds. For illustrative purposes let us suppose part of this sequence to be represented by

$$S_1 - S_2 - S_3 - - - - - S_m.$$

What do we know about

(i) the relation of this sequence to the physiological sequence?

(ii) the generation of the sequence?

We know from a number of studies, the most important of which are those by Schachter,[13] that the correct way of considering the S-sequence with respect to the P-sequence, is that the S-sequence consists of the *meanings* given by he who experiences that sequence to *some* of the items of the P-sequence. For example P_1 may not be experienced as a meaningful psychic state, but P_2, P_3 and P_4 may be experienced jointly as S_1, P_6 as S_2, and P_5 as S_3. In fact the sequences may be ordered very differently and correspond very unevenly.

Since the S-sequence is a sequence of meanings the organization imposed on that sequence will have something of the character of a *grammar*, and will involve relations which could hold between meanings. The most characteristic of such order-giving relations is 'reason for'. Since the P-sequence is a sequence of physico-chemical states organization will be imposed upon it by such concepts as 'oxidation of . . .'. This explains why the organizations of the sequences are, in general, a bad fit.

Applying the realist methodology of reason to the S-pattern demands the introduction of generating 'mechanisms' for that pattern appropriate to its nature. Typically these will be transformations of deep structures, and other suitable mechanisms, or in some cases, where the mechanisms elude detection, models of the unknown generators. It is here that Freudian concepts might have a place in a scientific psychology.

As to the metaphysics behind the two sequences of states, we accept the contingent identity thesis,[14] or 'Australian materialism',[15] that the differences between S-states and P-states are not differences in existence, that is they are not *numerically* distinct, but are differences in the mode of manifestation of the one existent. S-states and P-states differ pretty much as do statements and the marks or sounds of which they are the meaning. Detailed applications of this idea to psychology have been worked out.

The P-sequence is susceptible of a preliminary application of the parametric method, and the use of independent and dependent variables as analytical tools, but this is justified only because of the nature of the mechanisms which generate the pattern and sequence of P-states. The S-sequence is not susceptible of the application of this method, *in general*, because generative 'grammars' and their analogues produce patterns in such a way that those patterns are not susceptible of this method of analysis; cf. Chomsky, particularly *Syntactic Structures*.[16]

S-sequences are 'teleological' in the weak, Taylor sense,[17] in that they are ordered by such concepts as 'reason for' and 'intention', while P-sequences are non-teleological, in that they are organized by the concept 'physical cause of . . .'. S and P-sequences are not, *in general*, mutually convertible, because of the degree of mismatch of their respective organizations. This is vividly exemplified in Schacter's studies of hunger.

The structure of the S-system determines the structure which is sought in the P-system, when we are seeking an explanation of the S-system. Since it is a logical point that the criteria of identity for entities and systems on the P side *must* derive from the S side, in order to be relevant to the explanation of performance, psychology must necessarily impose its form upon physiological investigations. If the S-sequence is not only grammatically ordered, but is also seen to involve modelling and monitoring feedback, then it will impose a system-theoretical structure upon physiological hypotheses, since the neurological system must contain the necessary mechanisms for the performance of the higher order functions. And in so far as we inherit those mechanisms there will be deep structures in grammar and in the rules of social life. We have seen preliminary steps in the discovery of these structures for language by Chomsky and for certain aspects of the social behaviour of men by Levi-Strauss.[18]

A final point concerns the degree of generalizability of patterns found in the S-sequences. These are two ways in which these may be idiosyncratic, and unique to each person.

(i) The physiological items which bear certain meanings in two different people may be different. This corresponds to the way the same statement may be couched in French or English.

(ii) The meaning-structure is obviously strongly susceptible to minute differences in experience, so that there may be wide differences between what are taken to be intelligible connections. *A priori* one would expect to find families of patterns having common structures, as for example, elucidated by Levi-Strauss, but it remains an empirical question whether there is an underlying deep structure to meanings, and this would remain an empirical question even if the Chomskean grammatical thesis for languages was finally established.

REFERENCES

1. R. S. Peters, *The Concept of Motivation*, Routledge and Kegan Paul, London, 1958.
2. R. Brown, *Explanation in Social Science*, Routledge and Kegan Paul, London, 1963, pp. 71-2.
3. C. L. Hull, *A Behavior System*, Yale University Press, New Haven, 1952.
4. R. B. Zajonc and J. J. Taylor, 'The effect of two Methods of varying group task difficulty on individual and group performance', *Human Relations*, 16, (1963), 359-68.
5. N. Abrahamson, *Information Theory and Coding*, McGraw-Hill, New York, 1963.
6. G. Berkeley, *A Treatise Concerning the Principles of Human Knowledge*, London, 1710, Principle *c* ff.
7. D. Hume, *An Enquiry Concerning Human Understanding*, ed. L. A. Selby-Bigge, Oxford.

c

8. J. S. Mill, *A System of Logic*, Longmans Green, London, 1868, Bk. III.

9. L. Festinger and J. M. Carlsmith, 'Cognitive Consequences of Forced Compliance', *J. Abnorm. Soc. Psych.*, 58, 1959, 203–10.

10. R. B. Zajonc in G. Lindzey and E. Aronson (editors), *The Handbook of Social Psychology*, Addison-Wesley, Reading, Mass., 1954, Vol. I, Ch. 5, 320–3, 359–66, 373.

11. N. P. Chapanis and A. Chapanis, 'Cognitive Dissonance', *Psych. Bull.*, 61, 1964, 1–22.

12. D. Macfarlane, 'Behavioural Aspects of Homoeostasis', *Advances in the Study of Behaviour*, Vol. II, edited by D. Lehrman, R. A. Hinde and E. Shaw, 1970.

13. S. Schachter and L. Wheeler, 'Epinephrine chlorpromazine and amusement', *J. Abnorm. Soc. Psych.*, 65, (1962), 121–8.

14. J. A. Fodor, *Psychological Explanation*, Random House, New York, 1968, pp. 107–11.

15. D. M. Armstrong, *A Materialist Theory of the Mind*, Routledge and Kegan Paul, London, 1968.

16. N. Chomsky, *Aspects of the Theory of Syntax*, MIT Press, Cambridge, Mass., 1965.

17. C. Taylor, *The Explanation of Behaviour*, Routledge and Kegan Paul, London, 1964.

18. C. Levi-Strauss, *Structural Anthropology*, Allen Lane, The Penguin Press, 1968.

CHAPTER TWO

Social Psychology and its Recent Philosophical Basis

THE ARGUMENT

Foundations of Recent Psychology

1. The Mechanistic Model of Man requires

   a. that behaviour should be explicable in terms of external stimuli, either immediate in the S-R model, or latent in the S-O-R model;

   b. that the contribution of factors internal to the organism be minimized;

   c. that wherever a cause of the same type exists, the effect will be the same.

2. The Humean Conception of Cause requires

   a. (i) that causal laws be taken to express constant correlations of stimulus and response,

   (ii) that the mode of connection of cause and effect is not part of empirical science.

   b. A naïve determinism results from combining the mechanistic model with the Humean view of cause:

   (i) in radical behaviourism external stimuli are seen as approaching the status of efficient causes;

   (ii) analysis of the mode of connection of cause and effect is limited by the tendency either to ignore organismic factors, or to regard them as mere conditions, subsidiary to the primary impact of the external stimulus.

3. The Logical Positivist Methodology requires

    a. the verificationist theory of meaning, and

    b. the operationist theory of definition, which together imply

    c. the view that the role of theory is restricted to providing a logical organization of the given facts.

The Laboratory Experiment

1, 2 and 3 together imply a methodology restricted to simple manipulations of independent variables, themselves allegedly simple components of behaviour. One should note the important assumption that complex behaviour is an additive function of simple behaviours. (This assumption explains the primacy once given to animal studies.)

Current Doubts

    1. That the positivist methodology will not automatically yield a body of accredited and reliable scientific knowledge.

    2. That S-R and S-O-R paradigms yield only an illusion of objectivity.

    3. That animal and laboratory studies cannot be generalized in most conditions.

    Note. The Skinnerian movement represents the rearguard of the old style, rejecting only logical positivism. This position is made possible only by the use of very loosely defined concepts of highly variable meaning, e.g. 'control'.

    4. Social psychology has been studied without reference to its major phenomena, namely meanings, and without taking account of its main behaviour generating feature, namely the agency of people.

The Malaise Diagnosed

    1. In social psychology, insufficient attention has been paid to the concepts used. It has been assumed that the experiments will

somehow themselves define appropriate concepts and eliminate inappropriate ones.

2. A close examination suggests that, because of inadequate conceptual frameworks, the individual experimenter uses uncritical common sense to connect theory and empirical procedures.

The Remedy Outlined

1. Human beings must be treated as agents acting according to rule, and it must be realized that it is unscientific to treat them as anything else.

2. Social behaviour must be conceived of as actions mediated by meanings, not responses caused by stimuli.

3. The theory of movements, physiology, must be clearly separated from psychology, the theory of actions.

4. It must be clearly appreciated that most human social behaviour cannot be made intelligible under the mechanistic, causal paradigm.

5. Reasons can be used to explain actions, and not all reasons can be treated as causes in the mechanistic sense, though in some special cases causes may be cited as reasons.

6. Lay explanations of behaviour provide the best model for psychological theory, and properly considered they can be seen to be actually more in accordance with the actual methodology of real natural science than is the positivist methodology which provided the old models of science which psychologists have copied.

For about a half century three fundamental ideas have been taken for granted as providing a sound methodological and theoretical foundation for a behavioural science. These are: a mechanistic model of man, a Humean conception of cause that places stress on external stimuli, and a related methodology based upon the logical and epistemological theories of logical positivism. The more a behavioural science has fitted itself to these conceptions, the more scientific status it has believed itself to deserve. These conceptions are perhaps most clearly realized in a behavioural science which places the laboratory experiment at the centre of its quest for knowledge. This has controlled much of what has been attempted in the field of psychology. As we shall make clear a subscription to these three ideas leads to an emphasis on experiments with animals rather than humans, and to the restriction of empirical research to the kind of experiment where the phenomena are analysed into dependent and independent variables, and the investigation consists in the manipulation of the independent variable and the observation and correlation of subsequent changes in the dependent variable or variables.

The specific content of the three conceptions we have identified as being at the base of much psychological science will be discussed below, and we shall elaborate on the way in which adherence to these ideas has placed severe constraints on the possibilities of discovery in psychology. We intend to contrast these conceptions with views on the nature of human action that have emerged both from recent investigations in philosophical psychology and from current trends in that part of sociology which is closest to psychology. We shall also try to make clear how new ideas about the nature of science, associated with the 'realist' school of philosophy of science, dissolve many of the constraints imposed upon psychological science by the logical posivitist methodology within which it has been too long confined.

In the following chapter we will show specifically how the three basic conceptions we have referred to have shaped the psychological experiment into a particular form. It will emerge that this is not the only possible way of developing an empirical basis for psychology.

Psychologists are prone to view a human being as a complicated mechanism whose behaviour can be fully explained, in principle, by a combination of the effects of external stimuli and prevailing organismic states. People are viewed as objects which are passively affected by events in their environment. This point of view becomes institutionalized even in the very terms by which psychologists refer to the people who cooperate with them in 'experiments'. Psychologists seem to prefer to call the people they are studying 'organisms' or 'subjects'. They think of their subjects as mechanisms that, like less complex physical objects, respond to the push and pull of forces exerted by the experimenter or the environment. In the classical exposition of this point of view an organism is regarded as being subjected to a certain *stimulus* situation, and it *responds* to it in a predictable manner. This is a familiar S-R (stimulus-response) model. The necessity of incorporating the effects of learning and experience into psychology led to the S-O-R (stimulus-organism-response) model in which changes in the organism led to modifications of the form of the response. At least as controlling ideas in the design of experiments these models are still very much alive.[1] Even when debating the details of this or that S-R or S-O-R model psychologists seem to have taken very much for granted the necessity of some form of mechanistic model, if psychology is to be a science at all.[2]

The psychologist's view of 'cause' follows the general lines of the 'regularity' theory of David Hume. Hume thought of causation as essentially a statistical relation between independent events, analysable in terms of the constant conjunction of pairs of events, one of each kind, under varying conditions and circumstances. Causation is nothing but the regular sequence of one kind of event and another of the kind which usually follows. In the understanding of causes the things in which the cause-effect relation occurs play the part only of bearers of the externally applied impetus. The fact that the natures of things do influence the effects produced is assimilated to this paradigm by referring to changes brought about in the things by previous impressed forces. Any spontaneity or generative power in the mediating things is discounted. The Humean view is thus associated with the most naïve form of determinism. Further, any connection there may be assumed to be between the cause event and the effect event is treated as a psychological phenomenon produced in the observer by the repetition of the causal sequence, and of no interest to science.[3] The prototype of Humean causality is the occasion of one billiard ball striking another. The impact is followed by the movement of the second ball, but does not produce it. This causal theory is associated with a deterministic and indeed mechanistic view of human responses. Its consequences are vividly sketched by Melden in his book *Free Action*,[4] as follows:

'Not only choice, but all of the other psychological factors that issue in action are themselves enmeshed in the bonds of causal necessity: my perceptions, desires, interests, motives, needs, no less than the character traits I now have or had at any other time in the past. My past choices, like my present character, had to be what they were: for given their causally antecedent conditions they could not have been other than what in point of fact they were . . . whatever does happen, happens necessarily as it does, for given the conditions of its occurrence, the happening is causally necessary. Trace the causal antecedents of my conduct and my character back into the past as far as one pleases, to the conditions of my birth and my training, what happens now when I act as I do must happen in precisely the way in which it does' (pp. 4–5). We have the picture of the human actor as a helpless spectator carried along on the flood tide of physical causes.

As the formative idea of their methodology most psychologists have tacitly adopted a logical positivist metaphysics and the methodology that goes with it. As formulated by the members of the Vienna Circle in the early nineteen twenties, logical positivism stressed operationism as a theory of definition, and the principle of verification as a theory of meaning.[5] This amounted to the idea that the meaning of the terms appearing in a science is given by the way the statements in which they figure could be verified. Ordinary language was viewed as unfit for scientific use, and attempts were made to develop systems of concepts, satisfying these principles, that would be appropriate for science. The general theory of science proposed by the positivists took the form of what has come to be called 'logical atomism'.[6] Propositional assertions were to be reduced to their elementary constituents, or logical atoms, which were thought to correspond to absolutely simple observational facts. In most forms of the theory the basic facts were taken to be 'atoms of experience', and these were assimilated to the sense-data of empiricist epistemology. From the logical atoms, which described the simple facts, more complex propositions could be constructed using the apparatus of elementary formal logic alone. The heart of this system was the idea that the very meaning of a proposition could be expressed in the form of elementary statements, its truth conditions. This was the origin of the verification principle. By reducing complex concepts to simple logical functions of simple concepts, related to unambiguous experimental operations, science, it was thought, could be built upon a solid foundation of indisputable facts.

These three conceptions, the mechanistic model of man, a Humean and externalistic idea of cause, and science conceived in the logical positivist form, are, we believe, still the unconsidered foundation of a very great deal of modern psychology, particularly at the experimental level. They are so deeply rooted in the thinking of the majority of psychologists that it is if we were wearing blinkers, or moving about in a two dimensional world. Let us go a little further to show just how much a part of psychology these assumptions are, before we remove the blinkers, open a new dimension, and take psychology, at least on its social side, out into the light of day.

It is easy to see how adherence to these three conceptions leads to an emphasis upon the laboratory 'experiment' as the prime source of scientific data. It is in the laboratory that events can be produced by arrangement in simple, correlated pairs. It is there that operations can be performed which would verify the causal link between an antecedent and a consequent event, conceived as a mere regularity of sequence. It is easy to see how these ideas restrict the form of experiments in a particular way. We get the most vivid picture of this psychology if we examine the earlier days of behaviourism, say from about nineteen twenty to nineteen fortyfive, the years from John B. Watson's day[7] to that of Clark L. Hull.[8] In this period the three themes that we have identified as still lying at the base of much psychological work were stated explicitly. Behaviour was ideally defined in terms of a series of movements that could be easily observed. Laboratory situations were created in as schematized a form as possible. Fragments of behaviour, torn from their larger context in everyday life, became the focus of study. People's actions were, and indeed in distressingly many laboratories still are, restricted to the pushing or pulling of buttons, or to the saying of *yes* or *no*, *larger* or *smaller*, 'I like it less' or 'I like it more'. It was assumed that complex behaviour is made up, in some fairly simple way, of various, independent, simpler behaviours, and that if we dealt with the most elemental movements, we could be more objective, more certain and more scientific. Eventually we could build upon a gradually acquired and certified knowledge of Humean regularities, to develop a science of more complex behaviour. The study of animal behaviour, under carefully contrived laboratory conditions was preferred to the study of human life, on the grounds that the procedure was simpler and more manageable, and produced more surely the certified knowledge of the basic elements out of which all behaviour was assumed to be composed.

Despite the pervasive influence of these ideas in laboratory psychology to this day, there have been some voices of dissent and some loosening of views. Sigmund Koch, commenting on the first three volumes of the series, *Psychology, A study of a science*,[9] finds striking agreements on the following points:

1. That psychology has moved from a period of optimism, where investigators were confident that formal theory construction linked with definitional experiments and operational methods would rapidly and surely build a substantial science of psychology, to the view that the path to an adequate science was tenuous at many points, and that many turns must be taken before it would lead to even modestly adequate theory.

2. That the 'intervening variable' and the stimulus-response paradigms are illusory as means towards the objectivity required for an adequate behavioural science.

3. That the generality of knowledge gained from studies of animals and from studies confined within the narrow context of the laboratory, is severely limited.

Despite this consensus of opinion there can be little doubt that in the practice of psychological enquiry the early views still have a dominating influence. Perhaps the most popular form of the point of view we repudiate, even today, judged by number of adherents, is the 'radical behaviourism' of B. F. Skinner.[10] Though he eschews the official tenets of logical positivism Skinner embraces more tightly than anyone the other two ideas that make up the basis of modern psychology, the mechanistic model of human action, and the Humean conception of cause. His subscription to a mechanistic conception and to Humean notions of cause restricted to external stimuli are revealed in the ubiquity of the concept of *controlling variable* in his psychology. Skinnerians repeatedly emphasize his view that behaviour, including the verbal behaviour of a scientist, is under the control of variables which are primarily environmental. The only important function for a scientist, for the Skinnerian, is to make observations that further his knowledge of the concommitances between behaviour and controlling variables, that is which control the emission by the scientist of 'verbal behaviours' which sound like the statement of laws of concommitance between controlling environmental variables and behaviours. Unfortunately the theory is shot through with almost intolerable vagueness, and it is, in our experience, impossible to find out what is meant by the statement that behaviour is *under the control of environmental variables*, nor, indeed, is it at all clear what 'environmental variables' are. Skinnerians give us such examples as the lever-pressing rat, or the spot-pecking pigeon, but since they do not explain what they mean by the concept of 'control' we are unable to see how to apply it sensibly to other situations, particularly those in which human beings are involved, and where understanding and other higher order powers are involved.[11]

Even social psychology, with its avowed interest in *social* behaviour, has not freed itself from the pervasive influence of these conceptions. Social behaviour is meaningful behaviour. It involves an agent with certain intentions and expectations, an agent capable of deliberating and choosing from a variety of courses of action, and whose words and actions are understood by his fellows. A central part of this whole process is communication between people. But much social psychological research is framed in terms of concepts that do not recognize these properties and powers of an agent, and communication in much laboratory work is restricted to little more than mere stimuli. Little effort is expended in any direct examination of processes that arise from the status of the subject as an agent, or from the central fact of human social life, the mediation of all human action and interaction by language.

For example, in research on attitude change suggested by the concept of cognitive dissonance, the experimenter creates a laboratory situation that he believes will arouse dissonance in the participants which, if present, will have certain behavioural consequences.

The experimenter focusses upon his manipulative situation and the ensuing behaviour with little attention to the intervening *process* of the creation of dissonance and its ramifications as it occurs in a particular person. The experimenter treats the experimental paradigm as if its operations represent the concepts themselves. *Dissonance* remains unanalysed. And in the absence of a clear account of what dissonance *is,* there can be no set of precise rules that a scientist can use for generating a series of dissonance-inducing experiments. Without such rules he can not tell whether his experiment has succeeded or failed. The statement that 'dissonance occurs when the obverse of one cognitive element follows from another' is singularly uninformative, as the ambiguity of the words 'obverse' and 'follows' in this context vividly shows. In Festinger's original monograph on the topic,[12] this statement is fleshed out mainly through example, rather than by careful conceptual analysis. The multitude of investigations that have been carried out since then have provided us with further examples in the form of a variety of experimental operations. But the conceptual work remains to be carried out. What constitutes a 'cognitive element' is not at all clear, and what it means for 'the obverse of one cognitive element to *follow from* another' is still unspecified.

We might well ask how experimenters do proceed in the face of such ambiguities. What they in fact do is to fill in the conceptual gap by inventing experimental operations through the use of their *common sense.* But since the conceptual leap from the theory to the operation is accomplished through the scientist's intuition, the results of such experiments necessarily have an uncertain, and indeed controversial interpretation.

In a more general sense, what many psychologists and some other behavioural scientists are doing is overemphasizing empiricism at the expense of conceptualization, or fact at the expense of ideas. They are acting as if observation and experiment *by themselves* can create a science. This misplaced emphasis stems from an approach to science via logical positivism, with its stress on operational definition and its relegation of theory to a merely organizational role. But the fact is that operations can never be a *substitute* for the concepts to which they are related. They can relate to them only in some specified fashion that leaves the one conceptually independent of the other. Operations may define the measure of a certain property, or they may identify the effect of a certain cause and so on. Clear accounts of the concepts themselves are needed, along with precise statements of the relation of the properties and states described by such concepts as dissonance to the phenomena which can be observed, and which 'operations' are designed to detect or measure.

We turn now to a preliminary discussion of a more adequate model of man, and of the mode of genesis of his actions, to be elaborated throughout this book. We are particularly indebted to T. Mischel[13] for making us aware how the philosophy of Kant can be seen as providing a model quite different from the mechanical conceptions in vogue of late. Apparently Kant anticipated some of the central points in current thinking on the philosophy of action, points that we particularly wish to emphasize.

For Kant, perception and thought are to be construed as activities we perform, rather than responses produced in us. To describe experience as the passive reception of sensory inputs is, on the Kantian view, to misdescribe it, because seeing something is constructing a spatio-temporal object from the inputs on the basis of rules. Neither experience nor thought can be understood as things that happen to us, but only as things that we do, because they are synthetic activities that involve construction according to a rule. But most importantly, Kant insisted that we must distinguish between the different 'standpoints' from which agents and spectators view behaviour. Each standpoint involves a different system of concepts. From the standpoint of the actor or agent who consciously controls his performance, desires, emotions or passions are not linked to behaviour like blind mechanical pushes, but are factors in determining what the agent takes himself to be doing. Kant argued that human beings have interests which they can state in rules and plans, and they act from the conception of a rule, and do not consider themselves to be blindly pushed. Actions are mediated by meanings, that is by considerations that arise from an understanding of the connections that actions have with one another, and with their consequences in complex patterns of social life.[14]

Kant acknowledged that bodily acts that involve movements can be explained in terms of the causal theories of physics and physiology. But as Mischel makes clear, he implied that if we consider people as agents, then we must connect their social behaviour to a network of concepts appropriate to the description of self-controlled actions in a world of agents who have interests and who follow rules and plans in their dealings with other agents. So, what we see in social reality, is not, for example, an arm moving upwards, but a man trying to attract attention, a man greeting a friend, and so on. When we see an action of a certain sort we thus connect what we see with a conceptual context utterly different from that involved in seeing movements, and this context determines the form of explanation that is appropriate.

We might also note that Kant thought that psychology could never be a natural science, in the sense of a description of the behaviour of bodies passively subject to external influences. While psychology could engage in the empirical study of the systematic order underlying human actions, this will not result in the kind of causal account that we are familiar with in physics and physiology. In this respect, perhaps, Kant made the same mistake that modern psychologists have made in identifying natural science with the paradigm of mechanics. Modern philosophers of science think of this model as far too simple to serve as an ideal form for all kinds of scientific enquiry. Scientists are not limited to the methods of mechanics, nor to mechanical models for their store of concepts and ideas of causal connections; in fact there is some question as to whether they are particularly apt in any science. Indeed it was Kant himself who introduced some of the most important, non-mechanical ideas into physics.[15] It might well be that psychology would be better modelled after some of the aspects of quantum physics, or geology, or meteorology, rather than mechanics. All of these sciences appear to provide models which could be a source of concepts that might better serve as the origin of more appropriate notions of human action, for the description and explanation of social behaviour.

What then is the model of human action suggested by Kant, and elaborated by such contemporary philosophers as R. S. Peters (*op. cit.*), A. I. Melden (*op. cit.*), Richard Taylor,[16] Charles Taylor,[17]

T. Mischel (*op. cit.*), A. R. Louch,[19] G. E. M. Anscombe,[19] S. Hampshire,[20] D. S. Shwayder[21] and others? No one denies that we may not occasionally make use of the mechanistic framework—this is appropriate when things happen *to* a person, which are not part of his ongoing, self-determined pattern of actions. He may make a slip of the tongue. He may accidentally drop a valuable vase, or inadvertently press the red button. But much of human behaviour, according to these philosophers, does not have the character of things happening to a person. Instead it consists of things that people have made happen for various reasons. A person is an active agent in much of his social life. He is, if you like, the efficient cause of his own actions. He monitors his performances and controls the manner in which he presents himself to others. He takes care of the meaning of his acts.

Action of this kind has significance and *meaning*, and it occurs in a *social* and not a physiological context. It is inextricably bound up with the nature and limits of language and with the fabric of society. There is no way of reducing action to movement, and so of setting it within a physiological context. To try to do so is to transform what was action into something else. Compare the following pairs of statements:

1a. His arm extended straight out through the car window.

1b. He signalled a left turn.

2a. Her arm moved rapidly forward and made contact with his face.

2b. She slapped him angrily.

These examples, though trivial in themselves, make clear that when we describe actions in terms of movements, we lose the real significance of the action as a part of human social life. The legacy of behaviourism is such that those of us who are social psychologists have too often failed to focus on human action in devising experimental studies and empirical investigations, and concentrated instead on the sounds or movements which are merely the vehicles of action. Too often, in consequence, our laboratory operations have had only the most tenuous relation to human action outside the laboratory. We shall be developing this point in several ways in later chapters.

The adoption of the concept of action, rather than movement, as the basic empirical concept, carries with it another idea that is very important in the search for appropriate forms of explanation for social phenomena. This is the idea that a person often does things *for a reason*. Suppose a person is seen to cross the street, enter a building and come back shortly thereafter. If he is asked why he performed the action, that is if an account is required of him, he may reply with a *reason*, for example that he went to buy a packet of cigarettes. In this case he could be said to tell us what his plan had been. In many contexts, a man's action is *adequately* explained by references to his reason or reasons for doing it. And this may direct us to quite a different structuring of reality from that revealed by the application of the concept of cause, in its mechanistic signification. It directs us to consider such items as the plan according to which the man acted, or the impression he was trying to create and so on.

In effect, the philosophers we referred to above are recommending a consideration of the kind of explanation of behaviour that is familiar to us as laymen, and that is naturally couched in the subtle and expressive medium of ordinary language. It is an explanation of action that is intentional and purposive. Actions are explained in terms of the ends for which they are performed. Objections to teleological forms of explanation that had once been considered definitive have been re-examined by philosophers and found to be neither as sound nor as final as they once seemed to be. This point of view also implies that the behaviourist programme of reducing complex actions to simple, independent behavioural elements, capable of independent explanation, is impossible, since psychologists would then be studying something quite different from the social life of human beings. It is complex and deliberate actions, unified through their contributions to the meaning of the total act, that constitute the true subject matter of human social behaviour.

Our view of man, which we elaborate still further as our investigation develops, may be summarized as follows:

1. A man is capable of initiating action, action that may take place only after deliberation and with a more or less clear end in view. The whole of the action sequence may be anticipated in a more or less clearly formulated plan.

2. Most human actions cannot be, and many need not be traced to antecedent events linked to the actions in a regular, chain-like fashion in order to be explained in a satisfactory manner. An explanation is not unscientific because it makes reference to such items as plans and rules, or because it assumes the social actor to be one who deliberately follows them.

3. Action cannot be described reductively in terms of movements which are the vehicles for action, without losing its character and meaning. Human action is by nature psychological, and it cannot be reduced to physiology or physics, or even to simply observed behavioural elements without destroying it.

The consequences of failing to adopt this point of view, and the new directions it suggests for research will be brought out in the discussion of psychological experiments in the next chapter.

Before leaving this topic some comments on the place of sociology with respect to the views contrasted in this chapter are in order. A great number of sociologists, particularly those who emphasize methodological 'rigour', quantitative methods and sometimes laboratory experimentation, subscribe to the same inadequate doctrines as the psychologists we have been criticizing. But sociology, like psychology, has many points of view and approaches. Another important group is the sociological theorists. By and large their work is too far removed from individual behaviour and indeed from any sort of empirical data to have much relation to our purposes.

Quite distinct from both of these groups of sociologists are the symbolic interactionists, who follow the tradition stemming from George Herbert Mead.[22] Sociologists of this persuasion will undoubtedly be highly sympathetic to the position taken in this chapter. The position is, in a general way, very close to their own, and in some ways represents the application of some of their concepts to the field of problems traditionally the province of social psychology. However, the symbolic interactionists have, in general not yet developed a really adequate and unified conceptual system for carrying out research from their point of view, nor have they perceived, for the most part, the connections that their ideas have with developments in the apparently remote and esoteric field of philosophical psychology. Much of the writing of symbolic interactionists,

D

though by no means all,[23] simply reiterates their basic viewpoint, and does not get on with the difficult task of developing more elaborate conceptualizations to be tested by detailed empirical study. The present book attempts to carry the more adequate conceptualization a step further, and points the way toward specific empirical research consistent with it.

Finally, anthropology bears on the present enterprise in only a tangential way. For the most part, social anthropologists are concerned with identifying and describing culture wide patterns in various societies, leaving the relation of the behaviour of individuals to such patterns to other behavioural scientists. Nevertheless the general standpoint of 'structuralism' has more than a little in common with the point of view we develop in this book.[24]

REFERENCES

1. R. B. Zajonc and Nieuwenhuyse B., 'Relationship between Word Frequency and Recognition', *J. Exp. Psych.*, 67 (1964), pp. 276–285.

2. D. E. Berlyne, *Structure and Direction in Thinking*, Wiley, New York, 1965, Ch. 1.

3. D. Hume, *An Enquiry Concerning Human Understanding*, London, 1777, §§ 48–81.

4. A. I. Melden, *Free Action*, Routledge and Kegan Paul, London, 1961, pp. 4–5.

5. cf. A. J. Ayer (editor), *Logical Positivism*, Free Press, Glencoe, Ill., 1959.

6. J. O. Urmson, *Philosophical Analysis*, Oxford University Press, Oxford, 1956, Part I and II.

7. J. B. Watson, *Psychology from the Standpoint of a Behaviorist*, Lippincott, Philadelphia, 1924, pp. 26–8, 38–42.

8. C. L. Hull, *Principles of Behavior*, Appleton-Century, New York, 1943, pp. 16–31.

9. S. Koch, *Psychology: The Study of a Science*, McGraw-Hill, New York, 1959, Vol. I, Ch. 1.

10. B. F. Skinner, *Science and Human Behaviour*, Free Press, New York, 1953.

11. cf. N. Chomsky's review of Skinner's *Verbal Behavior*, in J. A.

Fodor and J. J. Katz, (editors), *The Structure of Language*, Prentice-Hall, New Jersey, 1965, pp. 547–78.

12. L. Festinger, *A Theory of Cognitive Dissonance*, Harper and Row, Evenston and New York, 1957.
13. T. Mischel, (editor) *Human Action*, Academic Press, New York, 1969, Ch. I.
14. I. Kant, *Anthropology from a Pragmatic Point of View*, 1798.
15. I. Kant, *The Metaphysical Foundations of Natural Science*, translated J. Ellington, Bobbs-Merrill, New York, 1970.
16. R. Taylor, *Action and Purpose*, Prentice-Hall, New Jersey, 1966.
17. C. Taylor, *The Explanation of Behaviour*, Routledge and Kegan Paul, London, 1964.
18. A. R. Louch, *Explanation and Human Action*, Blackwell, Oxford, 1966.
19. G. E. M. Anscombe, *Intentions*, Cornell University Press, Ithaca, 1966.
20. S. Hampshire, *Thought and Action*, Chatto and Windus, 1965.
21. D. S. Shwayder, *The Stratification of Behaviour*, Routledge and Kegan Paul, London, 1965.
22. G. H. Mead, *Mind, Self and Society*, Chicago University Press, 1934.
23. E. Goffman, *Behavior in Public Places*, Free Press, Glencoe, Ill., 1963.
24. C. Lévi-Strauss, *Structural Anthropology*, Allen Lane, The Penguin Press, London, 1968.

CHAPTER THREE

Experimentation in Psychology

THE ARGUMENT

Loss of Verisimilitude due to Manipulative Restrictions

1. The experimental set-up destroys the possibility of the study of the very features which are essential to social behaviour in its natural setting.

2. This can be illustrated from another field, from the revolutionary studies in perception by J. J. Gibson.

    a. The traditional perception experiment required

        (i) a physically restrained person,

        (ii) that his attention be directed wholly to simple sensations, out of which, it was assumed, perceptions are built.

    b. Gibson showed

        (i) that simple sensations have little to do with how the world is actually perceived,

        (ii) perception is actually achieved by the apprehension of invariants in the environment through a process of active exploration.

3. Analogous restrictions appear in social psychological studies of personality judgement where the 'stimulus' person is presented in terms of absurdly limited information, such as bodily silhouette, or a few attitude statements purported to be his, and where the perceiver is severely restricted in the form of judgement he may make.

4. Common to all types of overly-restrictive experiments is the conception of people as information-*processing* machines, rather than information-seeking and information-generating agents. Thus information is deliberately restricted, and *inter*-action prevented.

But in judging personality in life situations, as in perception of the world of things, social exploration to discover or invent bases underlying the judgements is required.

Loss of Verisimilitude due to Conceptual Naïvety

1. Empirical Concepts: psychological reactance experiments are vitiated as possible bases for generalizing to real social life by failure to appreciate the immense complexity of the concepts involved, particularly in these experiments, the concept of free action.

2. Theoretical concepts: Dissonance studies also suffer from confusion and lack of clarity on the theoretical side.

a. The central theoretical concept, 'dissonance', oscillates in meaning between a feeling and a logical relation.

b. It seems that careful examination of the procedures used shows that in some cases the laboratory situation itself contains social factors of sufficient strength to produce the results of apparent 'forced compliance'.

Critique of the Analogy between Human Characteristics and the Variables and Parameters of Physical Science

1. Random assignment of people to treatments in effect relegates important person parameters to the category of the unknown, guaranteeing that the experimental results, even when positive, will be incomplete, and sometimes trivial or banal.

2. There are two senses of the word 'variable' with different logics.

a. that used when people are manipulated to experience differing amounts of some characteristic or state, e.g. anxiety;

b. that used when each person in a class has an attribute at a different level, but different people have the attribute in differing amounts, strengths or levels, e.g. intelligence.

Note. It is in sense (a) that the concept is used in physics, and upon which the logic of the classical experimental method rests,

while it is in sense (b) that a good many crucial human characteristics are variables, though there are some which are variables in
sense (a).

The relative importance of (b)-type characteristics compared
with the relative unimportance of (a)-type characteristics in generating readiness to social behaviour guarantees that much experimental
work issues only in banalities.

      c. The reduction of person-parameters to zero can vitiate a
whole field of experiment. For example, learning studies which
eliminate idiosyncratic methods of learning, effectively eliminate *all*
methods of learning which occur outside the learning laboratory.

The Psychological Laboratory as a Special Kind of Society

    1. Consequential difficulties:

      a. Participants in experiments try to fulfill the experimenter's
hypotheses, however cleverly he tries to conceal them.

      b. It has been established that experimenters subtly suggest
to participants how to behave (and by calling them 'subjects', delude
themselves into thinking that they are not taking part in the experiment as intelligent agents).

    2. Attempted solutions:

      a. Attempts to eliminate these difficulties by eliminating
experimenters or replacing them by machines must fail, since people
react differently to machines and to people.

      b. The stimulus conditions cannot be neatly correlated with
the behavioural results, but must be extended to include the participant and the experimenter and their views of what is going on, as
integral and idiosyncratic elements in each 'experiment'.

The Psychological Experiment as an Interaction between Strangers

    1. The general form of such interaction:
      a. Names are not known.
      b. Interactions fall into two classes.

      (i) Non-verbal interactions, which may be quite elaborate.

      (ii) Verbal Interactions.

2. Verbal Interactions:

    a. These often take the form of rituals.

      (i) This is possible when there are clear role definitions.

      (ii) This is necessary for the protection of honour and the concealment of self.

    b. Non-ritualistic interactions open up time perspectives through monitored disclosures of biographies and plans, and often take place within a game framework.

3. Interactions between strangers do not usually lead to permanent social relations. This permits

    a. deliberate falsification of biographies in self-presentation,

    b. inadvertent falsifications of biographies which are not worth correcting.

4. The formal character of much stranger interaction is probably the most important point for the critique of the experiment, in that in this mode of interaction selves are protected, or over-exposed. It is easy to see how this can affect the results of 'forced compliance' experiments, for instance.

Earlier we asserted that adopting a mechanical model of man, a Humean and externalistic view of cause, and logical positivism as a method had a profound influence on the way in which experimentation is carried out. The present chapter provides some documentation for this assertion. The most general effect of these conceptions is to introduce constraints that distort the phenomena being studied and that block out considerations that play a vital part in a naturalistic situation.

The Limitation of Information and the Inhibition of Natural Forms of Response

Experimental constraints take many forms, so many, indeed, that the concept has an open texture and can scarcely be defined.

However the following points are obvious and crucial. The amount of information provided the person may be severely restricted. The physical structure of the experiment may make certain responses impossible. The psychological structure of the experiment may inhibit certain responses and encourage others. In fact, the very capacities to behave in various ways may be created or abrogated by the laboratory situation.

The brilliant work of Gibson[1] on perception provides an excellent illustration of how certain experimental constraints operated for almost a hundred years to blind us to the true character of perception and its relation to sensation. This has occurred in apparently objective psychophysical experiments, because the person has been restricted to the role of a passive observer. Normally his head is held in a fixed position by apparatus, and he is asked to focus upon a fixed point in the visual field. Psychophysical investigations focus upon such simple stimulus variables as intensity, area or volume, and frequency. These can be neatly varied and correlated with sensory experiences as long as the person is assigned a passive role.

This research emphasis has led psychologists to conceive of perception as a complex process of interpretation in which simple sensations provide the basic information for the perceptual process. But Gibson has shown clearly that the kinds of sensations that a person experiences in psychophysical experiments have little to do with how he perceives the world outside the laboratory. When in his experiments, Gibson placed his subjects in an active exploratory role, he found that the crucial explanation of how we perceive lies in apprehending the invariances in our environment through *active exploration*. This activity, which has always been eliminated from psychophysical experiments by rigorous controls, allows the person to respond to higher order variables in the environment that provide the true basis for the kinds of perceptual experience that occur outside of the laboratory. If Gibson's view is correct, then no amount of experimentation in the framework of psychophysics would enable us to explain everyday perceptual phenomena.

According to Gibson, the useful dimensions of perception are those that specify the environment and the observer's relation to the environment. Perhaps this is clearest in his studies of the sense of touch. What he shows is the variable and chaotic nature of sensation in contrast to the clarity and simple order in the environment. For example, when pressing a rigid object with a finger there is an increase and then a decrease of sensation, actually a flow of changing intensities. But the perception is of a constant rigidity of the surface. Furthermore, a person can discriminate correctly between two protuberant surfaces, one rigid and the other yielding, when he presses them, but not when they are pressed on the passive skin.

Or, when one lifts an object, the judgment of its weight is easier than when it is allowed simply to press downward against the supported resting hand. In active lifting, a whole set of additional inputs is involved, stemming from the receptors of the joints of the fingers, wrist, and arm. Instead of presenting itself as a kaleidoscope of sensory information, this complex input from a dozen body joints is apprehended by the person as simply the weight or mass of the object. The person is responding to higher order, sequential properties of the environment as he interacts with it. He responds to the mass of the object with only the vaguest (if any) awareness of the complex set of sensations that theoretically occur.

The unhappy consequences of unconsidered psychophysical constraints for our knowledge of perception are not an isolated example. We have an analogous but largely unrecognized problem in many other areas of experimental research and even in the last place where it might be expected—social psychology! Because we social psychologists were also trained in a relatively narrow, behaviouristic tradition, many of the experiments we conduct have meaning only in a kind of never-never land of behaviour that is forever inapplicable to behaviour outside the laboratory, except in the most limited sense. In part this is true because of the manner in which the experimenter structures the behaviour of the person serving as a subject through the assumption that behaviour is a complex of simple behaviours. If we abandon the basic theoretical assumptions of behaviourist psychology, this prescription of the form of experiments is no longer tenable. This is why we must pay strict attention to the meaning of laboratory experiments and their relevance to ordinary behaviour. We must discover the strategy for making empirical studies and for designing experiments that permit the person to behave as he would outside the laboratory under similar conditions. For many areas of social behaviour we may even need to abandon the laboratory for the actual world.

In the typical psychophysical experiment, the person plays the part of an information-processing machine. The judgmental aspect of his behaviour is emphasized, and those other aspects of the perceptual process that operate in non-laboratory situations, such as exploration, are excluded. Such defects are not limited to psychophysical experiments. At the 1967 convention of the Western Psychological Association, a study was presented on judging personality from body-type silhouettes. The human figure was presented in silhouette form ranging from very fat through athletic to very lean, and the people serving in the study were asked to arrange the figures on various personality traits such as lazy, religious, and so on. Naturally the judges were able to carry out this task with considerable agreement. The fat types were lazy; athletic types were energetic. The thin ones were the most religious. The outcome of the experiment was predicted quite successfully by the experimenter, because he, too, was able to examine how he might process the same restricted information.

In this experiment and in many others, the information provided (body silhouettes only) is so limited that there is virtually only one way that the person can process it—a way that fits the hypothesis. Such experiments tell us little that we did not know in advance of the experiment. Such trivial experiments can be made more meaningful by providing more complex information so that the person has a choice of several alternative means of processing it. The treatment of a person as an information-processing machine does not necessary condemn our experiment as trivial. This will depend upon the degree to which the simplifying procedure falsifies the actual process. The role of silhouettes in forming ideas about another person has to be considered in relation to the real situation in a social context to answer this question.

The misuse of the information-processing model applies to many other studies in psychology. As one more illustrative case, we refer to a programme of published research on the relation between liking for a person and the amount of similarity between the liker and the person he is judging.[2]

The dominant experimental paradigm that runs through most of this research on interpersonal attraction and similarity is as follows: the person is asked to read a set of attitude items representing the responses of a hypothetical stranger, and to make a judgment about probable liking of him and probable enjoyment of working with him, as well as a variety of other attributes. For different hypothetical stimulus persons, the proportion of attitude statements congruent with the individual's own attitudes is varied. Byrne and his colleagues find that the larger the proportion of similar attitudes depicted as belonging to the hypothetical stranger, the greater the interpersonal attraction of the individual toward him, as deduced by them from the answers to another questionnaire.

In this paradigm, the judge is given extremely limited information, supposedly about another person, and asked to make quantitative ratings of his potential attraction to that person. He cannot act as would one person toward another outside the laboratory, for two main reasons. First, he is deprived of the rich input we normally receive concerning another person—the only information he has is a set of attitude statements and he is not, in fact, in contact with another person at all. Second, he cannot react with warmth and friendliness as he would in a face-to-face situation, but is limited to choosing a point on a quantitative scale of attraction from which, of course, no rewarding or discouraging feedback can be expected. Moreover, the context of judgment is one in which the experimenter specifically tells the person that the purpose of the experiment is to see how accurate he can be in making such judgments.

Placed in a situation like this, most people, but by no means all, indicate greater attraction toward the more similar stranger. Using mean ratings, a roughly linear relation is found. However, some individuals do not process the information in this way. Apparently some show that there is little relation for them between similarity and attraction, and others show a reverse relation.

What is glaringly wrong here is the contrast between the laboratory situation, in which the action of the participants is confined to a series of dispassionate judgments based upon written descriptions, and the face-to-face situation where a person reacts to another person with warmth and friendliness and a feeling of spontaneous liking which may be encouraged or inhibited by the meaning the other person's responses have for him. The dissimilarity between the life situation and the laboratory situation is so marked that the laboratory experiment really tells us *nothing* about the genesis of liking and friendship among real people.

Disparity between the concepts appropriate to natural situations and those defining the laboratory situation

A further aspect of the problem of generalizing from laboratory experiments to real life may be taken from the series of experiments on *psychological reactance* by Brehm.[3] 'Psychological reactance' is the name given to an effect that occurs when a person or a situation imposes some restrictions upon another individual's choices. The individual experiences an increased motivation to carry out the behaviour that is forbidden. Parents will immediately recognize this phenomenon. The mere banning of some activities is often sufficient to ensure that a child will engage in them.

The problem that we find with this line of research is the failure to make any careful analysis of the concept of psychological reactance, in particular as it is to be applied in naturally occurring situations. Instead, like any well-trained experimenter who has digested or absorbed in some way the themes of logical positivism, Humean causation, and a mechanistic model of man, Brehm *begins* by setting up a series of experiments. Participants are told that they are free to do certain things, and this freedom is later restrained or threatened. Increased motivation to carry out the restricted actions is tested for. Because the experiments involve explicit operations, the confirmation of the hypothesis is considered to validate the concept of psychological reactance, and the operations to clarify its meaning. But what has actually happened is that 'reactance' has been studied only in the very restricted form tacitly defined by the 'experiments'. *That* throws virtually no light on reactance outside the laboratory, that is bloody minded behaviour as it is known to parents, or the more general psychological phenomenon which is the theme of the proverb that the other man's grass is always greener etc.

A key problem in getting to grips with the variety of real life 'reactance' situations is the specification and application of the concept of free behaviour. This is done in a prescribed way in the experiment, and the concept defined by fiat, but outside the laboratory, it is not at all clear what it means for behaviour to be free, for behaviour to be restricted, and whether these concepts form an exclusive disjunction. Austin's analysis of the concept of voluntary action shows that the conceptual complexity in this area is very great.[4] What kind of behaviour is a person ordinarily free to engage in? Is he bound by social convention? Is he bound by his own standards? What structural constraints exist outside the laboratory? If other agents constrain his behaviour in any way, which of these create reactance and which do not? Brehm's experiments, like so many others, modelled after logical positivistic tenets, do not answer any of these questions.

As we noted in Chapter One, the popular dissonance theory experiments suffer from some of the same limitations. Like Brehm, dissonance theorists are attempting to introduce cognitive elements into the explanation of behaviour. But because of the constraints exerted by the tacit mechanistic paradigm, this move toward mentalism is handled gingerly indeed.

All of the proponents of dissonance theory try manfully to stay at the operational level. Scarcely a single study by any of the major dissonance experimenters appears in which they attempt to measure or ascertain the presence of dissonance in an experiential or phenomenological sense, that is as something a person might *feel*! They set up situations that should create dissonance, they deduce what changes would occur if dissonance were present, and they ascertain whether these changes do in fact occur. More than 200 studies of this kind have been carried out; an enormous investment of time and energy.

But the fruits of such work are more meagre than they need be, because the paradigm is mechanical and operational. In spite of the recent publication of the 900-page book, *Consistency Theory*,[5] much of which is devoted to so-called theoretical discussion of dissonance theory, no single writer or combination of writers have given sufficient specification to the theory, even on such an elementary matter as whether dissonance is a feeling or a logical relation, so that we can move from the idea of dissonance between two cognitive elements (a logical notion) to an experimental situation or a non-laboratory situation where we can say with any surety that dissonance (an emotion or feeling) will be aroused, and that it will have certain effects. Indeed we have no clear criteria for telling when a state of dissonance exists.

This state of affairs obtains because psychologists, by and large, still believe that the way to clarify concepts is to invent experimental operations and to do experiments. They overlook the fact that such procedures, if they are to be used at all, have still to be linked up with social situations outside the laboratory, situations that are described by the subtle and enormously refined terms and concepts of ordinary language. In the present state of dissonance theory, to do an actual experiment, one has to take a giant conceptual leap from the formal idea of two elements in a dissonant relation to some concrete situation which is employed in the experiment. There is little theory to guide us.

These theoretical problems have gradually come to light through the experimental work and subsequent analysis conducted by experimenters in this field. An outstanding example is the now-classical, early experiment on dissonance theory conducted by Festinger and Carlsmith.[6] Participants in the experiment were induced to tell the next participant (actually an accomplice of the experimenter) that the dull, boring task they had just completed was interesting, exciting, fun, and enjoyable. Those engaging in this attitude-discrepant behaviour for a small payment had fewer cognitions consonant with their behaviour than those receiving a large reward, and thus were expected to reduce this dissonance by changing their attitude toward the task in the direction of the behaviour. Thus, we have a situation where the smaller the incentive to engage in attitude-discrepant behaviour, the greater the attitude change in the direction of one's behaviour. Some subsequent experiments produced comparable results. Other investigators,[7] however, found just the opposite, obtaining an amount of attitude change directly proportional to the payments received.

This impasse led both to further experimental work and to more theoretical analysis of the meanings of these various experimental situations. For example, Carlsmith, Collins, and Helmreich[8] point out that in the original Festinger and Carlsmith experiment, the participant was asked to make a *public* statement which conflicted with his private belief, and furthermore, that the person to whom he made this statement was unaware that this conflicted with the private belief. But in one experiment obtaining opposite results, the participant was asked to write an essay in favour of a position he did not agree with. He was assured that it would be anonymous, and that only the experimenter (who knew that it did not express a private belief) would read it. They argue that the latter task may create no dissonance—the participant is co-operating for good reasons, clear to himself and the experimenter. Role play participants engaged in a face-to-face deception; essay writers carried out an intellectual task involving no deception. An analysis by Rosenberg[9] emphasizes the possibility that experimental situations such as the original Festinger and Carlsmith study induce anxious concern in the participant that his performance is being evaluated, and that the more he is paid, the greater his suspicion and concern, thus, the less his attitude change. Participants may assign any of a variety of meanings to these experimental situations, meanings that would presumably produce different amounts of dissonance and lead to different relations between the incentives offered and the amount of attitude change. This suggests not only that laboratory investigators must take into account the participant's interpretation of the experimental situation, but also that they must specifically work with theory that provides a place for the meanings that participants attach to experimental situations.

Variables, Parameters and Causal Mechanisms

In the most common form of experimental design, the independent variable is established by setting up levels of treatment, with people being assigned at random to the several levels. The object is to compare the several experimental groups with respect to the dependent variable, which is some form of behaviour of the people in the various groups. We are not concerned here with the problems arising in this procedure which have been competently treated elsewhere.[10] Instead, our objective is to point out certain logical and strategic limitations of this widely accepted method of doing psychological science.

In experiments conducted in the natural sciences, another class of operations other than the correlation of independent and dependent variables plays a vital part. These are operations involving parameters. These are factors that are held constant, factors that are *measured and specified*. For example, an experiment plotting the relation between the pressure and the volume of a gas might be conducted with temperature and every other possible relevant variable held constant. In this way the identity of all samples of gas is ensured, and so the inverse correlation of pressure and volume can be treated as a phenomena produced by the same causal mechanism, in every case. While this sometimes has an analogue in psychological experiments, in the latter there are certain important parameters which remain unknown. These are the parameters associated with the characteristics of a person. People are assigned at random to the various treatments. In this way it is thought that these unknown parameters are of no consequence, because they will have random effects on the dependent variable, from one treatment to another, random effects whose limits are known through the application of statistical theory. In this way, it is assumed, the same explanation of the behaviour can be assumed.

But there are circumstances under which this method of eliminating individual differences creates a serious problem, limiting the conclusions which might be drawn from an experiment. Most experiments produce only relatively small mean differences from one treatment level to another. Thus, while the general mean differences in the dependent variable relate in a systematic way to the treatments, only a minor proportion of the persons in each treatment group are clearly different on the dependent variable from those in another treatment group. The crucial limitation inherent in this state of affairs is that, since the person parameters are not identified, measured, or specified, those people in the treatment groups responsible for the positive outcome of the findings cannot be identified, other than nominally. This means that the experimental results yield a conclusion which is of value only in an actuarial sense, not a causal one. Having done an experiment on, say, the efficacy of two different drugs, and having obtained positive results, one might then say that one drug will work better than another in the sense that if it is given to a large number of patients, more will be helped than would be in the case for the other drug. But the experiment yields no information enabling the prediction of which persons will be helped by the drug, and who will not, and what the mechanism of action of the drug within the biochemistry of a person will be. That is statistical methods do not enable one to isolate genuinely causal relations.

The basic problem here is one of interaction between the levels of treatment and the unknown person parameters. Since the design makes no provision for assessing this interaction, the relation between the independent variable and dependent variable must be thought of as correlational rather than causal. For a causal statement to be made, we need to have some knowledge of the manner in which the experimental treatment leads the person to produce the behaviour observed. One of the minimal requirements for this knowledge is specification of the interaction between the independent variable and the relevant person parameters, i.e. we must have *some* idea of the causal mechanism at work, or, in the case of the social behaviour of people, of the meanings they perceive, of the plans they conceive, and of the reasons they have for their actions.

It might be argued that the carrying out of numerous experiments using different independent variables in relation to the same dependent variable would gradually yield results that could be added up to give us a comprehensive view of the causal factors producing a particular effect. But if all of the experiments have the structure described above, this does not follow. For each experiment contains unknown person parameters which are apt to interact with the independent variable to produce different effects. Since these parameters are unknown, we continue to have only correlational and not

E

causal information. Moreover, the assumption that the various independent variables would themselves be additive is gratuitous: the possibility of interaction among them must be assumed.

Another attempt to rebut this logic might lie in the argument that the independent variable of one experiment is the parameter of the next experiment. Now, this might certainly be true in some cases. But here we must recognize a fundamental difference between two uses of the term *variable*. The first and proper use of independent variable is found where persons can be manipulated so as to display varying amounts of an attribute, as where they are made to feel more confident or less confident through exposing them to a series of success or failure experiences. The other use of the term variable cannot appropriately be regarded as an independent variable; this pertains to those attributes which the individual possesses in some relatively fixed amount, such as intelligence, but which differ from person to person. It is these variables that constitute person parameters, and they are not dealt with in experiments.

One consequence of doing experimental work in which the person parameters are allowed to remain unknown would seem to be that the generalizations that are produced are apt to be banal—certainly of little use for understanding the behaviour of individuals. Those experiments that are replicable are the ones that will get published and that will receive the most attention. But the model guarantees that these findings will be banal or trivial, because the conditions have to be extremely general to hold across the idiosyncracy of persons. We end up not being able to say anything much about the conditions of social behaviour or about the behaviour of particular people in particular sets of conditions because most of specific social behaviour depends upon idiosyncratic features of people, such as their aims, beliefs and current emotional states. It is true that human beings have a certain degree of commonality in their physiological makeup, and even certain commonalities in their social experience. But only a small number of very specialized kinds of experiments can capitalize on this to yield useful generalizations. And when social behaviour is the object of study, the widely varying life experiences to which individuals have been exposed is simply too great to ignore. The theoretical solution to this problem would seem to be to develop a typology of individuals, so that experiments can admit individual variance as a part of the design.

This notion of person parameters allows us to obtain a somewhat clearer view of the effects of experimental constraints, discussed in the first part of this chapter. The effect of many types of experimental constraints is to *reduce the person parameters toward zero*. We previously illustrated this in connection with psychophysical experiments. Another example comes from the learning of nonsense syllables. Speaking of learning nonsense syllables through the use of associations, Woodworth and Schlosberg make the following statement:

'Such aids in memorizing are naturally regarded with much favour by O, but E would like to be rid of them. They make the learning task less uniform and introduce variability and unreliability into the quantitative results. Besides, E wants to study the formation of new associations, not O's clever utilization of old ones.'[11]

Miller, Galanter, and Pribram[12] point out that by arranging the experiment so as to eliminate these individual differences, the experimenter is changing the very character of the phenomenon he wishes to study—forcing it into a form that he finds more convenient, and thereby discovering nothing of how persons left to their own devices would learn a list of nonsense syllables. The apparent desirability of controlling person parameters is only an illusion; the most usual consequence is that the experimental relation studied has no counterpart outside of the laboratory. In the social world, the phenomena studied in the laboratory interact with numerous parameters, so that functional relationships are radically altered.

The Experiment as a Social Event

There is a subset of person parameters which deserve special comment because they have no counterpart in natural science. This set pertains to the participant's notions of what the experiment is about, and what his relation is to the experimenter. An interaction between any two people is guided by certain rules or expectations, and the laboratory situation is no exception to this principle. In any particular experiment, we have a radical alteration of the social structure and the rules of action that would prevail outside of the laboratory, and we have the invocation of some kind of social structure that characterizes the laboratory.

Surely the actions of participants in experiments are in part a function of this laboratory structure. To the extent that this is radically different from the social structure outside the laboratory in which similar behavioural phenomena occur, we are unlikely to discover anything that can be transferred to life situations. And surely we need to know how participants in an experiment construct and construe the social world of the laboratory, if we are to understand their behaviour and if we are to tie it up with the world outside the laboratory.

Some of the recent work on the social psychology of the experiment by Orne,[13] and Rosenthal,[14] is relevant here. Orne, for example, has shown that many experiments have what he calls *demand characteristics*. Acting as an agent, the participant perceives through various slight clues what behaviour is appropriate to the experimenter's hypothesis. And if he is motivated to co-operate, he helps the experimenter to get the right results. Rosenthal has attempted to demonstrate what he calls *experimenter bias*, by which he means that the experimenter, unbeknown to himself, subtly suggests to the participants that they should behave in a certain way.

But Rosenthal's solution to this problem is curious, and betrays an inappropriate model of human action. His solution is to eliminate the experimenter entirely, if possible, using tape-recorders, blind experimenter mechanical contraptions, and so on, to eliminate the human element from the investigative side. He fails to see that the participants, being human, are still going to construct certain meanings to provide themselves with a framework for interpreting the experiment, and that this construction of meaning is going to relate to the way in which they behave, and to the kind of personality they present.

We are reminded here of an experiment in which participants played a game with two kinds of opponents. One half of the participants were told they were playing the game with a computer, and the other half that they were playing the game with a person stationed in the next room. In both groups the moves made by the opponents were exactly the same. Yet the participants in the two groups used very different strategies and modes of play, depending on whether they thought they were playing with a person or with a computer. So a totally computerized experiment would itself provide a kind of experimenter bias that would prevent generalization to human interaction situations outside the laboratory. What leads psychologists into thinking that such an experimental situation would be desirable is clearly an unthinking assumption of the mechanistic model of man and Humean notions of causation.

A schematic model more adequate than the prevailing one might take the following form:

If $C_1, C_2, C_3 \ldots C_n$, then B by virtue of PxE.

In this model, C stands for conditions, including both physical and social ones, B stands for the ensuing behaviour, P stands for a set of person parameters, and E stands for a set of experimenter parameters. This model takes into account the nature of the person and his current state of mind and body, as well as the actions of the experimenter. Also included in the person parameters are the participant's views of the laboratory experiment. We cannot afford to continue thinking of the participant as an empty organism or a mechanical robot. We are going to have to investigate the phenomenology of people in experiments, and we cannot any longer think of the experimenter as a non-person. We are going to have to put the person back into experimental psychology.

While the logic of the experiment calls for a schematic model of the kind sketched above, its practical application is not an easy task. Specification of person parameters and person-experimenter interactions will require considerable conceptual and empirical work. We are not suggesting, for example, that conventional measures of personality would be fruitful for this model. On the contrary, as we shall see in more detail later, the dispositional or trait concept of personality fails to take account of the situational nature of human action. It may be necessary to develop a kind of typology of people in connection with each set of phenomena subjected to study. The central problem is to discover those person parameters that interact with a given set of phenomena. Obviously many person parameters will be irrelevant to particular phenomena and can safely be ignored, but others will have a vital significance.

Finally we would draw attention to the fact that the traditional psychological experiment, considered as a social interaction, is one of the kinds of interaction between strangers, and could be studied as an episode of that kind. It might well show certain important analogies with other situations in which strangers interact socially.

Let us begin by considering the general form of interactions between strangers. Typically they do not know each other's names. An *a priori* analysis of 'when strangers meet' yields the following possibilities of structure: The primary distinction will be between those interactions in which nothing is said, and those in which, to a greater or less extent, the medium of exchange is words. Non-verbal interactions may be very elaborate. One of the authors was entertained during a night-flight across the Atlantic by the interaction between a young man and a girl across the aisle. Convention decreed that while it was yet night no verbal interchange could take place, as being a good deal too intimate, yet by whistling complicated tunes and tapping with his fingers, the young man contrived to indicate his interest in music, while by studied indifference the girl was able to indicate her interest in the young man. When dawn broke they were at last released from the shackles of propriety and began to talk vehemently. We are happy to report that they left the plane together planning to share a taxi up to London.

A good many verbal interactions between strangers are constrained by highly developed rituals, as in many customer-salesman interactions, such as the rituals governing calls at service stations, purchases in a shop, paying conductors on buses and the like. In the cases just mentioned there is a clear role definition for each participant and that determines which ritual is performed. By adhering to the role definitions other aspects of the self are protected. Even when there are no clear role definitions interaction between strangers occurs under powerful conventions giving it a highly ritualistic character. Most, if not all cultures, have definite rituals by which this situation is handled. They have important features in common. These involve devices for the protection of honour, such as the elaborate methods embodied in Polynesian ritual, for finding out a stranger's name without asking him, and they have their informal counterparts in the West. They also involve devices for the regulation of the rate and degree of self-disclosure, and a general preparedness to go through a face-work ritual if one party oversteps the mark, revealing say, an embarrassing difference in social class. There is good reason to suppose that these devices come into operation automatically in psychological experiments, in that these have the social character of interactions between strangers calling for the following through of the appropriate ritual. Far from penetrating into the reality of social interactions psychological experiments which are deliberately restricted so as to be in fact interactions between strangers are practically guaranteed to lead to self-protecting rituals, which ensure only graduated and tentative self-disclosure.

This reasoning is supported by a series of experiments reported by Jourard, in which the experimenter varied the extent to which he disclosed information about himself, and obtained quite different results for differing amounts of disclosure.[15]

Any further interaction between strangers involves the opening up of time perspectives. The adjacent passengers may exchange biographies, thus opening perspectives into the past, or they may exchange plans, opening the future. Introducing new dimensions of interaction in this way can radically alter the nature of the interaction. It needs very little observation to notice that competitive, game elements make their appearance very early on in the developing situation, and biographies may be disclosed in a manner only intelligible from a game perspective. The authors have noticed this feature of psychological experiments when informally discussing their participation in experiments with people who have been 'subjects'.

A final, and indeed vital point concerns time perspectives. Interactions between strangers do not usually lead to permanent social relations. This fact has two important effects upon such interactions as those aboard planes. The first is that the authenticity of exchanged biographies is a matter of little importance. This has two different effects upon self-presentation. A biography may be deliberately falsified so as to present a more favourable picture, with the fairly certain knowledge that it will not be called into question, then or later. Much more common is the falsification that occurs through some early disclosure being misunderstood, and the subsequent effort to correct that misunderstanding being too bothersome to undertake. The fact the interactants will probably not meet again permits a degree of self-disclosure not generally risked by those who must allow for further social interaction with the people involved. Quite extraordinary degrees of intimacy are possible in these situations since they do not have to be paid for later, as it were. It is worth considering that both these features may be present in social psychological experiments. Whatever time perspectives are opened up in the course of the experiment may lack authenticity, and there may be degrees of self-disclosure unthinkable in apparently corresponding situations in real life.

From the point of view of the critique of the standard sort of experiment the formal character of interactions between strangers may be the most important feature of the experiment. In formal interactions the selves of the interactants are protected from each other, so if the scientist conceals himself behind a formal treatment of his 'subjects' they too will be protected by a complementary formal response. Consider, for example, the 'forced compliance' experiment, where P is asked to play a role which commits him to acting in accordance with opinions, which are not his own. If his response is to take a formal stand, it may well be that he is less committed to the attitude descrepant behaviour than he would be if he behaves in a less formal way, following the lead of a less formal complementary interactant, E. In the former case the dissonance aroused would be much less. This analysis of the character of interaction between strangers is consistent with an analysis by Friedman[16] of the behaviour of people serving in experiments who are unacquainted with one another. His study suggests that the results of much experimental work produces only a psychology of interaction between strangers.

REFERENCES

1. J. J. Gibson, *The Senses Considered as Perceptual Systems*, Allen and Unwin, London, 1966.
2. D. Byrne, W. Griffit, and D. Stefaniak, 'Attraction and Similarity of personality characteristics', *J. Pers. & Soc. Psych.*, 5, (1967), 82-90.
3. J. W. Brehm, *A Theory of Psychological Reactance*, Academic Press, New York, 1966.
4. J. L. Austin, *Philosophical Papers*, Oxford, 1966, Ch. 6.
5. R. P. Abelson, *et al.* (editors), *Theories of Cognitive Consistency*, Rand McNally, Chicago, 1968.
6. L. Festinger and J. M. Carlsmith, 'Cognitive Consequences of Forced Compliance', *J. Abnorm. Soc. Psych.*, 58, (1959), 203-10.
7. A. C. Elms and I. L. Jarris, 'Counter-norm attitudes induced by consonant v. dissonant conditions of role-playing', *J. Exp. Res. Person.* 1, (1965), 50-60.
8. K. M. Carlsmith, B. E. Collins and R. L. Helmreich, 'Studies in Forced Compliance', *J. Pers. & Soc. Psych.*, 4, (1966), 1-13.
9. M. J. Rosenberg, 'When dissonance fails', *J. Pers. & Soc. Psych.*, 1, (1965), 28-42.
10. D. T. Campbell and M. C. Stanley, *Experimental and Quasi-Experimental Designs for Research*, Rand McNally, Chicago, 1963.
11. R. S. Woodworth and H. Schlosberg, *Experimental Psychology*, Methuen, London, 1954, p. 708.
12. G. A. Miller, E. A. Galanter and K. H. Pribram, *Plans and the Structure of Behavior*, Holt-Dryden, New York, 1960.
13. M. T. Orne and L. A. Gustafson, 'Effects of perceived role and role success on the detection of deception', *J. Applied Psych.*, 49, (1965), 412-17.
14. R. Rosenthal and others, 'Data desirability, experimenter expectancy, and the results of psychological research', *J. Pers. & Soc. Psych.*, 3, (1966), 20-7.
15. S. M. Jourard and L. A. Kormann, 'Getting to know the Experimenter', *J. Humanistic Psych.*, 8, (1968), 155-9.
16. N. Friedman, *The Social Nature of Psychological Research*, Basic Books, New York, 1967.

CHAPTER FOUR

The Methodology of the Advanced Sciences

THE ARGUMENT

I. *The Method of the Advanced Sciences*

On Critical Description

1. Scientists try to explain non-random patterns in things and events.

2. Knowledge of these patterns is critical description.

    a. Critical description begins with common knowledge.

    b. Common knowledge must be extended by exploratory studies and corrected by experimental studies, yielding critical description.

Scientific Explanation

1. This is achieved by description of the causal mechanisms responsible for producing the non-random patterns identified in the critical descriptive phase.

2. a. Accessible Mechanisms: Some generative mechanisms can be observed with the senses, or the extended senses, e.g. joints and muscles, sap vessels in wood, etc.

    b. Quasi-accessible Mechanisms: The existence of the main elements in a quasi-accessible mechanism can be demonstrated to the senses or the extended senses, but much essential detail has to be filled in by the imagination by analogy with similar systems fully known, e.g. Harvey's theory of blood circulation required capillaries which he had to imagine.

c. Inaccessible Mechanisms: Knowledge of these derived wholly from the imagination under rational control, which creates models of the unknown generative mechanisms;

    (i) by analogy

    (ii) under the general discipline of plausability.

Models in Science

1. Iconic models are representatives of real or imagined things.

2. Sentential models are sets of sentences in 1–1 correspondence with other sets of sentences. Sentential models are of importance in science only if they reflect an underlying iconic modelling between their subject matters.

3. a. Paramorphs: source and subject differ,

    (i) Example of creative paramorph: the virus.

    (ii) Example of heuristic paramorph: electrical networks as models of hydraulic networks.

    b. Homoeomorphs: source and subject are the same. These are of heuristic value only, e.g. maps, schematic diagrams etc.

4. Real science is distinguished from critical description by its use of iconic paramorphs to stand in for the unknown generative mechanisms of non-random patterns in nature, and its persistent attempt to check the reality of these models.

It is our intention to construct an analogue of these processes for social psychology.

II. *The Conceptual Basis of Modern Science*

1. The traditional basis involved two main conceptions,

    a. Things were considered to be substances with qualities.

    b. Action was supposed to be impressed upon passive things, which merely passed it on, the model for this general concept being a passive, inert body passing on motion by impact with another like body. This was associated, naturally, with the Humean conception of cause.

2. The modern basis was developed in the late Eighteenth and early Nineteenth Centuries, under the pressure of discoveries of

electrical phenomena, and the critical philosophy of physics developed by I. Kant and R. J. Boscovich. It involves a radical revision both of thing concepts and of action concepts.

    a. Things are to be treated as individuals with powers.

    b. Action is to be treated as the realization of a potentiality created in space in the neighbourhood of active things.

    3. The analysis of the power concept.

    a. We say that a thing has a power when it is capable of a certain action either of itself, or upon another thing, in virtue of its nature.

    b. The conditions which have to obtain for a thing or person to have a power are called 'enabling conditions'.

        (i) Intrinsic enabling conditions are those which involve the identity of the thing having the power, e.g., the chemical composition of an explosive, the electron structure of an atom.

        (ii) Extrinsic enabling conditions are those which are not central to the identity of a thing, e.g., gunpowder must be dry to explode but does not cease to be gunpowder when damp.

    c. In general, intrinsic enabling conditions ensure the possession of long-term powers, while extrinsic enabling conditions ensure the possession of short-term powers or readinesses.

It is our intention to construct an analogue of this conceptual system for social psychology

In the course of our critical discussion in Chapters Two and Three, we identified a number of mistaken background assumptions in the way in which social psychology has been studied. Amongst these was the positivist methodology of science, in which the job of an experimental scientist is seen as the collection of correlations among observables and the job of theoreticians as the construction of deductive systems of laws from which these correlations could be deduced under the sole constraint of logical consistency. Real science is a much more complex and promising affair.

One must first be clear about what it is that scientists are trying to explain. The history of science shows a clear answer to this question.

Each generation of scientists from the very earliest times has been trying to explain those patterns in nature which seem to them to be non-random. These might be patterns among events, such as the regular risings and settings of the main heavenly bodies which the earliest scientific astronomers attempted to explain, or they might be patterns in things, such as crystals and organic forms. Anything, process or structure, which did not seem to be just the product of chance events is a suitable case for scientific treatment. First of all, one supposes the most obvious patterns forced themselves upon people's attention, so that a certain amount of critical description is just common knowledge. Some 'common knowledge' is not true. From here arise two tasks: 1. the task of extending what is known by common observation, and 2. the task of critically checking the authenticity of what is thought to be known. Each task is carried out by a different kind of empirical study. Perhaps they could be usefully distinguished as 'exploration' and 'experiment'. Much of empirical science is exploratory, and involves a methodology not at all like the traditional idea of hypothesis, prediction and test. In exploratory studies, a scientist has no very clear idea what will happen, and aims to find out. He has a feeling for the 'direction' in which to go (increase the pressure and see what happens) but no clear expectations of what to expect. He is not confirming or refuting hypotheses. This is the pattern of chemistry, and is beautifully exemplified in much of physics, as for instance in Gilbert's classical study of magnetism, the *De Magnete*,[1] or Newton's *Opticks*,[2] or Faraday's *Experimental Researches*.[3] The conjecture/experiment pattern is very much more rare. In the whole of the Nineteenth Century, it occurred only once in chemistry, in the prediction of new elements by Mendeleev, and testing of the hypotheses he formulated as to their likely behaviour.[4] Much of the work of anatomists and physiologists, ecologists and ethologists is similarly exploratory, and is very rarely experimental in the traditional sense. We propose to distinguish empirical from theoretical studies, and to use the terms exploration and experiment to distinguish the two main kinds of empirical study which we have distinguished above. We believe that the traditional methodology of social science which we took occasion to criticize in Chapters Two and Three is derived from the confused idea that all empirical studies must be experimental in the strict sense.

The upshot of exploration and experiment is what we shall call the 'critical descriptive phase' of a field. This is scarcely ever carried out in complete innocence of ideas as to the causal mechanisms at work in the production of a certain kind of phenomena, and indeed the direction of explanation may on occasion be very clearly and closely determined by such ideas. Nevertheless critical description is *possible* and is sometimes actually undertaken with no clear ideas as to the causal mechanisms involved. For instance the factual discoveries made by behaviourist psychologists are a partial critical description of behaviour of this kind since by a self-denying ordinance they deliberately eschewed any interest in the way patterns of behaviour were generated by such cognitive processes as self-directed rule-following, and the like, confining themselves wholly to the conditions in which and under which they occurred. It is not that behaviourists and other mechanistically oriented psychologists were not doing real science, but they were tackling only a very small part of what the logical extent of their field would be, had they applied the determining criteria used by chemists, physicists and biologists.

The task to which the activity of natural scientists has always been finally directed is the rational explanation of the non-random patterns of phenomena that have been found in critical descriptive studies. This they do by describing the causal mechanisms which produce the patterns. Chemists discover reactions, and by describing the interplay and interchange of ions they explain them. Geneticists discover non-random patterns in the distribution of animal and plant characteristics from generation to generation, a simple example of which are the patterns described in Mendel's Laws, and they explain the existence and persistence of these patterns by the mechanisms of gene transfer, dominance and recessiveness, and so on. Evolution is explained by random mutation and natural selection, diffraction is explained by the interference between waves, the aurora is explained by the mechanisms of ion formation high in the rarefied regions of the atmosphere, by electrons from the sun being drawn off towards the poles by the earth's magnetic field, and so on.

Phenomena which strike one as having no pattern, which seem to occur at random, are seen, from this point of view as being produced by a variety of different and unconnected mechanisms, while non-random patterns are taken to be the product of stable, relatively enduring mechanisms, whose productions have a strong common character, so that we can associate a good understanding of the generative and productive mechanisms of phenomena with a tendency to treat the description of their pattern as having the force of law, and the unfolding of the pattern may fairly be said to have something necessary about it.

How do scientists know what the productive and generative mechanisms are? Ions, genes, electrons, fields, natural selection, and so on are not things that can be observed, nor are the processes in which they are involved easily followed. The answer to this question is complex and takes us to the heart of scientific method.

The first step is taken by noticing that in some cases the generative or productive mechanism is as easily inspected as the phenomena it generates or produces. For instance, the mechanism by which the limbs have their characteristic motions is easily discovered by dissection, so that joints, tendons and muscles are laid bare and their interrelations observed. Of course, a deeper analysis of the mechanism is possible, but that is a later stage. Allowing a scientist a modest extension of his senses, such as he achieves with a microscope or stethoscope, or probe, it is possible to explain the syndromes of diseases as due to the behaviour of bacteria in the body, for example; or the way that the top of a cut into the bark of a tree becomes moist with sap before the bottom as due to the arrangement of vesicles within the wood, and so on. More powerful extensions of the senses allow scientists to include among their explainers such entities as viruses, dark members of star pairs, and the like.

There are some social matters where the generative or productive mechanism can be inspected with equal facility. An example is found in the relation between a printed litany and a church service, the non-random pattern of which is explicable as due to following the order of service and such supplementary rules as are printed in the missal. We can usefully think of all these items as generative or productive in character, and speak of them as being the whole or part of the mechanism which produces the pattern in the phenomena since it was by following these instructions that the people involved produced the service. We shall have much more to say about the function and status of rules as the substance of the generative mechanisms of sequences of action. In cases such as these, where there is no problem about inspecting what is taken to be responsible for the pattern in phenomena, we shall refer to 'accessible mechanisms'.

However, many explanations of patterns in phenomena make do with something a good deal less detailed in the way of observable mechanisms. For instance, when genes are referred to in describing the mechanism responsible for the exemplifications of Mendel's Laws, it is clear that, from the point of view of what can be observed, which is the behaviour of chromosomes, much essential detail is lacking. Similarly, in explaining the reaction of the pupil of the eye to light, the senses and their extensions do not penetrate to where much essential detail remains to be discovered. We shall refer to these as quasi-accessible mechanisms. A good deal more is known about reflex arcs than can be discovered by observation even with the extended senses. One could follow the positivists at this point and deny that there really is any further *knowledge* to be had, or one can attempt to develop an epistemology consonant with natural science. In short, at this crucial point one may attempt the reconstruction of natural science so as to fit an *a priori* epistemology, or one may try to construct an epistemology in keeping with natural science. Behaviourism was a psychology representing a choice of the positivist path at this junction.

There is little point in rehearsing the well-known arguments against positivism in general and behaviourism in particular. The next step can best be taken with the help of an example. Harvey made empirical studies of the course of the larger blood vessels, of the action of the heart, and of the quantities of blood flowing in and out of it. Partly on the basis of these studies he proposed that their explanation lay in the fact that the blood circulated and that the system of arteries and veins formed a complete *circuit*. This mechanism was only quasi-accessible. He was not able to carry out the empirical studies of blood-flow in sufficient detail to chart the flow adequately, nor was he able to make an empirical investigation of the system in sufficient detail to see whether in fact the system was a pair of completed circuits. He filled out the details by imagining what would be required to complete the mechanism, were it really a hydraulic system, and this is the source of the postulation of the capillaries. The epistemology of quasi-accessible mechanism involves an input to the knowledge of these mechanisms from empirical studies, usually from an exploratory study, and another input from an associated field of knowledge, channelled through an analogy. If the blood system is like a hydraulic system, then there should be capillaries. Harvey's conception of the system was completed just by imagining that there were just those invisible vessels.

Accessible mechanisms are discovered wholly by exploration, quasi-accessible by a joint method of exploration and imagination. Should there not be a place for a kind of mechanism our knowledge of which comes wholly from the imagination? The development of an understanding of 'inaccessible mechanisms' is in fact the most important part of natural science. Just to say that our knowledge of inaccessible mechanisms comes from the imagination is not sufficient for an adequate epistemology, since the imagination is as capable of speculation as invention, and indeed of fancy as of sober development.

The imagination becomes an instrument for the generation of scientific knowledge only under rational control. In discussing quasi-accessible mechanisms we have already had a glimpse of how this control is exercised through the analogy. The logic of analogy underwrites an epistemology of the imagination. It is this that makes science, which is not just critical description, possible. It is this that permits us to form ideas of the generative and productive mechanisms which are responsible for the non-random patterns discovered by empirical exploration of nature.

The key to the understanding of the epistemology and logic of creative science, and thus to understanding its methodology is to be found in the notion of a *model*. A model is a realistic representation of something, like its subject in some ways and unlike it in others, often leaving some of its relations with its subject uncertain. The term has been used in discussions of logic in two rather different ways:

F

1. in the sense above, in which a model of a subject is a representation of a real thing, or process by a real or imagined thing or process. Such models can be distinguished as *iconic* models.

2. 'model' has also been used in mathematics and logic for a set of sentences which are in some kind of correspondence to another set of sentences, the correspondence being determined by rules of transformation, which are in general arbitrary.

In scientific discourse there are sets of sentences which can be put into sentential modelling relations, but it is of crucial importance to understanding science to realize that sentential modelling is nearly *always* derivative from an iconic modelling between what is described by each set of sentences. Merely to achieve sentential modelling between two sets of sentences is neither here nor there in science. It is only significant when it reflects an underlying iconic modelling between the subject matters. Our attention will therefore be focussed exclusively on the modelling relations that can obtain between things and models of things, and processes and models of processes.

Let us begin with some examples:

Medical biologists were faced, in the years after Pasteur's and Koch's ratification of the bacterial theory of disease, with a number of well-established syndromes for which no causal mechanism based upon the idea of bacterial infection could be observed with the equipment of filters and microscopes then available. In short, the mechanism which was responsible for the observed disease entities was unknown. The disciplined imaginations of San Felice and Bordet produced the idea of the *virus*, an iconic model of the unknown cause of diseases such as influenza and poliomyelitis. The virus theory, looked at logically, can be reduced to two main propositions, one postulating the existence of viruses, and the other purporting to describe their nature. Their behaviour, of course, is already partially described in the syndrome of the diseases explained. How were Sanfelice and Bordet to tell what to say about viruses, how to describe them? For this purpose, they considered these imagined entities as analogous to bacteria, whose nature and behaviour were fairly well-known, at least in broad outline. The technological innovations which led to the construction of electron microscopes has enabled the creative imaginations of the originators of the virus theory to be checked, both as to the postulation of the existence of viruses, and as to the postulated behaviour and nature of these entities.[5] Here the function of the iconic model is to stand in for the causal mechanism which produces or generates the non-random pattern which has been observed. Models of this sort are one of the kinds of *paramorph*, that is, models whose source, the bacterium, differs from their subject, the unknown mechanism of the production of a certain disease.

Paramorphic models are used for another purpose, which has some application in all the sciences. There is a considerable similarity between the behaviour of electrical circuits and of hydraulic networks. This similarity can be exploited by using one as a model of the other. The degree of sophistication of the application of paramorphic models in this sort of case ranges between the purely heuristic in which the analogy between the systems is exploited at the purely formal level, by considering the correspondence between the set of laws describing the behaviour of the one kind of network with that describing the behaviour of the other, and the creative. It has often been pointed out that a paramorphic model exploited only to the rudimentary degree implied in the heuristic use, is dispensable in principle: the difference between discovering a new law directly in study of one kind of network and discovering it by anology with the behaviour of the other kind of network is no more than one of relative convenience of manipulation.[6] At a higher level of sophistication the paramorphic model can be used, even in this sort of case, rather as the virus notion was used in the first of our examples. We might see that the behaviour of such variables as pressure, fluid velocity, and so on in the hydraulic circuit could be seen to be a consequence of the flow of the fluid in that circuit. It would then be possible to make the creative step of supposing that there might exist an electrical 'fluid' whose flowing in the circuit was responsible for the observed pattern in the phenomena described in the laws. Here the subject of the model becomes the unknown mechanism generating the changes in the e.m.f. current and so on in the electrical circuit, and the source of the electric fluid model becomes the fluid in the hydraulic circuit.

Finally, mention should be made of a kind of model, much used in the biological sciences, that is at a yet lower level of sophistication than either of the exploitations of paramorphs that we have examined. For these models source and subject are identical. For example coloured wires can be used to make a model of the nervous system of an animal. The source *and* subject are the real nervous system. Such models have a certain utility of a purely pragmatic and heuristic sort. These could be called homoeomorphs. For instance, the great simplicity of a homoeomorph compared to the original may make it valuable as a source of understanding of the general geometrical and structural relations between the various sub-systems and individual nerves. Sometimes indeed relationships only become 'visible' as it were, by contemplation of a simplified model. Such models as these may be the ultimate products of the invention and testing of a creative paramorph. Should technological development lead to some kind of observational checking of the authenticity of the paramorph, it may be retained as a homoeomorph of the lately discerned real mechanism responsible for some pattern of phenomena. But of course its retention in such circumstances can be justified only on heuristic, pedagogical or pragmatic grounds.

The most important function of iconic models in science is as plausible analogues of the unknown causal, generative mechanisms of the non-random patterns discovered in critical explorations of fields of natural phenomena. In this role they serve as the basis both for existential hypotheses as to the reality of certain classes of entities, and further hypotheses as to their nature and behaviour. In this role they are indispensable, since if we depend only upon formal criteria for explanation, such as the deducibility from a theory of what is to be explained, then there will be infinitely many theories which satisfy that criterion for any given set of facts. Scientific method, as it is practised in the advanced sciences, consists then of the exploration of certain fields of natural phenomena in the attempt to discern non-random patterns in those fields, and critically to check them. This is followed, accompanied, or even preceded by the work of the creative imagination, in the course of which iconic models of the generative mechanisms at work in the field of natural phenomena are conceived. The invention of such models is essential to the scientific enterprise and their appearance is what distinguishes real science from critical description, for it is through them that we come to form some idea of why events happen as they do, and why things manifest the structures, powers and qualities that they do. Finally, consideration of iconic models directs the efforts of instrument makers towards new fields of possible observations which, when successful, lead to the final annihilation of the model by reality. At this point, a new set of models is adopted to represent the unknown mechanisms at work in the newly-discerned field of phenomena. The chemistry of substances demands the mechanisms of atoms, the physics of atoms demands the mechanisms of proton and electron structures, the physics of these entities demand the mechanisms of quarks, and so on, extending as far as technological proficiency and human ingenuity can lead.[7]

II. *The Conceptual Basis of Modern Science*

A radical change took place in the conceptual foundations of modern science between about 1770 and 1850. In that period the field-of-potential concept received its modern form, later translated into mathematics by Maxwell. Up until that time nearly all scientists of the late Seventeenth and Eighteenth Centuries had worked with a modified version of the classical conception of matter and form, in which material things were taken to be substances differentiated by their qualities. Changes in the qualities of things were supposed to be the effect of influences 'impressed from without', and it was taken for granted that in the ultimate analysis the thing itself was a passive recipient and transmitter, particularly of the mechanical qualities of motion, which appeared in later, more sophisticated forms of this general theory, as momentum and energy. It is an odd historical quirk that at the same time as this philosophy was being quietly abandoned in physics, it had received its most triumphant vindication as a general theory of the world, in the series of experiments designed to refute the idea that organic life was impressed upon matter which passed it on to the subsequent generations. Passivity of matter was institutionalized in Newton's First Law.

The idea that things were qualitatively differentiated pieces of matter served as one of the intellectual origins of the positivist way of thought. When philosophers and scientists reflected on the consequences of supposing the world to consist of matter with qualities they were inclined to draw the conclusion that these qualities were, in the last analysis, to be identified with peoples' sensations. The subject matter of science, it was agreed by Hume,[8] Berkeley,[9] Mach[10] and Russell,[11] was the sequences of sensory events in which the passage of change amongst qualities was marked. Notice, too, that qualities are outer manifestations, and serve to conceal the inner natures of things. It was not long before it came to be thought that there was something unscientific about reference to inferred internal states in giving an explanation of the sequences and coexistences of qualities, even in physics and chemistry. The Humean conception of cause as regularity of sequence amongst events, the behaviourist model of man as the passive respondent to stimulus, and the logical positivist conception of science as the task of finding logical order in generalizations from experience of sensory qualities, follow pretty directly and naturally from the adoption of the metaphysics of substances and qualities.

The metaphysical foundations upon which natural science was built in the early Seventeenth Century by English scientists were radically different,[12] and were revived again in the late Eighteenth Century[13a, b] to dominate the most advanced branches of physics to this day. Field conceptions in physics employ a range of concepts whose nearest common equivalents are expressed by a range of concepts: agency, potentiality, spontaneity and power. In the principles of quantum mechanics, for instance, spontaneity is institutionalized in the irreducibility of randomness in the final description of nature, potentiality in the concept of the field. We shall briefly sketch a general conceptual basis based upon the concept of a power, which will have sufficient generality to encompass both electrons and men, and by implication all degrees of complexity of entity between, and which will substitute across the board for the conceptual system based upon the idea of substance and qualities. Nowadays no serious person supposes that a science can be built independently of a metaphysical system which finds expression in the constraints that are felt upon the choice of systems of concepts.

Not all arrays of concepts are possible, and of the possible arrays not all are capable of universal and consistent application. For instance, the concepts associated with the mechanical view of nature cannot be applied universally without contradiction, a conceptual fact long known to physicists, and one of the origins of field theory.

The system of concepts, or metaphysics, which we will describe is subject to two constraints. It must enable us to treat of the natures of things as well as their surface manifestations and overt behaviour, and it must be, at the very least, compatible with the ascription of agency to some or all of the individuals with which it equips us to deal. Our system turns on the substitution of the conceptual pair 'individual/power' for the pair 'substance/quality'.

To say that an individual thing or person has a power to A is to say that it has a certain nature which, if the appropriate stimulus conditions were to obtain, would lead it probably to do A. This will be further explicated as we proceed. It should be noticed that there is no suggestion that an individual has in fact to have done, or be doing A in order properly to be said to have the power to do it, and indeed we shall find that it is a very important feature of this concept that it will be proper still to ascribe the power to the individual even if it never does A. This is because the ascription of the power really hinges upon the satisfaction of what have come to be called 'enabling conditions'.[14] Their status and variety can be made clear with the help of examples.

The enabling conditions have to do with the intrinsic state and nature of the substance and individuals to whom powers are ascribed, and sometimes to their extrinsic relations. A lump of dynamite has the power to explode by virtue of its chemical composition, a heavy weight has the power to crush an egg by virtue of its relative position above the earth. But notice how differently these enabling conditions are related to the individuals involved. The heavy weight preserves its individuality as a sphere of iron 10cm. in diameter, wherever it stands with respect to the egg, and may indeed have acquired that power with respect to the egg through a change having been made in the position of the egg while the iron ball remains poised upon the shelf. But to have a certain chemical composition is what it is to be nitroglycerine. The intrinsic enabling condition is related to the criteria of identity for the individual having the power, and the obtaining of the intrinsic enabling conditions are necessary to the maintenance of that identity. When the chemical composition of the lump has changed, it has not only lost the power to explode but it has lost its identity as that lump of dynamite.

We have already noticed that intrinsic enabling conditions are marked off from all other circumstances surrounding the possession and exercise of powers by their connection with the criteria of identity of the individuals who have the power. It is this logical fact that justifies us in asserting that powers are related to the essential natures of things.[15] If we treat the dispositions that a thing or material manifests as the exercise of its powers then we can make sense of the idea that the ensemble of dispositions (behaviours and tendencies to behave and so on) is not accidental, that is, that an account of the nature of the individual involved can be given which makes its possession of just this ensemble of dispositions intelligible. This is easily seen in a simple example from the natural sciences. Hydrogen has the power to radiate light of certain very definite wavelengths under appropriate circumstances. It also has the power to combine with other substances, in quite definite proportions. These powers are treated as being in fact specific powers of hydrogen atoms. A hydrogen atom has the power to radiate quanta of certain wavelengths only when appropriately treated, and the power to enter only into certain combinations with other atoms. This latter power is called its valency. By treating these dispositions as powers our attention is directed to the question of the nature of hydrogen atoms. This turns out to be capable of description as a certain spatial structure of a pair of charges. The existence of the very same nature is the intrinsic enabling condition for both the spectrum dispositions of hydrogen and its chemical dispositions. We can thus treat its electron-proton structure as its essential nature, and thus as what it is that makes intelligible the existence of just that ensemble of dispositions characteristic of hydrogen. In physics and chemistry the essential natures of things and materials are usually identifiable with their microstructures. The microstructure of an atom is a structure of entities which must also be characterized in terms of *their* powers,

Finally we notice that in the physical sciences the maintenance of the microstructure is logically related to identity, for instance in chemistry through Aston's conception of Atomic Number as the number of electrons in the microstructure of the atom, thus confirming our idea that the powers/natures connections lead to criteria of identity and thus to essential natures. For instance, the transmutation of an element into a different element is brought about by changing the microstructure of protons, electrons and neutrons of the atoms of the original element. The new microstructure is the essence of a different element, and different dispositions exist by virtue of it. The new element is distinguished therefore by possessing different and characteristic powers.

That the powers concept provides a way of dealing with the essential nature of individuals is of the utmost importance for behavioural science. For the latter has, for the most part, dealt with generic individuals, admitting into the system only those features of human nature that all men have in common, which in the context of the study of social behaviour, may be a very limited part of a particular person's make-up, and relevant only to a very restricted part of his social behaviour. The powers concept applied to individuals has the potentiality of bringing into the system the nature of individual people, in a manner compatible with a social interaction framework.

There is one more feature of the powers conception in the natural sciences to which we wish to draw attention because of the importance of the corresponding notion which we shall develop in the context of human sciences. This is the distinction between long-term powers and short-term powers or readiness. Causal powers like valency in chemistry are long-term powers. A change in a chemical element which would change its valency would change the essential nature of the material, that is, we would describe such a change as a transmutation of one element into another. The maintenance of the conditions for the exercise of long-term powers is properly identified with the maintenance of intrinsic enabling conditions. But the readiness of an atom to radiate electro-magnetically is due to the existence of a temporary energy state, a state of excitation, change in which makes no difference to the essential nature of the atom.

These conditions are related to extrinsic enabling conditions. Change into and out of such states does not upset the identity of the individual involved. It is a modification of the inner nature which does not change its essence.

We shall find that both creative model building and the identification of powers and natures must form essential parts of the methodology of the social sciences just as they do in the natural sciences. We shall undertake some creative model building for social psychology in Chapter Five, and we shall be developing a theory of human powers in Chapters Twelve and Thirteen. In the end we hope it will become clear that the human and natural sciences should in fact employ the same methods, and that much of the disappointment one must feel with the progress of the human sciences in the Twentieth Century derives from their imitating a false picture of the natural sciences, in particular the picture delineated by positivists and inductivists.

REFERENCES

1. W. Gilbert, *De Magnete*, new edition, Dover, New York, 1958.
2. I. Newton, *Opticks*, new edition, Dover, New York, 1952.
3. M. Faraday, *Experimental Researches in Electricity*, Everyman edition, London, 1951.
4. J. R. Partington, *A History of Chemistry*, Macmillan, London, 1964, Vol. IV, p. 896.
5. N. W. Pirie, *Scientific Thought, 1900–1960*, edited R. Harré, Oxford, 1969, Ch. 11.
6. C. G. Hempel, *Aspects of Scientific Explanation*, Free Press, New York, 1965.
7. For a detailed exposition of these points see R. Harré, *The Principles of Scientific Thinking*, Macmillan, London, and Chicago University Press, 1970.
8. D. Hume, *A Treatise of Human Nature*, London, 1739.
9. G. Berkeley, *A Treatise Concerning The Principles of Human Knowledge*, in *Works*, new edition, edited T. E. Jessup, Nelson, London, 1949, Vol. II.
10. E. Mach, *The Analysis of Sensations*, new edition, Dover, New York, 1959.

11. B. Russell, *Our Knowledge of the External World*, Open Court, Chicago and London, 1914.

12. J. Locke, *Essay Concerning Human Understanding*, new edition, edited J. W. Yolton, Everyman's Library, London, 1961.

13a. R. J. Boscovich, *A Theory of Natural Philosophy*, (Venice, 1763), new edition, M.I.T. Press, Boston, 1966.

13b. I. Kant, *The Metaphysical Foundations of Natural Science*, translated by J. Ellington, Bobbs-Merrill, New York, 1970.

14. M. R. Ayers, *The Refutation of Determinism*, Methuen, London, 1968, Ch. 5 and 6.

15. M. Fisk, *Nature and Necessity*, Indiana Univ. Press, Bloomington, Indiana, forthcoming.

CHAPTER FIVE

The Anthropomorphic Model of Man

THE ARGUMENT

The Basic Principle of Ethogeny

For scientific purposes, treat people as if they were human beings.

The Development of the Anthropomorphic Model of Man (following P. F. Strawson)

1. The model is derived from contemporary philosophical analyses of the concept of a person.

2. The essential features of the model derive from a transcendental argument based upon the assumption that the use of language is what distinguishes human beings from all other creatures.

The argument sets out the necessary conditions for something to be a language user.

3. These are:

a. People are material things (exist in space and time) and are capable of being distinguished from each other as objects by their physical features. This is a necessary condition for the use of names, and of other referring expressions.

b. They are material things with a certain range of powers, the most characteristic of which is the power to use language.

c. They share with other animals the powers
   (i) to initiate action
   (ii) to monitor their performances.

d. People, alone among animals, possess the power to monitor their monitorings, to be aware of being aware, etc. which power is probably identical with that which endows them with the power to use language.

e. The powers under (d) are most naturally exercised in the giving of monitoring commentaries upon monitored performances, and in the special case of acting by following a rule or plan, which is to act to make an anticipatory commentary come true.

4. The use of self-referring pronouns depends upon a person having been referred to as a person by other people, and so is logically posterior to the recognition that there are other people. Thus the problem of language is not how we can apply person predicates to other people, but how we can know that we ourselves are people.

5. The capability of self-commentary depends upon the commentator having a standpoint outside the field of the commentary.

a. It is a mistake to deny the existence of the commentator upon human action on the grounds that he cannot focus upon himself.

b. This logical feature of conscious self-monitoring has been illuminated by the metaphor of the eye and the eye's visual field.

6. At this point we simply note that the biological individual may be associated with several internally consistent but mutually contradictory clusters of dispositions, each cluster evoked by a different type of social episode.

The theory that each biological individual may be associated in 1–1 correspondence with a social persona we believe to be a myth, reflected in the 'trait' conception of human nature, which must be radically reinterpreted to survive. The theory is not based upon sound empirical evidence, but is a reflection of moral and religious ideas.

7. It follows that one of the chief problems of social psychology is to understand the conditions under which a biological individual presents the appropriate persona from a hierarchy of possible social selves.

8. In fact, commentaries are usually produced in justificatory contexts, and it is in these that rules and conventions are usually adverted to in explanation of social behaviour.

9. There is, no doubt, a neurological basis for all these powers, in the system-character of the biological organism, but for the purposes of social psychology, it is necessary only to take account of the powers with which that system-character endows each individual.

Summary of the Anthropomorphic Model of Man (following S. Hampshire)

To summarize our argument we first assert dogmatically what are a person's powers, and then show that he must be a material thing to be able to exercise them.

1. a. A human being has the power to initiate change.

b. A human being is capable of being aware of things other than himself and knowing what they are.

c. A human being has the power of speech.

2. The proof of the major contention is by the argument that an entity lacking any one of these three powers would not be accorded the status of a person.

3. a. One necessary condition for 1, a, b, and c above is that a human being has a point of view in space.

(i) Agents act upon things, and things have places.

(ii) Perceivers must be aware of the perceived as different from themselves, and a perceiver can perceive things, so must differ in a thing-like way from the things perceived.

(iii) Language using would be impossible unless it was possible to refer to the point of application of predicates, and this is in part dependent on the existence of self-reflexives such as 'here' and 'over there', so the language user must have a place in the same system of reference as that to which he refers.

b. A second necessary condition for 1, a, b and c above is that a human being has an existence in time.

(i) Agents must know what they are about to do, what they are doing, and what they have done, in the sense of being capable of giving the appropriate commentary.

(ii) Perceivers must endure to perceive the enduring.

(iii) Language, as an articulated sequence of sounds, is also in time.

c. (a) and (b) together make up the sufficient conditions for an entity to be a thing. So that whatever is agent, perceiver and language user must also be a kind of thing.

Having rejected the 'mechanical' model of man, as we have discerned it operating in the concepts and practices of social psychologists, we must now outline our own model of man in order to develop a methodology to supersede the positivist methodology so often associated with the 'mechanical' model. We shall find our model in the most recent developments in analytical philosophy which have centred round the elucidation of the concept of a *person* as this concept appears in ordinary language and in philosophy. The model we will construct on the basis of recent work in philosophy we shall call the 'anthropomorphic model' of man. It is the heart of what we take to be the most radical proposal of this book, that we should treat people, for scientific purposes, *as if they were human beings*, as we know and understand them in everyday life. Thus we shall find the source of our model in contemporary ideas about the nature of a person which are rooted in the way that concept functions in the grammar of our language, and in the forms and systems of our commonest thoughts.

We believe that a human being is a system of a different *order* of complexity from any other existing system, natural or artificial. We believe this to be evident in the fact of human self-awareness and in the characteristically human linguistic powers. Thus for the purposes of any science which deals with phenomena specifically associated with performances that depend upon these higher order capacities any model of less complexity is void. Thus, machines, computers in their present state of development, and animals, are *all* inadequate, though none are wholly useless, as sources for concepts with which to delineate a sufficiently powerful model of man, which can be of any real use in the scientific understanding of social phenomena. The only possible solution is to use our understanding of ourselves as the basis for the understanding of others, and our understanding of others of our species to further our understanding of ourselves.

In order to discover the main lineaments of our ordinary conception of a person so that we can set about constructing the anthropomorphic model of man we can begin by looking for those features which are necessary to the application of this concept to an individual. The form of argument we will be using for this purpose is one long familiar to philosophers, but no doubt considerably less familiar to psychologists. It is a form of 'transcendental' argument. Its force is something like this: we choose some feature of human life which is common to all theories of man. We hold the use of language to be the most characteristically human attribute and that most universally admitted to be unique to men. We shall show that language-users must have certain properties, and certain capacities and powers, without which it would be impossible for language as we know it to exist. One of these is the capacity to use names and similar expressions to make reference to individual people when they are not present, and to refer to them without pointing, when they are in the immediate vicinity. We then ask what are the necessary conditions for this use of language to be possible. And we find that these can be summed up in the demand that both the objects referred to and the entities doing the referring, must be in space and time, and capable of being differentiated one from another by their outward appearance. Thus we establish that, whatever else they may be, people are material things. Anyone who wishes to argue with us over this conclusion must use language to do it, and if he wishes to dispute our conclusion he will be disputing one of the conditions for using language, that is he will be disputing one of the conditions which make the dispute possible. So anyone who tries to counter a transcendental argument is, as it were, pulling himself *down* by his own bootstraps. So people, using language in the form they do, cannot be disembodied intelligences but must be things in a world of things.

But this is not all there is to being a person. Characteristically people are capable of various higher order performances for which they share certain capacities with other animals. The most important animate capability is that of monitoring and thus controlling actions with respect to the task to be achieved. Animals differ from one another not only in outward form, but also in the range of powers and capabilities they possess.

Thus people are a certain class of *things*, biological organisms, differentiated from other species of the same class by their character- istic physical form and by the possession of a special range of powers. In short, men are 'rational, featherless bipeds'. What is special about the powers of people has to do with features of people which they have in addition to those they have in common with other organ- isms. All animals are capable of monitoring their performances, and many, it seems, are aware of what they are doing. We believe that what differentiates men from all other organisms is that men are aware that they are aware of what they are doing, that is they are capable of monitoring their own self-monitoring. This differentium is easy to state, but is fraught with enormous and complex conse- quences. We shall argue that the powers specially manifested by people require at some stage in their acquisition, and from time to time, conscious self-monitoring of performance.[1] So there exists the possibility of a continuity of conscious self-awareness along with biological identity. That is since the exercise of a person's powers are in the performances of his organism, and these require conscious self-monitoring, there is an obvious and strict connection, between the one concept and the other. A person is then a logical unity, in that his consciousness exists in the self-monitoring of his organic performances, and in particular in his intentional actions upon things and other organisms.

The final step in establishing this part of the argument to the anthropomorphic model of man, is taken by looking into the condi- tions for the use of personal pronouns, particularly those in the first person, by means òf which a man refers to himself. How is it pos- sible for there to be such uses of language? The first condition is obviously that which we have already briefly referred to, namely the existence of an awareness of being aware of performances, that is the existence of a capacity to monitor our monitorings. We are aware of our performances, and we can also become aware of that awareness. But whatever is aware at that higher level cannot, on

G

that 'level', be aware of itself. But two levels of feedback are sufficient to establish the basis for all the specifically human powers.
Thus a person would have no idea of himself as a conscious individual unless he were being referred to as such by other people. This
is a most crucial step in our argument, and we shall return to
elaborate its consequences from time to time. It is this point that is
at the very heart of Strawson's analysis of the concept of a person,[2]
an analysis which though disputed on matters of detail,[3] dominates
much contemporary thinking on the subject. People form the idea
of themselves as individual *people*, as opposed to mere goal-seeking
organisms, and so become capable of making reference to themselves as people, because other people identify them as such and
treat them as people. It is clear that none of this would be possible
were a person without linguistic powers, particularly as Hampshire
emphasizes,[4] the power to use referential expressions properly.

This leads us naturally to a difficult conceptual problem to which
we shall give only passing attention, but recommend to the attention
of philosophers. How far are linguistic powers and the power of
conscious self-monitoring connected, and if they are connected,
what is the nature of that connection? It does seem a very striking
coincidence that only people (and perhaps that most favoured of all
apes, Washoe) seem to have both these powers. This makes one
strongly inclined to say that they are in essence different manifestations of the same power which people have in virtue of the same
feature of the system constituted by their neural organization. It
may be that systems of a certain structure and degree of complexity
are capable of monitoring their self-monitoring,[5] and that this is the
essence of the capacity to shape sounds into articulated symbols, and
to make marks meaningful.

Whatever is the upshot of more detailed study of this problem we
can identify as specific human powers the linguistic and related
symbol-using capacities. We share with animals the power to initiate
action, that is it is not only people who are agents, but our special
powers enable us not only to monitor our performances, but, because we are aware of our monitoring and have the power of speech
we can provide commentaries upon and accounts of our performances, and plan ahead of them as well. It is the existence of this

(plans), while they are going on (commentaries), and in retrospect derivative capacity to comment upon our actions, in anticipation (accounts), that is our most characteristic feature, and around which the science of psychology must turn. In the anthropomorphic model of man we not only have the person as agent but the person as watcher, commentator and critic as well. It follows from this that the most characteristic form of *human* behaviour is the conscious following of rules and the intentional carrying out of plans.

It is in being aware of being aware that people are centres of consciousness. We must turn now to reflect upon the nature of the watcher. The standpoint from which one monitors one's monitoring of a performance, from which one gives commentaries upon the way one is doing something and with what aim, is not itself capable of figuring in an account, given from that standpoint. The commentator himself is not capable of description as a part of the psyche. He must necessarily escape observation, since he is the observer. Thus the standpoint from which commentary is made must always be one remove from experience, and cannot have attention focussed upon it. It was this feature of self-monitoring, as much as anything else, that led the philosopher Hume to deny the self.[6] No matter how deeply and how carefully he scrutinized his mental processes and feelings he could never find the 'self'. That is hardly to be wondered at since he was attempting something which a little reflection shows to have been impossible, namely to scrutinize that with which scrutiny is performed. Because the standpoint from which we view our actions cannot be attended to, we are not thereby required to deny its existence. It is, as Kant saw, transcedental, that is it must be conceived of, not as something given in experience, but as something presupposed by experience.[7] Its existence is a necessary condition for experience of the kind we have, to be possible.

The relation of the commentator and the subject of his commentary has been illuminated by various analogies. Wittgenstein offered the analogy of the relation of the eye to its visual field.[8] The eye which does the visual seeing cannot be seen in its own visual field. Wittgenstein even denied that its existence is a necessary condition for there being any visual field at all. One can extend the analogy a little. One *can* see one's own eye, but only in a mirror. One might say, in the spirit of that analogy, that one becomes aware of oneself both as commentator and as agent monitoring one's own performances, in the responses to and influences of other people to oneself. This is particularly so when other people say things of the 'Buck up!' variety, when one's powers of self-monitoring and self-initiation of action are called upon by others.

It is because we are systems which can monitor our own self-monitorings that we can give commentaries, and it is because we can give commentaries that psychology is possible. The heart of our psychological method will lie in the exploitation of these powers, for it is in the self-commentary that the way to a scientific psychology must lie, because it is in that, that our plans and aims become manifest, both to ourselves and to others.

So far we have paid attention only to the biological individual and his powers and capacities. We have already drawn attention to the fact that in his social behaviour a biological individual may perform in a wide variety of ways, which taken together, do not form a consistent whole. The idea that a biological individual must always exhibit a consistent social self is institutionalized in the 'trait' conception of personality, which we shall have occasion to criticize in a later chapter. There is little to recommend it either theoretically or practically other than the eminence of its advocates. We shall not attempt the impossible task of trying to find an underlying consistency in the social behaviour of a single biological individual. Instead we shall begin by supposing that a normal biological individual is capable of manifesting a variety of possible social selves, each of which has some measure of coherence, and may resemble the personas presented on suitable occasions by other biological individuals. We shall treat a social individual as one who shows a fairly consistent set of inner and outer responses to his fellows and to the social situation which called him forth, and who accounts for his actions in terms of unified sets of rules and plans. In Western culture, it has been assumed that there must be a one-to-one correspondence between social and biological selves. We believe that this is a myth, which has been generated not by observation, or by well-founded psychological theory, or by psychological discovery, but by our conceptions of moral responsibility, and by our religious theory of the soul. It is clear that in Japan, for instance, social psychology would be seriously astray in basing its personality studies on the assumption of a unitary personality for each biological individual. In Japan a biological individual manifests several different, but internally consistent personas, each appropriate to a particular social circle and system of obligation.[9] Taken together they do not make up an ethogenic, or behavioural, or emotional or any other kind of unity. Were we to perceive social life in the West 'straight', that is in independence of our traditional moral viewpoint, we would also see, we believe, a multiplicity of social selves, associated with each biological individual. It follows that among the first steps in any empirical study of social interactions we must try to discover which of a human being's possible social selves are being presented. The way selves are presented and their presentation controlled then becomes a crucial factor in the understanding of social phenomena, and so the study of this feature of the performances of human beings must be a central part of a reformed social psychology. It is partly because of our conviction in this matter that we intend to draw attention with considerable force, to the pioneering work of Erving Goffman,[10] and to recommend strongly further development of the initial theoretical study of this phenomenon by Simmons and McCall.[11]

An entity which consciously self-monitors its performance and is capable of anticipatory commentary or planning, is bound to put that power to use in generating its own performances and in interacting with things of its own or other kinds. Thus we would expect those organisms which are capable of using language and of self-monitoring to be much inclined to the use of rules and plans and strategies in getting things done the way they want them. Indeed one way of saying that someone has got what he wants is to say that his anticipatory commentary has come true.

In summary then, the anthropomorphic model of man conceives of the subject of social investigations as a biological individual whose characteristically human actions are generated by the conscious self-monitoring of its performance in accordance with certain sets of rules which it represents to itself in the course of making anticipatory and monitoring commentaries upon its performance, and which it subjects to critical appraisal in retrospective commentaries. At the level immediately 'above' performance it can, therefore, choose different sets of rules for action, and this is why a multiplicity of social selves are possible, since a social self is the apparent unifying principle present in an organism's performance in some social episode. Retrospective commentaries are usually given in a context of justification in which the rules which an individual followed in the course of a performance, or the plans it carried out, have to be shown in a favourable light to others of its species. Social science is the study of the system of such individuals and of their performances and of their ways of monitoring those performances and of the systems of rules and the kinds of plans they use in doing this. As we have seen there can be no presupposition that there will be one and only one consistent set of rules in use all the time by each biological individual.

There are two basic powers upon which the possibility of all this depends, the power of conscious self-monitoring and the power of speech. We are inclined to think that the power of conscious self-monitoring is the most fundamental, since we can see some reason for thinking that that power is a necessary condition for the possibility of so controlling noises as to emit articulate sounds and so to organize them as to express what one means. Expressing what one means we regard as a special form of conscious self-monitoring. We are also inclined to believe that the power of conscious self-monitoring is related to the degree of complexity of the neurological system, and cannot be further defined with the system of concepts we are employing in this study. The *general* lineaments of a system complex enough to be capable of self-monitoring at the appropriate level has been sketched by Farrell.[12] For the purposes of social psychology the power to monitor the way one monitors one's performance is a basic power and is possessed by people in virtue of the system nature of their brains. So any further steps in the investigation of the origins of this power must be taken by neurophysiologists. However, it follows from the same considerations that their discoveries can have little intrinsic interest for social science as such, which is concerned with the exercise of the power of conscious self-monitoring and commentary upon performance, and need take no particular interest in its physical basis. Chemistry, within its own realm, has no need to consider the physical basis of valency. The valencies of chemical atoms are their basic chemical powers.

The most extended philosophical development of the system of concepts we have just sketched, is by S. Hampshire.[13] So important do we regard this conceptual basis that we propose to use his exposition as a summary of our argument. Indeed this type of logical analysis may well show that the mechanical model of man is logically impossible as a basis for a social science.

Hampshire identifies three major powers or capacities characteristic of people.

A. A human being is characteristically an agent, that is has the power to initiate change and control the manner and goal of his performances.

B. A human being can perceive things, that is can be aware of things other than himself, and is aware of that awareness.

C. A human being has linguistic powers, particularly the power of speech.

The proof that these are in fact necessary conditions for a thing to be a person derives from considering whether we would be prepared to identify as a person a thing which lacked any one of these powers essentially. This is a conceptual matter which has to be tested by considering some borderline cases.

A catatonic seems to be properly classifiable as a person, though he usually cannot speak or initiate action. If we reflect upon what makes us want to classify such a one as a person it seems to depend upon our thinking that his disabilities are merely contingent, and in theory at least, are capable of being removed. A lion, on the other hand, is necessarily not a person, in that we are inclined to think that the level of neural organization of lions is such that they could never acquire human powers without fundamental and radical change in their very being. Washoe, the chimpanzee, is an intermediate case, and forces us to think deeply about the borderline of the concept 'language-user' and indeed about the borderline of the language concept itself. How we should demarcate the class of people is no doubt a matter of convention, but it would be wrong to think that decisions on the borderline can be wholly arbitrary. We should be able to advance reasons in support of such decisions. Washoe poses a problem because we are puzzled as to whether an ape, articulate in the deaf and dumb sign language, is enough of a language user to be classified for a wide range of *other* purposes as one of us. Many of these purposes will involve moral issues, such as our right to kill such a creature for food, to hold such a being morally responsible for her actions, and the like.

What are the necessary conditions for a creature to possess the powers and capacities we regard as typically human? A common necessary condition for all three, according to Hampshire, is that each human being has a point of view, that is occupies a place and knows that it does so, so that it understands itself as viewing the world from that place and acting upon things from there. Notice that this is one of the necessary conditions for an entity to be a kind of thing. It should now be clear that we are approaching the same conceptual terminus as our previous transcendental argument, but from a different direction, in that we are now taking the person's basic powers for granted and establishing his thinghood as a necessary condition for his being able to exercise them. In our earlier general argument we tried to establish what must be the powers of a thing if it is to be capable of typically human performances. According to Hampshire, occupancy of place is a necessary condition for agency because it is part of the concept of being an agent that he can act upon things, and things have a place, so the actions of an agent must take place at certain places. And human agents, are, for the most part, where they act. Having a place is also a necessary condition for perception, since to perceive something is amongst other things to be aware of it as different from oneself, and in the relevant sense this has to be as another thing, that is as occupying a place different from the place occupied by the perceiver.

Hampshire argues that the connection between linguistic powers and occupancy of place comes about through the central place that referring has in language using. To refer to something is to identify the place where the referent is with reference to where the speaker is located. Thus for that to be possible the speaker must have a place in the same system of space as does the thing referred to. This point is exemplified in such very simple utterances as 'It's over there' whose intelligibility to a listener depends upon some understanding of where the person making the remark is speaking from.

Not only must a person have a place in space along with other things, but he must also endure in time. Endurance, Hampshire believes, can also be seen to be a necessary condition for the exercise of the specifically human powers we have identified in A, B and C above. For example, to be an agent I must know what I am about to do, know what I am doing and know what I have done. Thus action has a 'trajectory' in time. This does not mean that we must always be aware of our intended actions, but that we must have the power to give anticipatory, monitoring and retrospective commentaries if called upon to do so. Perceiving, too, must be in time, since we perceive enduring things. Finally, the organization of articulated sequences of sounds into speech is achieved by a structure whose components are differentiated in time. In a purely sonic medium there is no other way to achieve a differentiated structure of sounds. Now endurance in time is, with occupancy of space, one of the necessary and sufficient conditions for existing as a thing. So in order to exercise one's powers as an agent, as a perceiver and as a language user, in short to be a human being, one must be a kind of thing.

A man then is a mechanism, but one which monitors and controls the way he performs. We have seen how such a being will most economically control the manner of his actions by following rules, and by forming and attempting to realize plans. It follows from this that we should expect abnormal forms of social behaviour to appear for two distinct kinds of reasons. The ethogenic form of some recognized kind of abnormal form of behaviour would be due to a failure by a normally organized person to understand and employ the rules of social life correctly. It might even be due to simple ignorance of what those forms are, or a lack of training in recognizing the meaning of the social actions of others. There would be a pathological but complementary form of abnormal behaviour due to the malfunctioning of the organism as a neurological system. Failure to respond properly to a socially meaningful action might then be due to failure to recognize it as such, or failure to know the correct rule for responding; or it might be the consequence of a physical lesion in the feedback mechanism by which the higher order monitoring functions are performed.

Thus one would expect to find ethogenic schizophrenia and pathological schizophrenia, ethogenic paranoia and pathological paranoia, ethogenic autism and pathological autism, and so on. Some recent studies in the origins of certain kinds of neurotic behaviour do seem to suggest that this is indeed the case, a fact which greatly strengthens the force of the general argument of this book. This is particularly shown in the success of Argyle's work[14] in teaching the meanings and rules of paralinguistic interaction to patients whose disturbed behaviour seems to derive not from any breakdown in their 'machinery' but from simple ignorance of the meaning of social actions.

There should be certain intermediate cases, where long term emotional disturbances, originally the product of ethogenic failure, lead to the malfunction of the neurological system through longstanding abnormal levels of endocrine product concentration. If we are right, then it is a matter of the first importance for clinical psychologists to distinguish between those patients who need to have the rules made clear to them, and those who need to have their 'machinery' restored to normal functioning by chemotherapy and other physiological means. The patient whose trouble is basically ethogenic, but who is misclassified as in need of physiological restoration, is in a very dangerous situation, since he is physiologically normal. Of course the confinement and 'treatment' of such a person in the usual physiologically oriented mental hospital will soon lead to permanent changes in his physiology, thus shifting him from the ethogenic to the pathological category. Or he may learn the wrong rules and meanings from the other patients. The perception of these dangers lies behind the warnings of Szasz[15] and Laing.[16]

We can sum up our conception of the anthropomorphic model of man by exploring an analogy between the kind of self-monitoring system we take a person to be and such a control system as an automatic pilot. The essential heart of the automatic control system of an aircraft is a model of that plane, within a model of its environment. The ongoing model of the environment is created by the use of various sensors which sample the aircraft's situation and convey that information to the control device. The responses of the model to the model environment are used as a base for correcting the responses of the aircraft to its environment.

In terms of this analogy we are obliged to imagine a person as incorporating not only control systems of that type but a number of higher order models in which the plane and its environment together with its incorporated control system is modelled. Let us suppose that there are four such models. Within each the model plane and its model control system differs with respect to the ideal mode of functioning which its self-monitoring is designed to produce. One produces a straight path, another a sinuous curve, another a switch-back ride, another aerobatics.

In terms of the higher order control system, each of these modes of behaviour can be chosen by choosing among the four possible control systems. If the plane, as in a fairy story, were to be aware of the admiration of an earth-bound audience as its flight-path became more and more spectacular, or of the apprehension of its passengers as it began its aerobatic routine, this would constitute the monitoring of performance within a higher order environment. This would correspond to the way a person can choose different sets of rules and conventions according to which he controls his performance, and so presents himself in accordance with this or that stereotype of a social persona.

We believe that most characteristically human behaviour can be explained by the exploitation of the analogy of second order monitoring. We believe that human beings have this capacity or power because they alone amongst the animals have a sufficiently complex nervous system, for second order monitoring to be maintained steadily. It is because of this that people alone among animals can speak, and that only people can play-act both on and off the stage.

REFERENCES

1. G. Ryle, *The Concept of Mind*, Hutchinson, London, 1947, Ch. 11 §8, Ch. VI, Ch. IX.
2. P. F. Strawson, *Individuals*, Methuen, London, 1959, Ch. 3.
3. A. J. Ayer, *The Concept of a Person*, London, Macmillan, 1963.
4. S. Hampshire, *Thought and Action*, Chatto and Windus, London, 1965.
5. B. A. Farrell, 'The Design of a Conscious Device', *Mind*, 79, (1970), p. 321 ff.
6. D. Hume, *A Treatise of Human Nature*, London, 1739, BK I, Part IV, Sect. VI.
7. I. Kant, *Critique of Pure Reason*, Riger, 1781, translated N. Kemp Smith, Macmillan, London, 1952, A107-8.
8. L. Wittgenstein, *Tractatus Logico-Philosophicus*, 1921; translated by D. Pears and B. McGuinness, Routledge and Kegan Paul, London, 1962; §§ 5.632-3-31.
9. R. Benedict, *The Chrysanthemum and the Sword*, Routledge and Kegan Paul, London, 1967, Ch. 5, 6, 7, 8, 9.
10. E. Goffman, *The Presentation of Self in Everyday Life*, Allen Lane, The Penguin Press, London, 1969.
11. J. L. Simmons and G. J. McCall, *Identities and Interactions*, Free Press, New York, 1966.
12. B. A. Farrell, *loc. cit*.
13. S. Hampshire, *op. cit*, Ch. 1, 3.
14. M. Argyle, *Social Interaction*, Methuen, London, 1969, pp. 394-402.
15. T. Szasz, *The Myth of Mental Illness*, Secker and Warburg, London, 1961.
16. R. D. Laing, *Self and Others*, Tavistock, London, 1969.

CHAPTER SIX

'Why not ask them ... ?'

THE ARGUMENT

The Open Souls Doctrine

In order to be able to treat people as if they were human beings it must be possible to accept their commentaries upon their actions as authentic, though revisable, reports of phenomena, subject to empirical criticism.

1. In contrast to this are

a. the view that the reports are the phenomena themselves (verbal behaviour), and not statements about phenomena that are legitimate objects of scientific study.

b. the view that reports are irrelevant to psychology since conscious self-monitoring of action is merely an epiphenomenon.

2. The bases of the refusal to take reports seriously seem to be the following:

a. There is alleged to be no independent check on whether the reported states exist.

b. There is no check on whether the act of reporting generates artifactual memories, etc.

c. Reports are alleged to be vague, as for instance 'mood' reports are supposed not to give much physiological or cognitive information.

3. By contrast we emphasize

a. the fact that there are clear cases where relevant states of minds, e.g., beliefs and moods, are *shown* in the content and manner of what is said.

b. the impossibility of giving an account of a person's states of readiness without taking notice of transitory changes in his psychic states, e.g. of emotion, belief, and so on, because these changes are of at least equal importance with physiological changes, e.g., amount of alcohol in his body, as the basis of states of readiness.

4. Part of the reason for denying reports of states of mind, intentions, reasons, etc., scientific status, is the idea that the predicates appropriate to people fall into two mutually exclusive classes, bodily predicates whose attribution is capable of scientific study, and mental predicates which ascribe private states, and so are alleged not to be capable of scientific study.

    a. This whole approach is challenged by the idea that person predicates form a bodily-mental *spectrum*.

    b. The idea that there are *any* person predicates, other than explicit attributions of consciousness, which we would not ascribe unless we thought the thing to be conscious is surely mistaken, so consciousness as a condition cannot really demarcate the person-predicates. For example computers can play games, and robots can walk, though we would not ascribe consciousness to computers or robots.

    c. A revised criterion would make M-predicates those for the application of which any reference to states of mind, including states of consciousness, is irrelevant.

    d. We develop a weaker 'awareness' criterion for P-predicates.

        (i) awareness is a broader concept than attentiveness

        (ii) awareness can be identified, for our purposes, as *being capable of commenting upon an action*.

        (iii) the weak 'awareness' criterion allows for self-deception and self-correction in giving reports.

    e. It is important to remember that self-ascription of M- or bodily-predicates depends upon 'psychological' factors, e.g. the effect on judgements of relative height of the status accorded the person.

        (i) However M-predicates can be corrected by wholly non-psychological means, e.g. physical measuring equipment.

        (ii) There are no non-psychological means of correcting P-predicate attributions.

Logically Adequate Criteria

(e), (ii) does not imply that P-predicates are unscientific provided some can be applied in conditions which involve logically adequate criteria, i.e., where admitting the satisfaction of the criteria and refusing to apply the predicate would be logically incoherent.

1. Mentalistic-predicates do *not* change their meaning between sentences in different persons, e.g. between 'I am tired' and 'He is tired' when said of the same person.

2. For many mentalistic-predicates, e.g. puzzlement, a disposition to say certain kinds of things, such as 'I'm puzzled by this' is part of being in that state of mind.

Comment

On 1: The point can be defended by asking what sort of reasons could be brought forward for supposing that 'tired' changed its meaning between the two sentences, other than a generally discredited verificationism.

On 2: There is no harm in admitting that the 'logically adequate criteria' ultimately have an inductive basis, since the ascriptions based upon them are revisable, while the refusal to apply them in seemingly good circumstances can sometimes be justified by a special account.

3. We have shown above, in connection with arguments about the conditions for language-use, that a person could not learn that he was a person, knowledge which is shown in his capacity to use personal pronouns of himself, unless he was recognizable as a person, i.e. as one who is a consciously self-monitoring agent, by other people.

Attributions of Powers

1. Some powers and readinesses are *shown* in action.

2. Some tendencies, etc., are such that they have no overt

expression and are never shown. They are attributed, revisably, on the basis of the most reasonable assumptions as to the nature (kind) of the person involved.

3. Powers to acquire powers are manifested in the exercise of lower-order powers.

A Spectrum of Predicates

1. Person-predicates form a *spectrum*, not two or more exclusive groups. *All* are capable of empirical application.

2. Characteristics of a spectrum of predicates:

a. Ascribed to things of the same kind.

b. For some, correct application requires the satisfaction of two criteria, C1 and C2. C1 is an objective criterion based on overt characteristics or behaviour, and C2, one pertaining to more covert features of the person for which the actor is the usual authority, but which is often also accessible to other persons.

c. Some predicates can be applied correctly on the basis of the satisfaction of a C1 type of criterion alone, and others on the basis of a C2-type criterion alone.

d. C1 criteria can be used for the ascription of predicates to things different in kind from those to which the whole spectrum of predicates applies.

e. C2 criteria are satisfied only by things of the kind to which predicates from the whole spectrum can apply.

3. a. In the case of the spectrum of predicates appropriate to people, which we have called the Bodily-Mental spectrum, psychologists wrongly supposed that only C1-type criteria were scientific, because philosophers wrongly supposed that the satisfaction of C2 criteria must necessarily be private.

b. Philosophers were mistaken because they treated the authority of each person as to whether a C2-type criterion is satisfied, as meaning that only he had access to knowledge of the property attributed, the very meaning of which was impenetrable to other people.

Thus it is possible to treat people, for scientific purposes, as if they were human beings.

The account which we have developed so far depends a good deal upon a person's understanding and analysis of his *own* modes of action. Each person knows he is a conscious self-monitoring organism. That is our view of ourselves. But will it do as a view of the others? *Many* psychologists have supposed that it would not do for that purpose. We believe that their doubts about the anthropomorphic model of man really stem from a scepticism about the reports that other people give on the genesis and meaning of their actions. This scepticism seems to derive from some bad philosophical arguments of the past, which have filtered through to the practising psychologists. We propose to redress this state of affairs by a short development of the main lines of refutation of this argument to re-establish once again the 'open souls' doctrine, and to allow a man once more to be taken seriously as a commentator on his actions, and as the main contributor to their understanding. We shall approach the problem by examining the kinds of things that one might want to say of a person, which one would not want to say of any other kind of creature, that is particularly those things which are connected with the specific human combination of powers of commentary and conscious self-monitoring we have emphasized in the previous chapter.

The Open Souls Doctrine

It is an essential principle of the approach to psychology we are advocating that all or very nearly all the kinds of things we ordinarily say about ourselves and about other people should be taken seriously as reports of data relevant in a science of psychology. This is not to imply that such statements are to be accepted uncritically, but rather to say that the phenomena which they purport to report both *really exist* and are *relevant*. This is in contrast to two other points of view:

a. Statements purporting to be reports of a large class of kinds of phenomena, roughly those which include feelings, moods, intentions, plans, indeed states of mind generally, are not to be taken literally

H

as descriptions of phenomena, but are to be treated as phenomena themselves, as pieces of verbal behaviour. From this point of view, a social psychologist would not be interested in the meaning of the remarks exchanged in the course of an episode, say one in which attitude change occurred but in the correlations between the remarks themselves, and other remarks showing attitude change. This point of view can take extreme forms, as in the idea that remarks should be considered only as sounds, and their role in a social phenomenon considered solely as stimuli. There is a tendency to this point of view in Skinner[1] and followers, brought about partly by their use of the phrase 'verbal behaviour' for the saying of things in the course of an episode. A social psychologist of Skinner's persuasions might be interested in the fact that his subjects understood remarks made in the course of an episode but takes the occurrence of the understanding as the phenomenon, rather than whatever is understood by the statement.

b. It has been pointed out by Skinner,[2] that one of the origins of classical behaviourism was the idea that though the phenomena of feelings and other states of mind existed, they were not relevant data for a scientific study of men. Their inherent unreliability was supposed to be such that any way of studying behaviour which purported to be scientific, and which assumed or demanded the reliability of reports of states of mind was doomed through defective data.

To establish in principle the breadth of kinds of data that the growth of the phenomenological[3] and cognitive[4] movements in psychology demand, it is not enough to argue for the *accessibility* of states of mind as possible scientific data, but their *relevance* must also be established. If we can show that psychological studies are in search of knowledge of human powers, tendencies and liabilities, and that the states in virtue of which some of these powers are possessed are states of mind, and that the rules which a self-monitoring organism supposes itself to be following in its various performances are indispensible elements in the explanation of social (and linguistic) behaviour, then knowledge of states of minds is an indispensible condition for doing psychology properly. We intend to return to a discussion of this issue from various points of view. What is really at issue when the reliability of reports is questioned? There seem to be several different problems.

The feeling, mood or emotion, opinion, belief or intention avowed may not exist; or the feeling ascribed may not really be felt; or the opinion reported may not really be held. There seems to be no independent and universally applicable check by which doubtful cases of avowals or ascriptions, confessions or attributions can be decided and genuine reports distinguished from mistakes or lies.

The demand for retrospective commentary may lead to the identification of feelings, moods, emotions, opinions, beliefs, intentions, etc., as existing in the course of an episode, which were not attended to at the time or did not even exist during that episode. How can we tell which reports are of genuine states of mind which really did exist, and which report fictitious pseudo-memories generated by the demand for commentary in a justificatory context? It is sometimes alleged that, because of this, commentaries upon action are worthless in giving a scientific explanation of behaviour because that is supposed to be concerned only with *what really happened*. And there are apparently no criteria for deciding between a plausible invention and a genuine recall.

In dealing with the problems which derive from sceptical doubts about the authenticity of reports we want to emphasize the fact that there are many cases in which a certain sort of remark is not just a sign of, or a report of a state of mind, but is a manifestation of that state of mind itself. For instance to complain verbally is a part of being discontented, because part of what is ascribed to a person who is described as 'discontented' is a tendency to complain. Indeed complaining may sometimes be the *whole* of discontent, though usually there may also be feelings of resentment, thoughts about better states of affairs, and so on. It is here that the philosophers' idea of logically adequate criteria will prove invaluable. This is the simple but pregnant idea that one cannot consistently deny that a person is discontented after accepting what they say as a genuine complaint. Similarly, under some circumstances, a report of a belief or of an intention may be exactly the manifestation of that belief or intention itself.

Why is it so important to take the reports of states of mind and the expressions of intention so seriously? It is partly because the systems of rules and meanings under which social life is lived can only be grasped by studying the reports and commentaries of social actors. It is partly because we wish to place considerable emphasis on the changes in people's powers and capacities that are affected by changes in their psychic states. In many cases changes in a person's emotional state, or mood, and changes in his knowledge and beliefs, are changes in virtue of which different tendencies and powers of action appear. A person may be incapable of violence unless he is angry. It is part of our point of view that the study of changes in mood, emotion and belief, is as important for any practically possible psychology as is the identification of physiological changes, such as for example the amount of alcohol in the blood. Knowledge of either kind of fact may lead to revisions of judgements as to the certainty of changes in a persons' powers and capacities by virtue of these changes of state. It is obvious that in the case of alcohol, capacities are lost and liabilities acquired because of changes induced in the nervous system. If the science of social psychology is really concerned with the prediction of changing liabilities and tendencies, capacities and capabilities involved in human interaction, then any changes in state, which are supposed to be changes in virtue of which dispositions change, must be of critical importance as data. For this reason judgements of emotion and mood, such as 'too angry to think straight'; 'angry enough to commit murder', and so on, must find a place in a science of social action and not be reduced to statements about the outward signs of these and other emotional states. This is not to say that we may not ultimately come to see emotional changes as indicative of, or indeed as causes and effects of changes in the nervous system. But because of Schachter's results[5] and other studies of the relations between cognitive states and the emotions we may not assume too glib a connection. Certainly for practical purposes of scientific study we cannot assume any simple identity between physiological states and emotions or moods.

The M–P Spectrum

In any general theoretical account of the kinds of predicates that may be ascribed to people, and of the conditions for their ascription, refusal or rebuttal, it is wise to go over once again, from whatever point of view happens to be current, the arguments for the idea that the predicates appropriate to people form two distinguishable groups, lately called the M-predicates and the P-predicates, a terminology introduced by P. F. Strawson.[6] The two groups of properties which such predicates are alleged to ascribe are roughly distinguished as the corporeal and the mental. There is a tradition in philosophy, reflected in a good deal of psychological thinking, that there are no outstanding difficulties about ascribing bodily predicates to all and sundry. People, machines and stones share mechanical and chemical predicates. But there are thought to be difficulties, perhaps of an insuperable kind, in applying mental state predicates to anything other than oneself. And even their application to oneself has been scouted as a basis for a scientific psychology.[7] We propose to argue that there is no way of making any *one* principle do the work of demarcating the groups of predicates, and then to look into the arguments that have been and might be advanced for the idea that there are logically adequate criteria for the ascription of at least some of the predicates on the mental side to people other than oneself.

Strawson himself argues that bodily predicates are distinguished by the alleged fact that we not only ascribe them to people, but to many other kinds of things 'to which we would not dream of ascribing states of consciousness'. Weight and volume, for instance, are attributes of people as well as of rocks and trees. But, he alleges, mental predicates are ascribable only to those things to which we would ascribe states of consciousness. Bodily predicates can be ascribed to things to which we would not ascribe mental states, but then since predicates such as weight and volume can be applied to anything the alleged distinction between bodily and mental predicates must depend upon the restriction of what can properly be described by means of a mental predicate to those things which can also be said to be conscious. Now this is surely more than dubious, it is wrong, if the restriction is that mental predicates can be applied only to those things to which we are prepared to ascribe states of consciousness. The recent discussions about how far we can describe computers and automata in terms drawn from the person vocabulary, though often rather pointless, has at least shown how far it does seem reasonable to ascribe mentalistic predicates to things to which we would not dream of ascribing states of consciousness. There are machines which are good at games; robots can go for a walk and perform simple domestic tasks and so on. It seems very doubtful that there are any mental predicates, except of course those actually attributing states of consciousness, which could not be applied to things to which we would not ascribe states of consciousness, particularly those attributing skills which are sometimes manifested in public. If a wide enough range of mental and mentalistic predicates are found to be applicable to things which we were at first not inclined to rank as persons on the grounds that they did not seem to be centres of consciousness, we might come to think that it was proper to treat them as persons, and hence to apply many (or all) of the rest of the range of mental predicates. The most striking example is the chimpanzee Washoe. The success of her trainers in helping her to acquire sign language has forced them gradually to increase the span of mental predication they wish to apply to her. They are currently slowly moving into the ascription of intentions. This suggests that rather than trying to divide the totality of predicates that can be ascribed to people into clearly demarcated domains, it would be more useful to see it as a spectrum or ordered series reflecting more and more stringent conditions necessary for calling a thing a person. For example, if a thing cannot express an intention then it is *certainly* not a person. If it seems to have no flux of emotion then it probably is not a person. If it cannot move about then it might perhaps not be a person, and so on. The importance for social psychology of all this apparent logic-chopping stems from the different kinds of explanations that seem appropriate to the behaviour of things depending upon whether or not they are classified as people. For those things which are people, we have already shown that a scientific explanation of their behaviour requires the intentions and plans of the actors to enter into any account of what took place.

Rather than positively requiring that the things to which bodily predicates can alone be ascribed should be those to which it is somehow wrong to ascribe states of mind, let us consider a weaker but more plausible criterion. Suppose that bodily predicates are those for whose application to anything whatever (stones or people) any knowledge of or conjecture about the states of mind of the thing to which the predicate is applied are *irrelevant*. This looks as if it would make 'weight' a bodily concept.

To see whether there is still a clear line of demarcation even on this weaker criterion we must consider whether there is a corresponding positive criterion for identifying mentalistic predicates.

We might be tempted to offer 'awareness' as the appropriate necessary accompaniment of mental states. To test this idea, let us look briefly first of all at predicates of action. To put it colloquially this criterion would demand that a person should not be said to be performing an action unless he is aware of what he is doing, knows what he is doing or something of the sort. The problem for us in seeking a criterion is whether we are going to demand that 'aware of what he is doing' should be treated as equivalent to 'attending to what he is doing', i.e. being capable of describing at every moment what he is doing at that moment. There are several important distinctions to be drawn here.

i. The difference between the action performed and the act attempted. It would not be right to demand awareness of the action performed, in that in many cases we are quite unaware of how we are doing something, that is what actions we are performing, we are aware only of what we are attempting to do.

ii. The difference between doing something absentmindedly and doing it attentively. We cannot see that it is wrong to say that someone knows what they are doing even when they are carrying out the task absentmindedly.

If these two points are correct then the 'awareness' criterion must be something other than an 'attention to' criterion. We propose the following:

A person can be said to be aware of what he is doing if but not only if he is *capable of telling* what he is doing, either before he begins, or at any time during the performance, or fairly soon afterwards. Later we are going to generalize this criterion into a criterion for intentional action.

There is a problem here for philosophers to puzzle over. Does it make sense for me to ask 'What am I doing?' when what I mean by this is that I really don't know? Usually this question would be put to someone else to try to get them to guess what I am up to. Sometimes it may be used as an exclamation upon realizing the true nature of my actions. We believe that it does not make sense as a genuine question, in that whatever I think I am doing, however inappropriate the actions performed may seem to be, *is* what *I* am doing, that is, is the act I am attempting.

A further virtue of a pretty weak 'awareness' criterion is that it leaves room for self-deception and self-correction in the self-ascription of action predicates and state-of-mind predicates. As far as action predicates are concerned I may be persuaded that my avowals as to what I am up to are naïve or touch only on short-term intentions or something of the sort. For state-of-mind predicates my remarks may have to be revised as I come to see the situation differently, e.g. I may come to see that what I thought of as my righteous indignation was jealousy.

So far we have been arguing that mental predicates can be distinguished from bodily predicates by whether some consideration of the state-of-mind and/or of awareness in a fairly weak sense is relevant or irrelevant to the priority of ascription of the predicate. The same form of words may sometimes be used mentalistically, sometimes corporeally. Thus under some circumstances 'sleep-walking' becomes a purely bodily predicate when a person cannot describe their somnambulations, while 'strolling in a day-dream' can be mentalistic provided the stroller can give an accurate account of his peregrinations. Of course retrospective commentaries can be given on sleep-walking, and in those cases we have a mentalistic use of the predicate. Thus it is probably better and more useful to distinguish mentalistic and non-mentalistic *uses* of predicates, rather than mental and bodily predicates as such.

But there are cases which throw doubt on even these modest

proposals for a demarcation. These arise both in cases of ascribing bodily predicates to oneself and in ascribing them to others. It is well known that self-ascriptions of bodily shape can often be shown to depend upon the beliefs, emotional states and so on of the person self-ascribing. Studies in person perception[8] have shown similar phenomena in the ascription of bodily predicates to other people, as e.g. height or shape, or degree of distortion of the other person relative to the ascriber. But we might reply that the demarcation can be preserved since there are objective measures of shape and height, and that any state-of-mind dependence of the ascription of bodily predicates can be over-ridden.

Can self-ascription of a particular mentalistic predicate be over-ridden in this sort of way too? That is, in a way against which there is no defence? This seems doubtful. One of Schachter's beautiful studies is relevant here.[9] When he established that certain obese people did not have stomach contractions when they said they felt hungry and did have contractions at other times when they said they did not feel hungry, we would not be inclined to say that absence of the usual objective cause or correlate of feeling hungry implied that they did not feel hungry, only that they ought not to have felt hungry then. The self-ascription of hunger is not over-ridden by the absence of the normal bodily concommitant of hunger feelings. The over-riding of the self-ascription of mentalistic predicates does occur, but not by confrontation with any bodily fact. It occurs by a restructuring of meaning. When we try to persuade the person to 'see' his situation differently, to attend to other aspects of a situation than those he was considering, and so on, we are trying to change the meaning of the situation for him. We try to get him to ascribe different meanings to things and situations from those he ascribed before which influenced his past choice of mentalistic predicates. If this is true, it must be possible for our subject to counter-persuade us to see the matter his way too.

It follows that there is neither a clear line of demarcation between bodily and mentalistic predicates, nor is there a priority of the one over the other in the matter of empirical validity. We are as free to ascribe and to rebutt the ascription of mentalistic predicates as we are the more empirical use of bodily predicates.

Logically Adequate Criteria

The case for all phenomenological psychologies would be greatly strengthened if it could be established that there were 'logically adequate criteria' for the ascription of states-of-mind, of intentions and so on to the people involved in social phenomena. The strongest kind of logical adequacy of criteria would be where if the criteria are met for the application of a predicate then ascribing the denial of the predicate would be contradictory of whatever true statements constituted fulfilment of the criteria, and *refusal* to apply the predicate when the criteria had been fulfilled, would be perverse because it would be irrational.

An important assumption for many of the discussions of this and related points is the idea that whatever is ascribed by the use of a mentalistic predicate is the same when that predicate is self-ascribed as when it is other ascribed. For example, to ascribe emotions ('fear'), states of mind ('puzzlement'), moods ('discontent'), beliefs ('in fairies'), liabilities, tendencies, capacities, capabilities and powers, 'to jump six feet', 'to stumble', 'to recite Endymion', etc., powers to acquire powers 'the capacity to learn a language', etc., we are attributing the emotion, state, belief, power and liability to another in exactly the same sense as we are attributing it to ourselves. This point has been generally assumed even by Carnap,[10] though in his case his extreme physicalism led to the bizarre theory that self-ascription is as behavioural as ascription of mental predicates to others.

The assumption of identity of meaning of mentalistic predicates throughout their range of ascription seems to us unquestionably correct but difficult to prove. We merely offer here some suggestions as to possible lines of argument.

It might be argued that the following sentences all mean the same thing: 'I'm puzzled', 'You are puzzled', 'He's puzzled', 'R.S. is puzzled', because, though they are different sentences, they are obviously being used to make the same statement, since they are all asserting the same thing of the subject. In short when you hear me say 'I'm puzzled' that is not evidence from which you *infer* that

R.S. is puzzled, rather it is a different way of expressing what you express when you say 'R.S. is puzzled'. But notice that this already assumes that your hearing of my saying 'I'm puzzled' would, on this view of the matter, have to be the basis for a logically adequate criterion for the assertion of puzzlement of me by you. This seems a sensible way of looking at the matter and there are reasons for adopting it, but if we do adopt this view of the matter we cannot then offer the alleged identity of what is self-ascribed and other-ascribed as a reason for supposing that my confessions and avowals provide logically adequate criteria for certain of your assertions about me, on pain of circularity of reasoning.

The problem then becomes: why does your hearing 'I'm puzzled' provide a logically adequate criterion for your ascribing puzzlement to me? Puzzlement is a state of mind. When a person is in that state his behaviour and his thoughts are marked by certain tendencies, such as a tendency to say 'I'm puzzled'. Since puzzlement might be only one among several different states of mind which could be held responsible for someone having a disposition to talk like that, it looks as if the utterance is not a sufficient ground for the ascription. It is clear that merely hearing me say 'I'm puzzled' is not, by itself, enough to pass from hearing 'I'm puzzled' to asserting 'He's puzzled' rather than 'He's pretending to be puzzled'. More needs to be known about what sort of person is saying it, and the exact nature of the situation. What if a person says he is puzzled when he has been forcibly recruited as a guide by vicious invaders? In short it only seems to be proper to treat 'I'm puzzled' and 'He's puzzled' as making the same assertion in 'normal circumstances'. But normal circumstances boil down to those in which we have no reason to think that the equivalence does not hold.

We can assume then that provided no reasons are advanced for supposing that such predicates meant anything different when ascribed to me by another and when self-ascribed, they have the same meaning. Any such reasons would have to be very special since they would have to count against the very basic condition that I understand what is said to me of me, and how I understand what I want to say myself must be the same if there is to be a language at all. And surely anyway I understand what is said to me *of* me in the same sense as I understand and intend what I may say, using the same words, of myself. Even in the case of the different sentences all ascribing puzzlement to one and the same biological individual, 'puzzled' must mean the same when predicated alone as when predicated in such a phrase as 'pretend to be puzzled'. We shall assume that whatever philosophical problems there are in this region are clustered round criteria rather than around meaning.

At the beginning of this section we gave the strongest possible interpretation to 'logically adequate criteria'. It seems that it was just such an interpretation that Strawson originally had in mind, since he links the notion with the very possibility of identifying people, with the possibility of using a vocabulary of pronouns, and so with there being any mentalistic predicates at all. The fact that we depend a great deal on historical and situational information in ascribing such predicates, which can, of course, be indefinitely improved, suggests to us that the strong criterion—namely, that there be a contradiction between assenting to the statements describing the fulfilment of the criteria (even including what people say as well as what they do and how they look) and asserting the predicate of the people involved—is too strong.

The weaker position is established by Strawson's mini-transcendental argument. It runs like this: There must be positive and adequate grounds for ascribing at least some mentalistic predicates to persons other than oneself, otherwise:

1. People could not be recognized as such by other people, in particular the putative user of 'I' could not be identified by other people, as a person, and hence

2. Could not truly be a user of 'I' which involves the recognition that one is oneself a person, namely one of them, an individual, for whom *they* use 'you' or 'he'.

3. In that event one could not ascribe to oneself what they could not ascribe to one, and hence one could not ascribe to them what one could not ascribe to oneself.

In short a necessary condition for having the concept of oneself as a person is that others should have the concept of one as a person. To put this another way, a necessary condition for the possibility of self-ascription of mentalistic-predicates is that one can other-ascribe them. The latter possibility amounts to there being logically adequate criteria for the ascription of such predicates to others. Strawson certainly seems to think that these criteria will depend upon the appearance of certain sorts of behaviour.[11] We shall look into the details of this below.

At this point we want to take up the question of the strength of the criterion of logical adequacy. It seemed to be unrealistic to demand that it be obeyed with such stringency that violation generated a contradiction. We propose instead that logical adequacy of criteria be judged not on whether adequate positive criteria can be found (i.e. criteria whose satisfaction logically entails an un-revisable ascription of the P-predicate), but on what are the conditions under which we would refuse to ascribe such predicates. The follow-ing points seem to be true, though we are unable to provide a strict rationale:

1. If someone says that he loves dogs, is given to petting them etc. these phenomena by themselves do not provide the basis for logically adequate criteria for saying that the person loves dogs. The love of dogs is easily feigned, and dog-loving behaviour easily imitated. There are even cases where, when one is imitating a dog lover for an ulterior motive one momen-tarily comes to love dogs.

2. Confession and misbehaviour constitute dual criteria for refusal to apply a mentalistic predicate. The predicate 'dog-lover' would normally be refused application to someone who either confessed to disliking dogs or was cruel in his treatment of them. Cruel behaviour would probably be paramount over protestations in our refusing to call a man a dog-lover.

Why do we feel that a man who *really* loves dogs could not be cruel to them to conceal his love, even in exceptional circumstances, while we are happy to concede that petting may conceal fear or hate? Perhaps it is because dog-loving is a favoured attribute and dog-hating not favoured that it is easier for us to conceive of the dog-hater feigning love than the dog-lover feigning hate.

However there is a way out of these difficulties. Suppose we treat the idea of the logically adequate criterion as a rather roundabout way of making a more important distinction. Is it not the case that the unity of belief, feeling and behaviour is such that any such cases as verbal protestations of love in the face of cruel behaviour gives us a prima facie reason for thinking that unity is being violated, and that such violations call for special accounts. No one seems to be called upon to explain his petting a dog when he has confessed to being a dog lover, the fact of the confession is reason enough. What has to be explained is divergence from the usual unity of confession and behaviour. What Strawson wants to describe as cases where there are logically adequate criteria can be construed as cases where no special account of the way the behaviour fits in with a unity of opinion, feeling and so on seems to be called for. This allows us to incorporate the important truth that in special circumstances behaviour which seems to be indicative of one kind of state of mind or opinion or belief, can be reconciled with a confession of a discordant state of mind or opinion, with the help of a special account. It seems to us that there are no combinations of feeling, belief and action for which a special account is in principle impossible.

Some Specific Problems in the Attribution of those P-predicates which are used to ascribe powers to people

a. POWERS TO ACT (including powers to say various things). There seems to be little objection to saying that the performing of the appropriate sort of action is the basis of a logically adequate criterion for an assertion that one did have the power to perform the action. The problem with powers, which will be dealt with in detail in Chapters Twelve and Thirteen, derives from epistemological problems of projecting power ascriptions into the present (when unrealized) and into the future. For example, if it is argued that your having solved the problems directly shows your cleverness at mathematics rather than being a piece of evidence from which your cleverness may be inferred,[12] then one may argue that all that is *shown* is your present capacity to do just these problems, and is no guarantee of continuing capacity or your capability in differing problem fields.

b. ATTRIBUTIONS OF TENDENCIES ETC. VIA IDENTIFICATION OF KIND.
Consider the difference between 'admires' and 'secretly admires'.
For the former there are logically adequate criteria in our weakened
sense since behaviour of a hostile kind after a confession of admiration would need a special justification, whereas friendly, or sycho-
phantic behaviour would require no special account. The reasons
for saying that someone secretly admires someone else must, on the
face of it, be very different from those ascribing admiration. To
justify the ascription of secret admiration we are required to produce
just exactly one of those special justifications mentioned above,
since secret admiration can be ascribed only to one who appears
lukewarm, neutral or hostile. In giving a special justification we
depend upon such notions as the *sort* of man he is, the *kind* of
situations, relationship and so on, and our final ascription of secret
admiration to the man finally depends upon our belief that we have
identified a kind of man in the kind of situation where we can
expect him to have the same tendencies, liabilities and so on as the
man who expresses open admiration, only he does not express them
for some special reason. To ascribe secret admiration is to inductively ascribe a tendency or tendencies which have a basis in the
nature, beliefs and emotions of the man, but are so controlled that
they are never manifested openly.

c. POWERS TO ACQUIRE POWERS and powers to assume powers and
exercise powers. To say that someone is musical is to say that he is
the kind of person who can learn and acquire certain capacities
which are exercised in musical performance. Here the attribution
stands upon two steps of logical adequacy, though for the second
step one must have the capacity to do a good many different things
to be said to be musical, just learning Brahms' Lullaby by rote will
not do.

We have referred to the group of predicates which are used to
describe people as forming a 'spectrum', implying that they fall into
a kind of order and that they are distributed between two poles, or
extremes, which are fairly easily distinguished from each other.
To complete our survey of the conceptual matters relevant to

introducing states of mind, beliefs, emotions and so on into psychological science we must look briefly into the nature of the spectrum and the principles of order involved. Philosophers are familiar enough with the problems caused by a set of related concepts each of which requires the satisfaction of two or more criteria in different measure for its correct application. Psychologists are not so familiar, and indeed it is perhaps their unfamiliarity with this idea that has led them to try to treat the particular spectrum of person predicates in the unsatisfactory way they have.

We can identify a set of predicates as forming a spectrum when the following conditions are satisfied:

1. They are normally applied to things of a particular kind, and are identified in the first instance, as the predicates normally used to describe things of that kind.

2. In many cases their correct application requires the satisfaction of two different kinds of criteria, C_1 and C_2 say. C_1 is an objective criterion based on overt characteristics of behaviour, and C_2 one for which the actor is the usual authority, and pertains to the more covert features of the person. C_2 type characteristics may be, and often are, accessible to other people.

3. But some of the predicates in the set can be applied on the basis of the satisfaction of a C_1 type criterion alone, while others can be correctly applied on the basis of a C_2 type criterion alone.

4. The C_1 criteria are of a type with those required for the correct application of predicates to things other than those in the given class.

5. The C_2 type of criteria are relevant to the application of predicates only to things in the given class.

Characteristic examples of predicates requiring the satisfaction of both C_1 and C_2 type criteria for the person-predicate spectrum are 'proceeding cautiously' and 'elated'. In the former, one criterion is concerned with overt behaviour, and the other with the way in which that behaviour is being monitored by the person concerned. In the case of the predicate 'elated', one criterion is concerned with such external features as facial expression, rapidity of speech and the

like, and the other with the accompanying emotion. These examples
can also be used to illustrate the difference in weight which can
exist between the criteria. In a case of dual criteria the criterion of
greatest weight is that which, if it is *not* satisfied would lead to the
predicate being refused. So that weight is to be understood as relative readiness to refuse the predicate to a person. In the case of
'proceeding cautiously', the overt style of the movement, e.g.
obvious carelessness, would be paramount over avowals of care,
while in the case of the predicate 'elation', the confession of true
misery would be paramount, and we are equipped with such concepts as 'feigned elation' just because of this. Compare the relative
oddness of the concept 'feigned caution'. It is worth noticing how
in mock cautious behaviour the cautious style is greatly exaggerated.

The fact that a very great many of the predicates used of people
by people are of this dual criterion type has encouraged psychologists
to fall into a trap, from which they are only with difficulty emerg-
ing, led by those who work now under the banner of 'cognitive
psychology'. It is clear that different people are typically involved
in making the reports upon which the attribution of these predicates
depends. Anyone can, in principle, give an authoritative report on
whether an organism is proceeding or not, whether it is grinning or
not, but only that organism itself can give an authoritative report on
whether it has been watching what it was doing, feeling really
happy and so on. So it seems as if one of the criteria is public and
the other private. Satisfaction of the private criterion cannot be
checked by any other person, but the use of the public criterion is
open to scrutiny by all qualified observers. Many psychologists fell
into the trap of thinking that they need consider only the public
criterion and use its satisfaction as the basis of the attribution of
psychologically relevant predicates, to people.

The worry about the subjectivity and unreliability of the private
criterion which led to this mistake can be put to rest quite easily.
Access and authority are two quite different concepts. It may well
be that a man is the best authority as to what he is feeling and how
he is proceeding, but he is not the only one with access to information of this sort. There are always some situations for any state-of-
mind predicate where others have some degree of access to that

I

state of mind, even in another person. We have already shown how this is possible through the idea of logically adequate criteria, and through those cases where the report is not just a description of a state of mind, but its production shows or exhibits that state of mind, e.g. readiness to complain is part of what it is to be discontented. It nevertheless remains true that a person is the best authority as to his own states of mind, feelings and the like. Now this privilege is not absolute. What we take it to amount to is that in cases of dispute, if we wish to maintain the outside observer's point of view over against that of the person himself and his avowals, then *a special case has to be made out*. A Freudian explanation is an example of what might be taken to be a special case for discounting a person's own explanations as authoritative as to his reasons, states of mind and so on.

Philosophers have had their temptations too in contemplating this spectrum of predicates. They have tried to resolve the difficulties occasioned by there being dual criteria for many predicates, by turning their attention to the two poles, so to speak, at one of which are predicates like '150 pounds', which a person can share with a lump of rock, and at the other, predicates like 'conscience struck' which seem to have application only to people, and then only on the basis of a person's categorization of his own feelings. The classical philosophical move was to treat the poles as marking proper attributions of wholly different kinds of predicates to distinct substances. Those like '150 pounds' were to be applied to the corporeal substance which made up a person's body, and those like 'conscience struck' being applied to the mental or spiritual substance that made up his mind, or soul. The philosophers found that they could not find any satisfactory way of dealing with predicates like 'elated' or 'proceeding cautiously' which presupposed an interaction between the substances, which had been so defined originally that their interaction was impossible.

The resolution both of the philosophers' and of the psychologists' problems stems from seeing the predicates for what they are. A set of attributions, always to the very same entity, namely a person, but differentiated by the degree to which different kinds of reports figure in deciding the correctness of attributing them to a person.

We have established in this chapter, we hope, the conceptual foundations for understanding the nature of the community of people. If we are right, that community is essentially linguistic. It is the web of language that makes for 'psychic' continuity between people. We can open our thoughts to each other because we can use language to do it. In so far as animals and birds are in symbolic interaction they too form a psychic community.[13] Such communities are very different in character from the energy-exchange community, of which people and animals form a part, and they are different again from the more specific communities constituted by the genepool. In our view human social life is through and through linguistic, and the best understanding of it can be obtained, we believe, by the use of linguistic and quasi-linguistic concepts. It may not prove too fanciful to take this idea so seriously as to seek for the grammars of the social order, and perhaps even for the deep structure or social universals that may lie behind all human communities.

REFERENCES

1. B. F. Skinner, 'The Operational Analysis of Psychological Terms', *Psych. Rev.* 52, (1945), 270–7, 291–4.
2. B. F. Skinner, *loc cit.*
3. T. W. Wann (editor), *Behaviorism and Phenomenology*, Chicago University Press, 1964.
4. R. B. Zajonc, in G. Lindzey and E. Aronson (editors), *The Handbook of Social Psychology*, Addison-Wesley, Reading, Mass., 1954, Vol. I, Ch. 5.
5. S. Schachter and J. E. Singer, 'Cognitive, Social and Physiological Determinants of emotional state', *Psych. Rev.* 69, 1962, 379–97.
6. P. F. Strawson, *Individuals*, Methuen, London, 1959, p. 104.
7. R. Carnap, 'Psychology in Physical Language', translated G. Schick, in A. J. Ayer, (editor), *Logical Positivism*, Free Press, Glencoe, Ill., 1959, Ch. 8.
8. W. H. Ittelson and C. W. Slack, 'The Perception of Persons as Visual Objects', in R. Tagiuri and L. Petrullo, (editors), *Person Perception and Interpersonal Behaviour*, Stanford, 1958.
9. S. Schachter, in *Advances in Experimental Social Psychology*, edited L. Berkowitz, Academic Press, New York, 1964, pp. 49–80.

10. R. Carnap, *op. cit.*, §7.
11. P. F. Strawson, *op. cit.*, p. 106 ff.
12. G. Ryle, *The Concept of Mind*, Hutchinson, London, 1949, pp. 25–40.
13. N. Tinbergen and H. Falkus, *Signals for Survival*, Clarendon Press, Oxford, 1970.

CHAPTER SEVEN

Preliminary Development of a New Methodology

THE ARGUMENT

I. *Methodological Consequences of Admitting the Analogy with Real Physical Science*

1. a. Statistical methods in current use yield, at best, critical description, and weak causal laws only of a correlational type.

b. Social psychology has yet to find a way to incorporate study of what corresponds to *causal mechanisms* in physical science.

c. This step must be based upon knowledge or conjecture as to what animates individual people to behave the way they do. It includes:

(i) the meanings they assign to items in their human environment,

(ii) the rules and conventions they follow in monitoring their social behaviour,

(iii) the waxing and waning of powers and capabilities.

d. (i) and (ii) are the substance of the *accounts* people give of their behaviour.

Our aim is to develop a conceptual system for analysing these accounts.

2. The conceptual system we develop can be 'checked out',

a. by how far it makes overt behaviour intelligible,

b. by how far it enables us to analyse and construct accounts.

3. These points can be illustrated from a comparison of the logic of the statistical method, and an example of real science, e.g., the scientific treatment of Boyle's Law in the molecular theory.

4. It follows that in ethogenic social psychology, *precision of meaning* corresponds to *accuracy of measurement* in physical science.

5. Since accounts are given in ordinary language the starting point for developing a conceptual system for their analysis must be the analysis of the conceptual system of ordinary language. This has already been done by the linguistic school of philosophy and psychologists can draw upon the results of their painstaking and detailed researches.

II. *Methodological Consequences of Accepting the Anthropomorphic Model of Man*

A. *Self-Direction*

1. The idea of self-direction is in contrast to the theory of environmental contingencies and controlling variables.

2. Current introduction of 'cognitive elements' into theory has been vitiated by a failure to accord them realistic status and to explore them through the collection and analysis of accounts. For instance 'dissonance' theories have failed in this way.

3. Examples of behaviour seemingly appropriate to each paradigm of explanation can be found, and some social phenomena seem susceptible of either mode of explanation.

4. Despite the overlap of explanatory modes it is clear that each will turn attention to different features of the phenomena themselves. We have already argued that social reality can even be destroyed by mechanistic analyses.

5. Critique of the attempt to eliminate causal, mechanistic explanations entirely:

    a. By taking habits as a model one might be tempted to try to eliminate mechanistic explanations entirely, since habits seem to be a class of high-grade behaviour which can be given a rules account by reference to the processes by which they were learned.

    b. *But*

        (i) there are other high-grade routines which seem to be

produced by the maturation of the organism as a system, e.g., walk-
ing, talking and the like, as well as social phenomena like facial
expressions.

(ii) In some accounts the causal paradigm is employed as,
for instance in those accounts sanctioned in Latin countries, in which
lust is cited as a quasi-mechanical cause of behaviour outside the
conscious self-monitoring of the helpless individual.

B. Explanation of Apparently Inconsistent Social Behaviour

1. The mechanistic model assumes a person identity to go with
a biological identity.
2. The self-monitoring and rule-following conception of social
behaviour allows one to consider the possibility of the biological
individual following different and incompatible rules of behaviour
from time to time, and thus presenting inconsistent social selves, or
personas.
3. Only within this conceptual system can the social psychology
of the Japanese be made intelligible, since, in Japan, consistency is
role-dependent and not biological person-dependent, and so a single
biological individual may have many roles to play, each of which
requires highly monitored rule-following of different sets of rules
which could not be combined into a single consistent system.

The Methodological Consequences of the Analogy with Natural Science

Social psychology can be considered a true science only to the extent
that it goes beyond the identification of patterns of overt behaviour,
and the conditions under which they occur, i.e., critical description.
As is well known, correlational findings can be given cause-effect
interpretations only within the unsatisfactory, Humean, metaphysical framework. Moreover, as we demonstrated in Chapter 3,
the neglect of person parameters in experiments guarantees that

relations between independent and dependent variables will be statistical only, and non-causal. As we have described, the established sciences are distinguished by the fact that they always seek to answer the question as to *why* the observed patterns among phenomena obtain. And they always proceed to answer that question by discovering or imagining the causal mechanisms which produce the phenomena. Social psychology shows only sporadic attempts to reach this stage, and has yet to pass confidently from critical description to science. Part of our purpose is to develop a method by which this transition can be achieved. The study of that which in the phenomena of social interaction corresponds to causal mechanisms in physical science we have called *ethogeny*.

As we have already observed, the mechanisms responsible for many of the observed patterns of social interactions essentially involve the inter-relations of meanings as perceived by the interactors. The way people respond is certainly *sometimes* determined by the way in which they have understood the meaning of the situations in which they find themselves.

The structure of the meaning relations can be discovered by studying the accounts that people give of social interactions in which they have taken part. It follows that, in order to discover what those meaning relations are, accounts must be collected and analysed, and for reasons which will emerge, these come usually in a justificatory context. Philosophical psychology has shown that a great many episodes in human life are best understood as the performance of certain patterns of action, in the course of which, and by the performance of which certain acts are performed. People taking part in such episodes understand their actions as the performance of certain acts. There are conventions or even explicit rules which serve to determine which actions are required for the performance of this or that act. These may be the formal rules of a ceremony, such as marriage, which determine which actions have to be performed in order that an act of marriage should be carried out, or they may be the informal conventions which determine which words, in which tone, and with which gestures, are the actions by which an insult is delivered. A description of the interaction which sets out the actions performed and the acts achieved we shall call a description of the

Act-action structure of the episode. The ethogeny of a formal episode like a marriage ceremony is easily uncovered, in that the people involved need refer only to the explicit rules in giving an account of what they each did. We shall be developing a methodology and conceptual system for the discovery and description of the ethogeny of less formal social interactions.

In the first instance we shall be trying to devise a system of concepts for understanding social interactions and to check this system against reality. It may be that after generations of human ethogenists have studied the lives of men, women and children, they may come to see that certain very subtle patterns of interaction do have the force of causal laws. But though our methodology cannot assume this, it must be such that it may ultimately lead to knowledge of laws. But the analysis of episodes should not be undertaken in the hope of discovering laws of nature immediately, but of identifying patterns in human life against which and with the help of which the adequacy of a conceptual system can be checked.

Looked at in more detail, 'checking-out' of a conceptual system can be seen to involve two stages. In the first stage, exemplified in such cases as those of the structure of a quarrel-pattern, only the broadest categories such as those implied by questions 'Did he do it?', 'Did he mean it?' and the like are involved, since one must first establish that this is an episode in which what happens is moderated by the perception of meanings. A movement, such as a hand coming into contact with a face, is fitted into a quarrel-pattern if the striker can be said to have meant it to hurt, and the sufferer to have understood it as being meant to hurt, and the like. At this stage we offer nothing by way of a justificatory account of the reasons for the action. In the second stage the justificatory context is invoked to produce an account which is then subjected to examination and analysis.

We have already noticed in Chapter Two that most social psychological experiments produce only descriptive information, albeit in quantitative form. The results of such enquiries are the proportions of similar interactions classified as to outcome, say cases of attitude-change which exemplify a certain pattern. At the critical description stage, the pattern is not explained. The significance levels of the results of doing many experiments on, say, the hypothesis that [PQ] is a pattern of inter-action in which there is the upshot Q, are not necessarily a measure of the degree of belief we should have in the proposition 'P caused Q'. For instance, finding that by engineering an inconsistency between behaviour and belief we can bring about an attitude-change to a certain significance level does not entail that cognitive dissonance *causes* attitude-change. That would involve construing the cases in which [PQ] is *not* exemplified as cases in which it *would* have been exemplified had there not been inter-ference in the background conditions. Instead we are perfectly at liberty to construe the cases in which the pattern [PQ] is not exemplified as ones in which some other pattern is exemplified, the occurrence of the pattern [PQ] being impossible in that type of situation. This point has been made informally by S. Hampshire.[1] High significance levels suggest the regular and dependable occur-rence of patterns of phenomena under specified conditions, but they have no direct causal implications. Such descriptive information, from experimental or other sources, provides no idea as to the mechanism of social interaction, nor could it provide it. Interpreting the parametric, mechanical model as a device for designing experi-ments that enable one to assign degrees of belief to causal hypotheses makes one think that the outcome [Q] of an episode can be ex-plained by instancing its temporal antecedents [P]. But what is wanted beyond critical description is the *explanation* of why the pattern [PQ] occurs, that is why and by what mechanism in those circumstances [P] produces [Q]. At least one of the answers may be that in that society there exists a convention by which the doing of [P] is the action for the achieving of [Q], for example it may be that a certain sequence of actions is, by convention, the performance of a marriage. More generally what is required is some understand-ing of the mode of *connection* between [P] and [Q].

Some of these points can be illustrated very clearly from the physical sciences. The experimental work of Hooke and Boyle by which they established the empirical patterns in the behaviour of confined samples of gas that we express as $PV = K$, were doing high-grade critical description. Their work was proto-scientific. We do not have real science until we know why P varies inversely as V, knowledge which became available only after the molecular theory of gases was formulated to provide us with an idea of the causal mechanism by which this pattern is produced.

So, too, in chemistry we begin with the critical laboratory checking of such statements as 'Blowing bubbles through a clear liquid prepared by shaking up lime and water and allowing it to settle, produces a white precipitate'. Much of practical laboratory chemistry is the extension and checking of 'rules of thumb' by which new information as to the patterns of reaction is discovered and false information from the common tradition weeded out. This is the first stage of science, and produces a number of protolaws. Science proper starts when the question 'Why?' is put and theory develops to answer it. By describing the causal mechanisms at work in a reaction in statements such as '$Ca(OH)_2 + CO_2 = CaCO_3 + H_2O$' we account for the pattern of reaction we observed, and connect it up with many other things that happen. This is the second stage of science.

The second stage has sometimes been attempted in social science, and the failure of particular efforts should not be the occasion for counsels of despair. L. Festinger's 'cognitive dissonance' theory was a bold attempt to advance to the second stage.[2] Empirical studies have revealed a number of patterns of attitude-change which the concept of cognitive dissonance was meant to explain. Unfortunately, Festinger's theory was too vaguely stated and the concept of cognitive dissonance too inadequately specified to serve as an adequate basis for explanation. A better understanding of attitude change which would incorporate what is meritorious in the theory, can be obtained by adopting an ethogenic approach by collecting a great many accounts of what people felt and how they understood their situation when they changed their minds at various times about various matters, and analysing these accounts by the use of the Role-rule set of models to be described later.

In fact, the ethogenic way with its readiness to blend the causal and the conventional, is the only way to pass to the second stage of science while preserving the conceptual integrity of the first stage in which descriptions involve the giving and grasping of meanings. This fact stands between the irreducible character of the patterns of human social life and the use of biochemistry and physiology to pass to the second stage. No doubt there are biochemical and physiological mechanisms at work in the giving and grasping of meaning, but they are at yet a third stage. They are related to linguistic powers and capacities as the theory of the electron structure of atoms is related to the atomic theory of chemistry, that is, they are always at one remove from the mechanisms of the patterns of reaction observed in the laboratory.

Since the giving and grasping of meanings is the mechanism of much of the patterns of social interaction, greater *precision* of the delineation of *meanings* is what corresponds in the social sciences to the development of greater *accuracy* of the *measurement* of parameters in the physical sciences. For instance, Argyle's studies of non-verbal behaviour[3] involve more and more precise delineation of the meaning of facial expressions and the like. His exercises in definition correspond to a physicist's exercises in *accuracy* of measurement.

Whenever it seems that the explanation of some pattern of social interaction should be sought in the reasons, rules, meanings and the like taken into account by the participants, it is clear that the description of the interaction would naturally in the first instance, at least, be expressed in language drawn from that commonly in use. The phenomena of social life are well-known, and a very elaborate system of concepts already exists in ordinary language for their description and explanation. This system has been extensively studied by linguistic philosophers, both in philosophical psychology and in modern ethics. It is a very powerful system, encompassing a great many kinds of social and individual phenomena, and showing great subtlety and refinement. Its present stage of sophistication is the product of a long historical process, in which it has been affected partly by the practical needs of social life, and partly by the refining effects of the need to express the subtleties of human interaction felt by dramatists, novelists, poets, lawyers, doctors, teachers and other practical people. We contend that ordinary language and its conceptual system is a much more refined instrument for scientific purposes than any terminology which can be produced *a priori* and *ad hoc* by a psychologist, though, of course a psychological vocabulary of great sophistication *could* develop by the same processes as have produced ordinary language. Comparative studies have borne this contention out with some force.[4, 5]

We shall not ourselves undertake any extended comparative studies of the effectiveness of ordinary language versus an *ad hoc* technical vocabulary in social psychology, though we shall from time to time draw attention to certain specific defects of technical terms. Rather, we shall make the more modest claim that no serious study can begin without paying careful attention to the conceptual system developed by philosophers for a particular field, and their understanding of the force of the vocabulary already at work there. It is one of the major contentions of this book that, while the statistical method is, with certain reservations and safeguards, a reasonable way of trying to discover and extend the critical description of social behaviour, it is impossible to use it as a method for discovering the generative mechanisms at work in social life. It could only do so were one to accept the Humean conception of cause and the positivist conception of science according to which causality means no more than regular concomitance, and explanation no more than subsumption of a particular case under a general law. We have already pointed out how these ideas are associated with a stimulus-response, or stimulus-organism-response model of human action, and a corresponding simple mechanistic model for the nature of human beings, which eliminates both spontaneity and idiosyncracy from its model, leaving human beings passive.

The processes that are productive of social behaviour occur in individual people, and it is in individual people that they must be studied. It is there that the vitally important dimensions of spontaneity and idiosyncracy occur. To achieve full scientific status, then, social psychology must make room for attempts to unravel the modes of generation of social behaviour 'within' the person. And this can be achieved only from the basis of an intensive study of particular cases, in which one may hope to discern the productive and generative 'mechanisms' at work, such as the evaluation of reasons, the making concordant of beliefs and so on. It is precisely this kind of study that the statistical method makes impossible, since it is concerned to eliminate idiosyncratic features of people by the use of controls, and by the method of random assignment to classes.[6] This is usually coupled with the assumption that changes produced externally and extrinsically to a person are determinative of his performance, attitudes, and so on, an assumption which effectively eliminates the dimension of spontaneity, and the vitally important capacity to consciously monitor performances, which is very characteristic of human behaviour and plays a very large role in determining the form the reactions take. It is in the detailed study of particular cases that we shall make progress towards discerning the patterns of reasons, feelings, beliefs, impulses, and so on that are responsible for the external relations and overall patterns discerned by the use of the statistical method. We have shown in Chapter Six that the arguments of philosophers which purported to show that information gleaned from people about their states of mind, beliefs and so on was unreliable for scientific purposes have little force, and can safely be ignored. At this point, we make contact with the phenomenological tradition.

Two cardinal principles of method thus emerge, which we shall illustrate in some proposals for empirical research along ethogenic lines. These principles are:

I. The conceptual system embedded in ordinary language should provide the basis for the concepts employed in a study, and should serve as the model for their logical interconnections. Thus, any serious study should begin with a careful conceptual analysis, using the results of the conceptual studies by linguistic philosophers as a guide, the product of which we shall call the O-system of concepts. Information already known by psychologists may lead to modifications both of the concepts and of the logical structure of the O-system.

II. Given the existence of some item of critical description, the detailed exploration of particular cases by the analysis of accounts should be undertaken with the aim of finding what cognitive and emotional structures are operative in producing the behaviour. A beginning in this direction has been made by the interesting work of Kelly.[7] For this purpose the accounts that people give of their behaviour, in a justificatory context, are an indispensable tool, and their critical analysis and the further study of the individual cases an ineliminable part of the method. In this way we shall start on the project of discovering just how behaviour is monitored. There are further features of individual human beings, the awareness of which demands a greater degree of sophistication in empirical explorations. Let us look a little further into what it is that really defines a human situation. Here we shall only sketch matters that will be given thorough treatment in later sections.

Most actual situations have to be described in two rather different kinds of terms, distinguished by the logically minded as the categorical and the conditional, or by the empirically minded as qualities (and relations) and powers. In studying aggression it is a commonplace to take account both of the degree of propinquity of the individuals involved and other such qualities and relations as well as of their dispositions to act aggressively, i.e., of their readiness to fight, shown for instance in the occurrence of threats. Mere descriptions of behaviour are apt to emphasize categorical or qualitative attributes to the neglect of the conditional properties or powers that underlie the behaviour sequence. In ordinary social life, an episode may be of great surface simplicity, but actually be of considerable complexity when looked at from the point of view of the waxing and waning of capabilities and readiness to act. For instance, a skilled hostess may manage to preserve an air of total calm throughout a difficult dinner party by being good at spotting the growing readiness to quarrel amongst one or more of her guests and skilfully circumventing it.

Thus, the reality of the episode may be largely confined to items which can only be described conditionally and in the subjunctive mood, such as 'might have happened', 'would have said', 'was spoiling for a fight', and the like. The actions and sayings of the people involved in an episode may be intelligible only on various assumptions as to the short and long-term powers of the people involved. It would be absurd to try to describe the waxing and waning of people's states of readiness as either dependent or independent variables, even though they are indeed something that varies. There are, of course, states of the persons involved that do indeed wax and wane in such form that might be metaphorically described as 'variables' (adrenalin concentration would be an example), but these are not the powers and states of readiness of a person, they are the states of that person by virtue of which he has that power or is in that state of readiness. This is a very simple logical point often overlooked by those who use a simple correlational methodology and investigate only the structure of interaction of external factors.

II. *The Methodological Consequences of Admitting Agency*

The Development from the Critical Descriptive Phase

The regularities observed in the behaviour of people may be explained according to several different schemata. One of the most interesting and natural dimensions along which these explanatory schemata may be contrasted is the extent to which the person is regarded as an agent directing his own behaviour. At one extreme he may be seen simply as an object responding to the push and pull of forces exerted by the environment. At the other, he may be seen as an agent guiding his behaviour toward some explicit goal by some means of which he is thoroughly aware. We may think of the former as focusing upon *environmental contingencies* and biological mechanisms and the latter as emphasizing *self-direction*, often by such means as following a rule.

Under the dominance of a behaviouristic framework incorporating the themes of logical positivism, a mechanistic model of man, and a Humean model of causes as efficacious external stimuli, explanations in terms of environmental contingencies have been much favoured, while explanations emphasizing self-direction have been castigated as unscientific, subjective, ambiguous and solipsistic. If, however, the assumptions on which behaviourism has been based are abandoned as untenable, then the way is opened for a reconsideration of explanations which involve self-monitoring as an essential element. The favouring of explanations involving environmental contingencies is the primary reason why psychology has often been subjected to severe criticisms by philosophers, scientists, and humanists. Much human behaviour can be quite simply explained and understood by supposing it to be the result of conscious direction by the individual himself. But in their zeal to adhere to what they conceived to be correct scientific principles, psychologists worked hard to explain this very behaviour in terms of environmental contingencies. The results of such extensive research efforts often appear banal or bizarre to non-psychologists who do not accept the assumptions which underlie the research.

The most persistent advocate of a psychological science based upon environmental contingencies has been B. F. Skinner.[8] His radical behaviourism stresses the manner in which responses are modified by various patterned contingencies of reinforcement. It is this paradigm which has generally been regarded as most deserving of the appellation of *mechanistic causal explanation*. Although his early work was conducted with rats and pigeons, his more recent interest has been in verbal behaviour,[9] and contemporary followers have extended his views to the study of children and mental patients.[10]

Those psychologists interested in social behaviour have for the most part adopted a form of explanation which falls somewhere between the extremes of environmental contingencies and full self-monitoring and self-direction. Currently popular among social psychologists, for example, are various cognitive explanations of behaviour. Such explanations generally postulate the operation of certain unobservable processes occurring in the individual. The causal chain is thought to begin with environmental contingencies which are perceived or interpreted by the individual. These perceptions in turn are thought to produce a certain cognitive state which affects his subsequent behaviour. For example, an individual who, under pressure from an experimenter, commits himself to some behaviour contrary to an attitude he holds is expected to experience *dissonance*, which might be interpreted as a state of discomfort arising from an inconsistency. One way of reducing this dissonance is to change his attitude to conform to his behaviour. It is important to note that this explanatory model lies at some middle point on the dimension characterized by the extremes of environmental contingencies and self-direction. Although it postulates the occurrence of certain processes in the agent, such as perception and a state of dissonance, these are not dealt with in any direct way, nor are they

K

obviously physiological in character. Emphasis in such research remains focussed upon the input of the contingencies or experimental treatments and the resulting output of behaviour. Although verbal reports are sometimes obtained from the participants in such experiments, they seldom play any important part in the explanatory schemata.

If explanations in which self-directing and self-monitoring play a part need no longer be excluded as unscientific, then a more sensible view than that hitherto taken by social psychologists would be that various behaviours, depending on their nature, are best explained by different schemata, or by combinations of schemata. Some forms of behaviour are perhaps best explained in terms of environmental contingencies. Certain emotional moods, such as depression for example, may well be produced by environmental contingencies in which self-direction has no part and the mechanisms of which are clearly biological. Many forms of habitual behaviour fall in the same category. In the exercise of skills, such as driving a car, playing tennis, or typing, the more elemental properties of the actions are under the control of environmental contingencies. These kinds of habitual behaviour are in a class characterized by the fact that their earlier history did indeed involve more self-direction during the learning stage. Awareness of means and intermediate goals characterizing these earlier stages gradually disappeared as the skills were acquired, leaving them in a semi-automatic stage. No doubt other habits, however, are learned without self-direction, such as stylistic aspects of expressive movement, and certain speech mannerisms.

There are also modes of behaviour at the other extreme which are best explained by schemata involving self-direction. For example, one may examine just those episodes where conscientious and meticulous rule-following is the origin of the sequence, as, for instance, in the sequence of actions or mock actions made by an actor, the behaviour of musicians in playing a piece, and in those episodes in ordinary life where there is an explicit and widely-accepted etiquette. Etiquette may extend not only to actions and facial expressions and the like, but may include feelings and emotions too.

Thus, when empirical investigation of a certain kind of social episode and a certain mode of conduct reveals regularities in the behaviour of the people involved, in the accounts they give of their reasons for conducting themselves in those ways and so on, the regularity may be accounted for either in terms of environmental contingencies or in terms of self-direction, or in terms of some combination of the two schemata. In some cases it is perfectly clear which treatment should be adopted. But, as we shall emphasize in Chapter Eight, a very great number of kinds of social episodes cannot be placed in the appropriate category straight away. It should be clear, too, from these considerations alone, that the discernment of a regularity is insufficient grounds for the declaration of the discovery of environmental contingencies and thus, of a causal relation. The difference between explanation in terms of self-directed elements and environmental contingencies is marked in the first instance by a difference in the concepts used in the description of the phenomena: e.g., the 'flatness' of the speech and other social performances of Nisei, i.e., second generation Japanese, discerned as a regular feature of their behaviour by Lyman,[12] could be described as the adoption of a self-protective *convention* or it could be treated as the *effect* of the change in certain social parameters. At the descriptive level there is little to choose between these modes of description except perhaps familiarity, simplicity, etc. But each leads off in a different direction in attempts to solve the problem of what to identify as corresponding to the causal mechanisms of natural science. The ethogenic view looks to systems of beliefs, attributions of meanings, adoptions of rules, codes of etiquette and the like, while the environmental contingencies view looks to a causal mechanism, which might also involve the *invention* of entities and states like cognitive dissonance, or sometimes looks to ungrounded assumptions about possible physiological mechanisms, quite unpursuable empirically in the forseeable future.

Unfortunately, the matter is not so simple as the above account might lead one to suspect. The difference between the several ways of approaching the task of understanding enigmatic episodes is not just a matter of the mode of explanation one should seek. If the scientist is committed in advance to a particular explanatory scheme, this will determine to a considerable extent what he identifies as the phenomena, and what he discerns in ambiguous reality to be the pattern of the episode. The *very descriptions* of the phenomena themselves are thus strongly coloured or biassed. Taking the rules-metaphor seriously would direct him to look for a pattern in the cognitive structures of the people involved, in their beliefs and in the kinds of reasons they might give in justification and explanation of the action. A quite different pattern might emerge by taking one of the more naïve causal approaches in which the pattern would be sought amongst the conditions and changes in circumstances which surround the people involved.

One might well ask whether it did not follow from all these considerations that the causal approach was redundant. An argument to that effect might be constructed in the following way: the result of using critical description to explore social phenomena is the discovery of certain patterns which are claimed by their discoverers to be discernible in the phenomena. In some cases these will be found to have their origin in the deliberate following of rules or conventions by the people involved. In those cases a simple causal account is redundant, if not absurd. But there are many other patterns which are not so clearly discernible as the product of the deliberate following of rules or conventions, even by those whose behaviour exemplifies them. Should not these be treated, *faute de mieux*, as cases of the production of effects by causes and their causal mechanisms sought, or paramorphic models of them conceived? But precisely the same feature of regularity of action with lack of awareness of rule-following or monitoring is found in a wide range of patterns of behaviour we call 'habits'. And habits are often the ingrained products of one-time explicit following of rules and self-monitoring of sequences of actions. The explanation of habitual sequences *must* in many cases include reference to the rules which had been followed during their ingraining. Thus in the concept of 'habit' we are presented with a paradigm for dealing with those cases which show regularity of sequence, but which are not, when fully formed, carried through by rule-following or any of its related ways of acting. Now habits originally based on rule-following, and genuinely causal sequences whose origins lie in the unthinking operation of biological mechanisms, are distinguishable empirically.

For a sequence of actions to be explicable as this type of habit, it must be possible, at least in principle, to identify the performance of that sequence, knowingly and with awareness, as a case of self-monitoring and perhaps rule-following actions.

So there are two dimensions upon which an empirical check can be made of the propriety of treating an enigmatic sequence under the rule-following metaphor. One lies in the collection and analysis of accounts by the actors in the sequence, and we shall devote considerable attention to how this check is carried out scientifically. It corresponds to the use of the microscope or the X-ray machine by a natural scientist. There is also the possibility of studying the manner of origin of certain sequences in social episodes, to see how they come into being. Are they taught through coaching and the encouragement of self-monitoring? If so, they are appropriately treated according to the rule-following paradigm. Are they the unthinking products of the operation of biological mechanisms brought into play by the maturation of the organism? If so, then they are appropriately treated according to the causal paradigm. The argument for the redundancy of causal hypotheses in the study of social phenomena depends upon the assumption that these alternatives are an exclusive disjunction. There is reason to think they are not.

It is by no means clear that there may not be some cases where an account of behaviour in terms of reasons and rules might not be profitably subsumed under a causal paradigm. Lyman and Scott, for example,[13] have noticed how in accounts of social behaviour amongst Latin people it is assumed that a person is simply carried along helplessly by such powerful forces as lust. Here what is clearly a cause is offered in a justificatory context, that is as a reason for a certain kind of behaviour. Finally, the fact that the mechanisms responsible for high-grade behaviour are biological leads to the *final* complication, that the biological maturation of the organism may lead to the development of competences, capabilities, capacities, liabilities, in short, of various powers, whose exercise occurs through rule-following. This is one of the important new insights into the nature of language using which we owe to Chomsky and his colleagues. So in the end, and we shall return to detailed discussion of the scientific consequences of this for social psychology in our chapter on human powers, only a rather complex blend of the biological causal model with the social rule-following model will give us an adequate treatment of the ethogeny of enigmatic episodes.

At this point it may be useful to show how the rule-following model of human behaviour can provide special illumination of certain puzzling types of social phenomena. We choose Ruth Benedict's analysis of Japanese social behaviour as an illustration.

The Humean positivist methodology makes an investigator look for the explanation of human behaviour in the 'controlling conditions', and to make two important identity assumptions about the people involved. One is that persons in experiments are identical to one another except for individual differences which are regarded as 'error' or unexplained, uninteresting, idiosyncratic variance. The other is an identity of the single person over time, a continuity in his behaviour. In this second identity, the invariant, which is necessary to any science, becomes something like a person's character, or personality. This choice of invariant encourages the application of concepts like consistency to all the thoughts, beliefs, emotions, acts and actions of a person, and the use of associated concepts like dissonance, in the explanation of changes in any of these items. So long as a person's behaviour, including verbal behaviour, is seen as an assemblage of responses to stimuli, however subtly these are differentiated and sophisticatedly distinguished, any attempt to introduce concepts such as agency into the scientific conception of man seems to be gratuitous. For an agent is apt to be considered capricious and unpredictable, quite unlike a robot. And it seems more likely that we can develop 'laws' of behaviour without this concept of man as an agent.

But it can hardly be denied that we *are* rule-following, self-monitoring agents. The most central fact in support of this view is that we could hardly be *scientists* unless we were! The difficulty has been to find a way of incorporating this central fact into a scientific psychology. It is our contention that the difficulty lies in an inadequate conception of what a science is, and of what it is to be scientific. We see nothing unscientific in the explanation of certain classes of human actions as lying in the following of action-generating rules by conscious self-monitoring agents. We see the origin of social behaviour in terms very similar to those in which Chomsky sees the origin of linguistic performance,[15] and with certain reservations, as Miller, Galanter and Pribram suggested many years ago,[16] one should see individual psychology.

In the case of the Japanese, we can hardly begin to understand their social behaviour on any other basis than that of the conscious following of different sets of very well-defined and independent sets of rules. The fact that the Japanese do not live according to one set of integrated rules, but have several quite independent rule-systems for different social relationships prevents us slipping into the idea that their behaviour can be understood on the positivist paradigm. We are inclined to think that that conception is partly a product of uncritical acceptance of philosophers' arguments about the epistemology of 'other minds', a feature even of sophisticated studies like that of Miller, Galanter and Pribram, but partly too a product of the fact that Westerners do indeed have fairly integrated 'personalities', and do follow a somewhat unified set of rules. It is then tempting to think that the regularities observed and described in stimulus-response terms are laws of human nature, whereas they are no more than the shadows cast upon the world by the relatively unified set of rules which each Westerner adopts. The same criticism can be offered of Western conceptions of personality in terms of traits or dispositions. But there is no single integrated mental system within *a* Japanese. For the Japanese, consistency does exist, but it is *role*-dependent, not *person*-dependent. To us, Japanese *people* seem to behave inconsistently. But this perception reflects a conceptual mistake. The concepts of consistency and inconsistency and related concepts just do not have application to a Japanese person as a biological individual, but have application only to each of his roles, each a system of rules. In Japan, it seems clear, the social individual does not coincide neatly with the biological individual, as he is assumed to do in the West.

This point has been made extensively by scholars of Japanese social behaviour. For instance, Ruth Benedict[17] describes the feature of Japanese life as follows: 'The Japanese view of life is just what their formulas of chu and ko and giri and jin and human feeling say it is. They see the "whole duty of man" as if it were parcelled out into separate provinces on a map. In their phrase, one's life consists of "the circle of chu" ["duty" to the State], and "the circle of ko" ["duty" to parents], and "the circle of giri" [e.g., "duty" to one's good name], and "the circle of jin" ["honour" in a group] and "the circle of human feelings" and many more. Each circle has its special detailed code and a man judges his fellows, not by ascribing to them integrated personalities, but by saying of them that "they do not know ko" or "they do not know giri". Instead of accusing a man of being unjust . . . they specify the circle of behaviour he has not lived up to. Instead of accusing a man of being selfish or unkind, the Japanese specify the particular province within which he violated the code. They do not invoke a categorical imperative or a golden rule. Approved behaviour is relative to the circle within which it appears'.

In a society in which meticulous rule-following is the stuff of life, one would expect a wholly different emotional scene. And this is related to the high degree of self-monitoring demanded in a system in which behaviour is generated by very detailed rules several independent systems each of which must be mastered. Japanese are very much aware of minor failures in fulfilling obligations. For them, obligations are not seen as derivatives of a categorical imperative, but as specific repayments of specific forms of *on*, a concept for which we have no real equivalent, though perhaps 'social indebtedness' might catch something of its flavour. The sanction which ensures that people do follow the prescribed rules for each 'circle' is public opinion, *within that circle*, so that failure within one circle does not carry opprobrium into other circles, which are wholly independent. Thus the concept 'bad man' cannot be applied to a man generally in a moral sense, condemning him as an individual, but has application to a biological individual only in the sense of 'unskilful'. As Ruth Benedict puts it:[18] 'the good player is the one who accepts the rules and plays within them. He distinguishes himself from the bad player because of the fact that he is disciplined in his calculations and can follow other players' leads with full knowledge of what they mean under the rules of the game'. In short, the good man is he who shows the highest degree of conscious self-monitoring and awareness of the social world and its meanings in following the detailed rules of each 'circle'. Failure produces shame, not guilt. 'Shame is the root of virtue' say the Japanese. Shame and guilt are very different emotions, and function very differently in the genesis of action. For instance, guilt is relieved by confession, shame is exacerbated by it. Thus, what a Japanese is ready to do in social situations that he defines as widely different, will be quite different from what a Westerner might do in the same social situations, which he may see as similar to one another. The emotional states that are felt by a Japanese in virtue of which he comes to have this or that short-term tendency or liability, show a different pattern, a pattern which can only be understood by reference to the particular rule-system, and the particular 'circle' of obligation in which he finds himself.

It seems to us, then, that, in giving a scientific account of Japanese social behaviour, the generative element is the set of rule-systems as understood and deployed in self-monitoring action by each Japanese. By pursuing the study of the rule-systems as understood by each person, a social psychologist will be doing just exactly what a chemist is doing in studying the behaviour of ions, whose inter-relations are responsible for the observed behaviour of chemically interacting materials. In short, only by reference to the complex systems of rules can we explain the facts of Japanese social life, and its differences from the social life of the West. Once one admits the need for explanation, over and above the discovery of critical natural history, one is driven to search for the rules, for they are what must guide the behaviour of self-monitoring organisms.

REFERENCES

1. S. Hampshire, *Thought and Action*, Chatto and Windus, London, 1965.
2. L. Festinger, *A Theory of Cognitive Dissonance*, Harper and Row, New York, 1957.
3. M. Argyle, *Social Interaction*, Methuen, London, 1969, pp. 92–110.
4. R. M. Kurtz, 'A Conceptual Investigation of Witkin's Notion of Perceptual Style', *Mind*, **78**, (1969), 522–33.

5. D. Hamblyn, *The Psychology of Perception*, Routledge and Kegan Paul, London, 1957.

6. A. Cicourel, *Method and Measurement in· Sociology*, Free Press, New York, 1967.

7. D. Bannister and J. M. M. Mair, *The Evaluation of Personal Constructs*, Academic Press, London and New York, 1968, Ch. 1.

8. B. F. Skinner, *Science and Human Behavior*, Macmillan, New York, 1953.

9. B. F. Skinner, *Verbal Behavior*, Appleton-Century-Crofts, New York, 1957.

10. T. Allyon and E. Haughton, *J. of Exp. Analysis of Behavior*, 5, (1962), 343–52.

11. R. P. Abelson *et al*, *Theories of Cognitive Consistency*, Rand McNally, Chicago, 1968.

12. S. L. Lyman, personal communication.

13. S. L. Lyman and M. B. Scott, 'Accounts', *Am. Soc. Rev.*, 33, (1968), 46–62.

14. E. H. Lennenberg, *The Biological Bases for Language*, Wiley, New York, 1967.

15. N. Chomsky, *Cartesian Linguistics*, Harper and Row, New York, 1966, pp. 59–73.

16. G. A. Miller, E. A. Galanter and K. H. Pribram, *Plans and the Structure of Behavior*, Holt-Dryden, N.Y. 1960, especially Ch. 1 and Ch. 4.

17. R. Benedict, *The Chrysanthemum and the Sword*, Routledge and Kegan Paul, London, 1967 (1st Edition, 1946), p. 137.

18. Benedict, *op. cit.*, p. 154.

CHAPTER EIGHT

The Analysis of Episodes

THE ARGUMENT

The Principles of the Analytic Scheme

1. Social behaviour is mostly consciously self-monitored rule-following.
2. In social situations people present themselves under what they take to be suitable personas.

The Similarities and Differences between Animal Ethology and Human Ethogeny

1. Similar in their emphasis on the careful observation of real life.
2. Different in that by means of language the genesis of human action in the plans and intentions of the agents can be investigated directly.

The Concept of an Episode

1. *Any* natural division of social life is an episode.
2. The content of a social episode includes not only overt behaviour, but the thoughts, feelings, intentions and plans, etc., of the participants.

Preliminary Conceptual Distinctions

1. Between things done *to* a person, and things done *by* a person.

a. The fundamental concept of Skinnerian methodology is 'things done *to* a person'. Our fundamental concept is 'things done *by* a person'. This modifies our conception of the way things done to a person affects him. 'Things done by a person' brings meanings to the centre of the system, and thus 'Things done to a person' are effective, in modifying social reality, in so far as they are understood by the person as having this or that meaning.

b. There are things that happen to people, e.g., disease, but their effect is profoundly influenced and modified by assignments of meaning, e.g., the Christian Scientist's conception of disease.

c. Most episodes include both kinds of impressions upon people.

d. The concept 'Things done by a person' is most closely related to the traditional conception of a person as an agent.

2. Between movements and actions.

a. Movements and emitted noises are parts of social reality, but count as *actions*, only in so far as they are directed towards the accomplishment of acts.

b. Movements, actions and acts are not in 1–1 correspondence conceptually.

3. Between causes and reasons.

a. (i) In the analysis of ordinary language, as it is used in raw accounts, this is a major conceptual distinction.

(ii) The same event may be offered as reason and as cause, in natural science.

(iii) Reason is that from which a description of a happening follows logically, but some adequate premises do not describe causes.

b. (i) In the accounts of human action reasons appear in a justificatory context, and logically imply the propriety of a happening, as opposed to its existence, which would follow from the description of its cause.

(ii) For 'propaganda' purposes some justificatory reasons are passed off as causes, as e.g., in the substitution in common speech of 'need' for 'want'.

c. The same happening may get a reasons account in a justificatory context, and a causes account in some other context.

It is the reason in the justificatory context that often generates the social action in real life.

d. The several accounts derived from a multi-person episode may differ, but authenticity demands concordance of accounts.

The Principles of Unity of Episodes

1. An episode may be structured because it is the following out of a plan by consciously self-monitoring agents. We treat plans as a special class of *ad hoc* rules, and assimilate intentional action to action according to rule.

2. An episode may be structured because it consists of the sequence of actions necessary to the performance of an act.

a. Habitual actions: These are performed unselfconsciously but are often capable of retrospective commentary.

b. Actions which are meant: Actions which are capable of any or all of retrospective, monitoring or anticipatory commentary.

Note. (i) Purposive actions are those for which, anyone, actor or bystander, can provide an anticipatory commentary.

(ii) Intentional actions are those purposive actions for which the actor can provide an anticipatory commentary.

c. Commentaries are normally produced in real life only in contexts of justification, so we are concerned in ethogeny often with readiness to comment rather than with commentary.

Formal and Causal Episodes

In seeking the basis for models for the ethogeny of social episodes we choose *formal episodes*.

1. Formal episodes: Reference is made to explicit rules in

accounting for the sequence and type of the actions performed, e.g. a marriage is explained by reference to the litany.

2. Causal episodes: Reference is made to physiological, chemical or physical mechanisms in accounting for the sequence and type of the happenings, e.g., gestation and parturition.

Considered with respect to either 1 or 2 most social episodes are *enigmatic*. Traditionally, psychology has chosen the causal model. Our choice is to understand the enigmatic on the model of the formal episode. This solution has been brilliantly demonstrated by E. Goffman, although in a rather casual, unsystematic fashion.

3. Unlike H. Garfinkel, we treat the question of the extent of the power of the formal rules model to explain the genesis of social action as an empirical matter. However we recognize the importance of two of his technical innovations.

a. 'garfinkelling': the technique of disrupting the social fabric to discover in the consequent reaction, its generating rules.

b. The study of people 'passing' in deliberately acquired social roles to discover what rules they are following to present themselves in the role.

Overt and Covert Structures of Episodes

1. Overt Structures: these are described in terms of acts and actions, and are called by us the Act-action structure.

2. Covert Structures:

a. The waxing and waning of powers and states of readiness, not all of which may appear overtly in actions, but reference to which may be necessary to making the episode intelligible. This will be called the Powers structure.

b. The flux of emotions, treated by us as the meanings assigned to states of arousal, will be called the Arousal structure.

The ethogenic point of view conceives of the paradigmatic form of overt social behaviour as the following of rules and conventions in a self-monitoring process of which the social actor may be conscious. Social behaviour is to be explained through the collection and analysis of participants' accounts. Through this channel, we hope to be able to discover what leads people to follow the particular social ways they do. In this way we hope to discover the rules, plans, conventions, images and so on that people use to guide their behaviour.

We now proceed to the development of a general conceptual system for the analysis and critical understanding of accounts, so that from them we can draw knowledge of the genesis of social actions, knowledge that will function in this sphere analogously to the way knowledge of causal mechanisms functions in the sphere of the physical sciences, explaining the observed non-random patterns in nature. By this means we hope a start can be made in discovering the dynamics of social behaviour.

Two general principles have emerged from our study up to this point, which we believe, must lie behind any serious theory of social behaviour. In general social behaviour is the result of conscious self-monitoring of performance by the person himself, in the course of which he contrives to assess the meaning of the social situations in which he finds himself, and to choose amongst various rules and conventions, and to act in accordance with his choice, correcting this choice as further aspects of the situation make themselves clear to him. This is the basis of our conception of social behaviour. Participants' accounts are accounts of this process. Our second general principle distinguishes the biological individual from the social individual, and we hold that most biological individuals are associated with a plurality of social selves or personas. The presentation of an appropriate social self is one of the important products of the self-monitoring of social performance. In the remaining chapters, we develop a conceptual system for the practical application of these two principles in a reformed social science. The first step must be the development of a rather general set of concepts for bringing some preliminary order into the mass of rules, conventions and so on which we refer to in justificatory accounts, and make use of in following plans.

The enormous developments in the science of animal behaviour which have inaugurated the 'new' biology, derive from one major change in method. The ethologists left the laboratory and the zoo, and watched the way animals, fish and birds ordinarily lived.[1] They observed modes of behaviour undreamt of by scientists in laboratories and curators of zoos. Unlike humans, the animals, fish and birds whose lives they studied, had no way of describing what they did, or accounting for it, so the ethologists have had to invent a new conceptual system to cope with the problem of the description and representation of what they saw, and more recently with its explanation.[2]

Only if social psychologists can be persuaded to turn their attention to life situations, of which life in the laboratory is a very small and restricted part can justice be done to the richness and complexity of the daily life that is familiar to all of us as lay persons, and for which our language is a well-adjusted conceptual instrument. Those who wish to study people as they really live their lives have a ready-made conceptual system for expressing the results of their observations in the accounts people ordinarily give of their behaviour. This is why we have emphasized the essential rightness of the discoveries of the linguistic philosophers for psychology. And since one important feature of the conceptual scheme is that it allows for the explanation of the behaviour of people from the point of view of the actors themselves, something which the conceptual scheme of Lorenzian ethology cannot, in the nature of the case, provide for animals, some insights into the genesis of that behaviour can be obtained by studying the accounts that are given by the actors themselves. At this point the ethogenic way merges with the phenomenological tradition. Any form of social psychology which makes essential use of actor-based understandings and construals of situations cannot be assimilated into ethology. Thus if we take the accounts of people involved in social interaction seriously, as reports of phenomena significant in the explanation of social behaviour, we have taken a step beyond ethology. It is for this reason, amongst others, that we have insisted that the scientific study of the social behaviour of human beings should be distinguished from ethology, and have coined the name 'ethogeny' for the more broadly based method we are advocating.

To an ethogenist, everything of interest that occurs in human life, happens in the course of, or as the culmination of, or as the initiation of an episode. We think the term 'encounter' unsuitable, since it suggests that people bring a fixed personality or nature to an episode, and that the episode is the interplay of enduring individual natures. In fact the powers and liabilities a person has in an episode are highly episode dependent. An episode is any part of human life, involving one or more people, in which some internal structure can be discerned. The vast majority of episodes can be seen to have a beginning, and to come to an end. The beginning and end of episodes are often marked by a ceremony, such as the extended episode of studying at a University, which begins with matriculation and ends with graduation. A dinner party has a less formal, but no less well defined ceremonial initiation and closure, completed by the 'bread and butter' letter or telephone call. A quarrel can be followed through to a final situation which the combatants resolve by disengaging, after which there is a longer or shorter tailing-off process, marked by the persistence of certain feelings towards the other, the quiet rehearsals of verbal or even physical revenge, and so on. This example shows that the choice of markers for the beginning and end of an episode is not absolutely determined. For certain analytical purposes, the moment of disengagement could be taken as the end of the quarrel, while for other purposes it might be necessary to take account of the aftermath in each participant. A person's change of attitude towards some subject is also an episode, marked by the initial disturbance of the tenability of a belief, and culminating in the manifestation or avowal of the new and different attitude. Ethogeny will provide us with a methodology and a related conceptual system, by means of which episodes can be identified, classified, and their internal structure unravelled.

Social psychologists and other social scientists are concerned not only with the study of the processes by which people interact socially, but also with the investigation of the nature of the products of that interaction. Their subject matter overlaps with that of novelists, biographers, historians, dramatists and poets, but they wish to study this same subject matter *scientifically*. In a previous chapter we have outlined the structure and methods of the natural sciences, and

L

pointed to the equivocal character of much of social psychological theory when examined with the structure and function of theory in the established sciences in mind. We noticed too that though certain theories, e.g., 'balance' theories, and particularly the theory of cognotive dissonance, meet certain of the desiderata of the established scientific methodology, social psychologists have paid insufficient attention to the demand that the mechanisms of social behaviour should have a high degree of plausibility in the context. For this reason alone the explanatory part of social psychology must contain reference to the thoughts, feelings, construals, social perceptions, and so on of those participating in the given interaction, or, by developing an adequate conceptual analysis, must provide good reasons for not incorporating reference to a particular common feature of human mental life, traditionally thought to be relevant to the explanation of some piece of social behaviour.[3] It should be noticed that this demand does not exclude physiological and biological facts from the explanatory armoury of social psychology. However, the correct way to incorporate facts of these kinds into social studies is a tricky matter, to be given a detailed account later in the book. This, we noticed, was connected with the tendency we drew attention to in Chapters Two and Three for there *still* to be underlying assumptions of positivist views of science, confused notions of causality, and assumptions of the essential identity of human beings as participants in experiments, despite lip service to individual differences. Part of this we saw to be due to the continuing use of grossly misleading technical terms, such as 'variable', part to simple ignorance of the method of the established sciences.

The many strands of argument developed so far must be drawn together now into a positive theory of method. The theory we now develop refines and integrates tendencies already in existence in social psychology and the other social sciences. We have already spoken of human life as consisting of 'episodes'. By this term we mean *any* sequence of happenings in which human beings engage which has some principle of unity. It might be that the happenings take place within a defined place and during a certain time as in a church service; it might be that they occur to and among a certain group of people, as in a student demonstration; it might be that they

issue in a certain discernible result, either by way of natural causation, or by convention, or by some combination of causation and convention, as in a marriage ceremony; it might be that they are unified
in some other way. We shall come to see that certain episodes have
such a principle of unity that they can come to the attention of social
psychologists, and other social sciences, while some merit the attention
of human biologists. Later we shall see how paradigm cases of these
distinct kinds of episodes are distinguished. For the moment we wish
only to make clear the extreme generality with which we wish the
notion of an episode to be understood: we do not propose a finite list-
ing of characteristics by means of which episodes can be identified.
Here are some examples of episodes: buying a chocolate bar in a small
shop; bumping into a passer-by, apologizing and going on; reading
a book and discussing it with several other people, some of whom
have not read it and one of whom pretends to have read it but has
not; a change of attitude; the emergence of a leader; a trial; a strike;
a playground game, and so on. There are any number of dimensions along which episodes can be classified.

The episodes which are of interest to social psychologists tend to
be face to face rather than mediate, to involve something less than
full communication between the people involved, and to be concerned with individuals, and with groups only in so far as these
bear upon the performances of individuals. But despite the fact that
the behaviour of institutions is not part of the field of social psychology, facts about highly structured institutions may figure in certain
accounts, if, as in the elucidation of, say, a case of 'role-conflict', the
discordant roles are thrust upon an individual by virtue of his
position in an institution. It is not possible to delimit a field of
enquiry for social psychology which does not involve paying attention both to wider social considerations, and to narrower considerations of individual psychology.

Before a conceptual scheme for classifying and analysing the
structure of those episodes studied by social psychologists is introduced we must go somewhat more deeply into two distinctions of
quite crucial importance to getting the method of a true social
science right. These distinctions have been much discussed in philosophical psychology but are usually tacitly assumed and not clearly

understood by social scientists, psychologists being particularly prone to get them wrong, through an uncritical use of the words 'behaviour', 'control', 'response' and the like. The first distinction is that between the things that are done *by* a person, including the things he says, and the things done *to* a person, or that happen to a person. Much of psychological research has been done under the uncritical assumption that the most fundamental concept is that of 'things happening to' a person. This is, for example, very marked in Skinnerian methodology. For example, in behaviour modification studies of psychotherapy the therapist's response 'Uh-hmm' was at first treated as an impersonal reinforcement, in a mechanistic causal framework. The view was advanced that these could be counted and in proportion to their frequency the associated patient behaviour would increase in frequency. But studies by Spielberger[4] have shown that the results are in fact more variable than would be predicted by a mechanistic cause-effect framework, and that the patient in fact is responding in terms of a meaningful *interpretation* of the therapist's behaviour, rather than to the *number* of 'Uh-hmms'.

The understanding is actively involved even in episodes such as becoming embarrassed in a certain social situation since one must know what the embarrassing words and gestures *mean* before they can have that effect. There can be no such qualification to what happens when one is pushed off a log. We shall be concerned from time to time with these intermediate cases, since they mark the shadowy boundary between the social sciences and human biology. How a person catches a cold is a biological question, though, once he has it, meanings, rules, conventions and the life games he is engaged in and the like may begin to intrude in the actual course of a real episode. For instance, anyone playing the life-game identified by Berne as the game of 'wooden leg',[5] must have suffered some injury which in a perfectly straightforward way causes certain subsequent states in him, which can be the basis for his self-pitying claim 'What can you expect of a man with a wooden leg?'

The intermediate region between things done to a person and things done by him is really the nexus of three dimensions of difference, that between patient and agent, that between being acted upon and taking action, and that between being the effect of a cause and being the result of a rationally guided action. The connection between the three dimensions is so close that any one will serve to partition episodes appropriately. When a person is genuinely subject to a causal process explained in terms of the biological mechanisms at work then he has to be treated as a patient who is acted upon rather than an agent who acts. The sequence of states that make the syndrome of a physical illness are the states of an individual who suffers them. But no real medical episode is purely physical, in the sense that all of its features can be explained by immediate advertance to biological mechanisms, though there are many other games than 'wooden leg' open to the ill. Thus immediate reference to biological mechanisms is appropriate to those cases when we are inclined to see a participant as a passive sufferer of the action of causes, whereas in those cases in which he appears to be acting as an agent the reference to biological mechanisms is at the best mediate, and often, in the present and forseeable state of the art, impossible. Thus the intermediate region can be identified either as those cases where it is not clear whether it is advisable to treat the participants as acting or being acted upon, or as those episodes in which a good deal of what happens seems to be capable of immediate biological explanation, but not all. How a person changes his attitude towards some matter is a social psychological question but is in the intermediate region, since though it is not strictly something that he *does*, it is not something that happens to him either. It is not like giving orders to subordinates, nor is it like breaking one's arm when caught by a swinging gate. We shall be developing some concepts for helping us to get a grip on this intermediate region directly below.

There is no single term for the things that people do including what they say, when we mean to include things done from habit, things done reflexively and things done deliberately. So we shall illustrate the distinction by an example. One of the things that people do is to make bodily movements. We shall discuss the distinction we are making here in terms of this case, though the distinction applies quite generally to anything that people can do, while it does not apply at all to the things people have done to them. In the intermediate cases we shall not be able to say without careful study and negotiation whether the distinction should or should not be applied. A person makes all sorts of bodily movements in the course of an episode, contracting and relaxing muscles in various sequences. Some of these movements can be seen or heard or felt by others, some are known to others only through their effects. Some of these *movements* we wish to treat as *actions*, and in some of these actions we see *acts* performed. We watch a man's hand move towards the extended fourth finger of the hand of a woman and slip a gold ring on that finger. If this movement meets certain criteria it is an action in the performing of which, together with certain other actions, a marriage is achieved, that is, an act is performed. A *movement* is given *meaning* as an *action* by being identified as the performance or part of the performance of an *act*.[6] This is a special case to illustrate a more general distinction which can also be reached from another direction.

Before we leave the special case of [*movement, action, act*] it is worth noticing that with respect to a given act, all sorts of different movements may constitute the actions in the performance of which the act is carried out. Holding hands and jumping over a fire, then smashing a glass, are the movements which, seen from the point of view of bringing about an act of marriage amongst gypsies, are the actions required for the successful performance of that ceremony. It follows from this very elementary consideration that the episodes of human social life can neither be treated wholly as sequences of movements, for under that description alone their significance and social meaning is lost, nor is it sufficient merely to state the act performed, since the performance, which is after all the true social reality, is a sequence of actions, that is movements and sayings and so on, given meaning by reference to that act. It is a very general truth that most, if not all, acts, correspond to a wide latitude of movements. Notice also that a closer look at the movements will not resolve the problem of their identification for an old-fashioned type of behaviourist, or indeed for any behaviourist who eschews meaning, e.g., Skinner, since on closer scrutiny the latitude of possible movements under even such a specific description as 'leaping over the fire hand in hand' becomes enormous. Reference to inner states is of no help either since we meet once again enormous latitude, for one can leap over the fire joyfully, resentfully, fearfully, nervously, unintentionally, unwillingly, unwittingly, drunk or sober, etc., etc., and *still* find oneself married. Compare the variety of inner states to the accompaniment of which one may buy something at an auction, where a careless movement, if it has a certain meaning to the auctioneer may land you with a Vermeer you can ill afford.

We can also consider the things that a man does from the point of view of the accounts that he gives of them, either spontaneously or when encouraged or pressed to do so. An account may be anticipatory, retrospective or contemporaneous with the sequence of things done to which it refers. Others may also give accounts of what he does. These accounts may refer to causal mechanisms, when, as in the defence of the man accused of ogling schoolgirls in a tramcar in Auckland, New Zealand, it was shown that he suffered from a tic in the eyelid; or more usually accounts may offer reasons in justification, explanation or excuse for what has been done, or is being done now or is going to be done shortly or later. Whenever someone, self or others gives an account consisting of reasons then what is, was or will be done is an action. The distinction between reasons and causes has been thoroughly debated by philosophical psychologists and has, it seems to us, reached a definite conclusion. There can be no doubt that the concepts are distinct.

For our purposes the conceptual issues raised by the relations between the concepts of reason and cause can be resolved through the following distinctions:

1. Both reasons and causes can appear in the explanation of happenings, whether these happenings are the actions of people, the movements of animals, or even inorganic natural phenomena. 'The reason why the avalanche fell was the sudden increase in wind pressure' seems to cite the same facts in the same relation as 'The cause of the falling of the avalanche was the sudden increase in wind pressure'. Should we conclude from this, as some philosophers have done, that reasons are a special class of causes, or should we say that causes are a special class of reasons? If we are inclined to see a strong conceptual connection between explaining and giving reasons, and are inclined to suppose that causal explanations are not the only way of explaining happenings, then we should be drawn to taking the

latter point of view, and suppose that citation of causes is one of the many ways of providing reasons. Reasons seem to be differentiated from causes by the fact that only some of the facts cited in explanation of happenings could be classified as causes. This argument seems to have force even for a quite strict positivist sense of explanation in which from a statement of the reason (or cause) one should be able logically to infer a description of that which it explained. We owe to S. L. Godlovitch an elegantly economical case from ethology where the reason for a phenomenon could not possibly be its cause, i.e., an explanation meeting the positivist criterion, but in which the explanans could not possibly be contrasted as describing a cause of the explanadum. The reason why a predator does not eat a moth is that it does not see the moth. The fact that it was not eaten implies that it was not seen. But of course these facts could not be causally related. Though, of course, we may quite properly say that a visual moth-stimulus (being seen) caused the predator to eat the moth, and so explain that fact causally.

2. A partition of greater ethogenic interest can be made by seeing that reasons are usually offered in human affairs in the course of providing a justification or excuse for some action.[7] Justifications may be extraordinarily varied. For instance, the justification for a certain action may be provided by reference to the act which is done by the performance of the action. Or, in accounting for an action, one may cite what one was trying to do, one's aim or end, as the reason for doing that thing. The logical point of importance here is that accounting for the action is citing something from which the *propriety* of the action is supposed to follow. In short, reasons are offered in justification of actions, and so are logically related to the propriety of the actions and not to the existence or occurrence of the action, which in one and the same episode may be causally explained. What is deceptive here is that both reason and cause are answers to a single question, 'Why did he do it?' What is overlooked is that this question can be answered in two conceptually independent contexts. In terms of reasons, the consideration is of an active agent making a decision in a normative or justificatory context; in terms of causes, the consideration is of a passive agent exposed to certain circumstances and conditions, both internal and external. That both

are answers to the same form of question—namely 'Why?'—sometimes leads the two forms of explanation to be confused with each other.

It would be a serious mistake to treat reasons offered in a justificatory context as if they were causes. This could be looked upon with some justification as one of the most serious defects of the methodology of traditional psychology. This treatment is implicit in the various attempts that have been made to treat both motives and intentions as special classes of causes. We shall not go any further into this matter at this point, since the problem of the correct treatment of motives has been thoroughly discussed by R. S. Peters,[8] while the conceptual impropriety of a thoroughgoing identification of intentions with part of the causal conditions of action seems to be a clear consequence of the study of intentions by G. E. M. Anscombe.[9] We shall have a good deal to say about motives and intentions construed as readinesses to give explanations, in the chapters on human powers. The scientific methodology of those reasons which are causes is natural science. Our aim is to make explicit a scientific methodology for the kinds of reason, some of which are quite certainly not causes, that figure in accounts. The zero-reason in this group is represented in the account 'I just wanted it'. Note that for propaganda reasons a person may try to pass off one of the second class of reasons as one of the first class, and instead of giving the above account of her decision to buy an unnecessary object, say instead 'I just had to have it'. There is a large slice of accounts which have this feature, exemplified by the use of 'need' as propaganda for 'want', and exemplified, for instance, in the often-heard claim that one needs a drink proper only when spoken by an alcoholic. We shall return to the analysis of this distinction in accounts later.

It is possible, therefore, for a movement to be accounted for by one commentator by reference to reasons while another commentator refers to causes. The social sciences have emphasized the causal framework to the neglect of the naturalistic mode of explanation in terms of reasons. The adherence to a causal framework has most often been tacit, and followed from an explicit adherence to such apparently neutral concepts as 'variable'. But of course to treat the state of the factors at work in a social episode as values of variables is precisely to beg the question as to the nature of the ethogeny of social life. In fact, social scientists are concerned with just those human interactions in which action is mediated by meanings, rules and the like, and these are just the concepts for which the explanatory framework is the system of reasons and justifications. However, we are not claiming that a causes account cannot be useful in certain cases, or is never relevant, but that the analysis of social episodes and the explanation of their genesis involves reference to principles of order for the sequences of happenings different from those which are used to order items causally which derive from the immediate reference to biological mechanisms for their explanation. There are very many cases, as we shall bring out below, where it is uncertain, at first sight, into which realm an episode falls. However difficult it may be to decide the case of a particular episode, and however complex may be the interweaving of the strands of cause and convention or the relative importance of biological mechanisms and rule following, the distinction between the *realms* is clear enough, and hence the distinction between modes of explanation and kinds of empirical exploration associated with the realms. Many episodes lie in both realms.

Of course not all episodes will be capable of being given an account by all the actors. Episodes in which habitual movements figure would be an example of this, in that they call forth what one might call the zero-account, 'I did it from habit', which indirectly refers to the historical origin of the tendency to make the movement or movements in that particular sequence. There are yet again intermediate cases, which serve to bring out the structure of the extreme cases. In the standard case of accounting there will be a concordance between the anticipatory commentary, the monitoring commentary and the retrospective commentary, and in the extremal case these commentaries will differ only in tense. When that occurs we are inclined to accept the commentaries as authentic. The notions of 'truth', and even 'verisimilitude' will prove to be too strong in the context of the human sciences, and their uncritical adoption has caused some mischief. It has been unthinkingly assumed that since they cannot be met in a *wholly* unproblematic way, commentaries have no authenticity and can form no part of science. This is *exactly* parallel to the problem of induction in the natural sciences, which is created by supposing that if general laws cannot be proved to be true from the restricted kind of evidence which *can* be collected, then they have *no* title to belief, a supposition which, if accepted, would make natural science impossible. Perfect authenticity will be said to have been achieved when there is full concordance between *all* accounts, both between anticipatory, monitoring and retrospective commentaries, and between the accounts of all the people involved in the episode. Concordance does not of course imply identity. We should expect in many cases that some people's accounts will contain items not in those of another, but authenticity is preserved when the idiosyncratic items are concordant with the items in the accounts of others. When accounts are first obtained there will be disparities both between the anticipatory, monitoring and retrospective commentaries, and between the accounts given by different people. There are various technical reasons that could be offered as to why accounts need never be concordant (e.g., the discrepant positions of the different observers, the different references frames they use, etc.). Authenticity is arrived at by negotiation between the people involved. The procedure of negotiation will occupy us later, since its structure and standards are crucial to the ethogenic way. Typically, an account of an episode in which much that happens is done from habit, will lack an anticipatory and monitoring commentary, but may be capable of being given an account in a retrospective commentary. Not only habit, but more diffuse notions like 'style of life' will occupy this important region of intermediate cases, between fully authentic accountable episodes, and those for which no reasons-account at all can be given or asked for.

So far we have briefly discussed only one of the many possible ways in which a principle of unity can give structure to a sequence of happenings in which human beings interact. This was the case in which the sequence constitutes a set of actions in the performance of which a certain act is carried out. The happenings, for instance movements, are given meaning as actions by reference to the act attempted, whether or not it is actually successfully performed. An Act-action structure is most characteristic of formal episodes and of those informal episodes which can be made intelligible by treating them as like this or that kind of formal episode. But there are other ways in which happenings can be given meaning with respect to something else, and so unified. These other ways have to do, one way or another, with the idea of the following of a plan or the carrying out of a purpose, with respect to which component items in a sequence of happenings constitute an episode. Movements given meaning as actions in this way, are one of the cases of intentional action most commonly discussed by philosophers. We see the carrying out of a plan as a special case of rule-following when the rule is one which one sets for oneself. We shall speak of what the plan is meant to accomplish, as the purpose of the actor, and its achievement as the achievement of an end. This case has been extensively discussed by C. Taylor in his *Explanation of Behaviour*,[10] but for our purposes it is enough to identify it as a special case of rule-following, but one which, though the plan has a purpose, we should nevertheless wish to classify under our head of routine (see later), since the relation between the purpose to which the plan is directed and the actions by which the plan is carried out are not given meaning by convention, but are determined by the laws of nature as the necessary conditions for the bringing about of the purpose. Compare the relation between making a contract and signing one's name, and the relation between putting on the light and pressing the switch.

The discussion of the analysis of episodes has given us the threefold conceptual distinction between movements, actions and acts while the discussion of reasons has introduced the idea of a commentary given in justification and thus in explanation in social terms of the actions performed. We shall assume for the moment that there is a clear distinction to be made between those episodes whose structure calls for a biological explanation and those which are to be explained psychologically. And we shall further assume that it is with the latter that we are at present concerned. With this in mind, a threefold distinction between kinds of actions can be developed, simply by their temporal relation to the commentary that their performer gives upon them, though we shall make some supplementary distinction by referring to who gives the account, if it is someone other than the actor.

1. HABITUAL ACTIONS: There must be occasions when a sequence of actions are capable only of retrospective commentary, by their performer, since they cease to be properly identifiable as habitual just as soon as their performer begins to monitor them consciously, that is, just as soon as he is capable of a monitoring commentary. A necessary condition for monitoring commentary is reflexive awareness which is also a necessary condition for self-control. Of course people other than the actor may give contemporary commentaries, and may, knowing the man and his habits, be capable of anticipatory commentary too. One qualification which should be entered here is that a man with great self-knowledge may be able to make an anticipatory commentary knowing himself what his habits are. Thus habitual actions and sequences of actions are those which at one time must have been capable of monitoring, anticipatory and retrospective commentary but are now such as to be performable without there being the possibility of either monitoring or anticipatory commentary.

2. ACTIONS WHICH ARE MEANT: an actor can give any or all of the three kinds of commentary upon the action or sequence of actions. Cutting across this distinction between actions which are open as far as commentary is concerned and those which are not, we can give our own criteria for distinguishing two classes which have caused much philosophical trouble in their identification:

Purposive actions will be identified as those actions which, whether or not they are open as to the possibilities of commentary, are such that when they are given commentary, by actor or bystander, the end, outcome, upshot or aim of the action is mentioned in the commentary. Thus a sequence of movements made by an animal may be commented upon by an ethologist by mention of the aim or upshot of the sequence, just as a sequence of movements may be so commented upon by the passenger in a car when they are performed by a distracted driver in the course of guiding the car. The distracted driver's actions will thus be both habitual (*he* is not able to give any kind of commentary), but purposive in, that in commentary upon them their order and significance is referred to whatever they are seen by the commentator as directed to achieving. When the actor himself provides a commentary, and includes among his reasons for being about to do, for doing or for having done the action, the aim, upshot, outcome or end, i.e., frequently the act attempted, then we shall call these intentional actions. We shall say that someone intends to do something when he is ready (has the power) to give such a commentary upon what he is about to do. In contrast, we shall speak of people being ready to do things when certain enabling conditions are fulfilled, but when they are not ready (do not have the transitory power) to produce an anticipatory commentary of the appropriate kind.

It is worth noticing, and will be a matter of some importance when we come to discuss the dynamics of small group interaction, that the commentaries of which we have been speaking are usually only *produced* in real life when the action has been queried, or is thought to be liable to be queried, that is commentaries are usually produced in the context of justification and excuse, and will generally show a logico-grammatical structure appropriate to that function, such as that elucidated by J. L. Austin[11] and utilized by Lyman and Scott.[12] On most occasions all that actually exists is the readiness to give a commentary, and it is upon that that we hinge our distinction between intentional and other kinds of action. The problems of the ascription of such powers and states of readiness will be discussed in great detail in a later chapter, but we believe that these are among the most important objects of scientific psychological research.

To sum up the discussion so far:

A movement is given meaning as an action by being identified as the performance or part of the performance of an act.

Meaning is elucidated in the accounts of sequences of actions, and these accounts are often commentaries, produced in real life for the purpose of justification, explanation or excuse. An intentional action is one for which in the anticipatory or monitoring commentary upon the action the act attempted figures as a reason for doing the action. (Where the action is not part of a conventionally rule-bound sequence, but part of a causal process, then it will be the outcome expected that figures in the commentary, making the action taken intentional). We noticed that in real life a good deal of action has to be classified not with respect to commentaries actually made, because in many cases none are, but with the commentaries we are ready to make. This important fact raises serious methodological issues.

Finally, a movement, e.g., a casting down of the eyes, a head nod, etc., acquires a place in social reality by being given accredited meaning. The description of a sequence of actions identified with respect to the act or acts performed in an episode we shall call the description of the Act-action structure of an episode. In real life, excuses, justifications and explanations, sometimes given under pressure, describe the putative Act-action structure of episodes. And of course we all know that, in those conditions, the actual accounts produced may be lacking in authenticity, and their divergence from authenticity is itself an interesting psycho-social phenomenon.

We have referred casually to the distinction between those sequences of happenings whose principle of order is a causal law or laws, and those sequences whose principle of order is a rule or rules, or, where the principle lacks explicit formulation, a convention or conventions. It is this distinction which is at the heart of the ethogenic way, since the ethogenist believes that what is really happening in social life is often best explained as the adherence to certain rules and conventions, rather than simply as the production of effects by the action of causes. For example, Newcomb's ABX theory[13] supposes that the attitude of one person, A, to another, B, depends upon a kind of 'balance' between A's perception of B's attitude to him, A's attitude to some third thing, 'X', and the attitude that he supposes B has to X. This might be looked upon as a causal theory, since the appearance of liking in A might be assumed to be an effect upon A into the genesis of which A, as an active participator, simply did not enter. However, it hinges upon quasi-logical consistency between A's understanding of B's remarks, actions and so on, both with respect to him, and with respect to the object X, and this involves A's givings of meanings to the various relevant items. Thus rules, conventions and meanings must also be taken into account in using this model of the generation of liking, since A's assumptions about the rules and conventions which guide B in his expressions of preference and so on are going to be crucial in A's assessment of the state of 'balance' obtaining between the various factors in the situation.

Just the same general considerations apply to those theories of liking which hinge upon 'consensual validation'. Notice that the introduction of alleged 'drive states' whose production is alleged to produce liking, as e.g., by Aronson and Linder,[14] entirely prejudges the issue as to the appropriate mode of explanation of the structure of an episode in which one person comes to like or dislike another, since the application of such concepts is only intelligible on a causal model. Similarly efforts by such investigators as Lott and Lott,[15] to develop an account of liking on classical conditioning lines is open to the fatal objection, pointed out by Secord and Backman,[16] that the results of empirical studies by these investigators can be explained only by introducing the idea that some of those involved are acting in *expectation* of reward in certain conditions, and thus depend upon shared conventions i.e. as to what is to count as a reward, with the person who is expected to give the reward. Under these conditions liking cannot be construed on the model of salivating, since once again the necessity both of understanding the relevant situation and of conventional construal of this or that response as rewarding intrudes. The causal model is appropriate only where the necessity for an intermediate act or sequence of acts of understanding can be ruled out, i.e. only where the person can be treated as the passive recipient of this or that effect. Rule-following, convention-obeying, meaning-giving or any other form of self-monitoring by the individual involved is fatal to the idea that the heart of an explanation lies in the causal story.

FORMAL EPISODES: These we distinguish as those sequences of happenings, in which reference is made to explicit rules in accounting for the type and order of the component actions. A set of explicit rules might be written, or printed, or known by word of mouth. Component actions within the sequence do not in general lead to later members of the sequence through the causal action of biological mechanisms, but are related through their meanings, and the following of rules. For instance, the sequence of actions which several

people perform which lead to two people coming to be married
constitute a formal episode, whose principles of order are in fact
explicit rules as to what must be done by the occupant of each role
and in what order. As with many formal episodes the point of
following the rules is to do the actions pursuant upon the performance of an act. Similarly, the sequence of actions that certain role-
holders perform which lead to a man's death may have a principle
of order imposed by legal convention, and comprise crime, arrest,
trial, judgment, sentence and execution.

CAUSAL EPISODES: in these there are sequences of happenings which
are related by the action of a causal mechanism. Compare the two
person episode in which a couple become parents, with the two
person episode in which they become married. Compare the one person episode in which a man catches an infection which leads to
his death with the formal episode of judicial execution. This rather
simple distinction has been developed by several authors, notably
R. E. Park[17] as long ago as 1921, and more recently by Simmons
and McCall.[18] It is not the same as the distinction between the
sequence of happenings which are explained by reference to reasons,
and episodes whose sequences are explained by causes, since the
distinction we wish to make is marked by a very specific kind of
reason which could not at all be confused with any kind of cause.
Part of the difficulty of trying to mark off psychology as the study
of the operation of reasons, from physiology as the province of causes
is that it does not take too much philosophical ingenuity to persuade
someone that *some* reasons are causes. But it would be drawing a
very long bow indeed to try to maintain that in an episode in which
there was explicit following of printed rules, the rules and the
determination to follow them were the causes of the subsequent
sequence of actions. It is perfectly clear though that what 'controls'
a marriage ceremony is the liturgy, while what controls gestation is
a complex of biochemical mechanisms. There are various dimensions
along which intermediate cases can be found, which make up the
field of social science.

If the ethologists are substantially correct then there are animal
routines having something of the character of ceremonies which

M

operate through meanings, but the power, or, as Chomsky calls it, the competence, which is exercised or manifested in the performance of these routines has its origin in the inherited mechanisms of the brain and nervous system. Following this line of thought, it would not be unreasonable to look for something in social life correspond- ing to the deep structure discerned by the Chomsky school in all human languages. We shall return to this point in discussing the hierarchies of rules. There is some ground for thinking that some, at least, of the paralinguistic elements in social interaction are of an ethological character. Facial expressions, for example, are effective in setting the tone of an episode through their meanings, that is through how they are understood. They may, of course, be mis- understood. Therefore they should not be offered as causes of which the tone of an episode is the alleged effect. Normally, though, the passage from understood meaning to emotional tone is not the product of a routine set of actions, whose principle of unity is some rule or convention. The sequence is the product of the working of an inherited mechanism. However, it has been discovered that some forms of mental disturbance are consequent upon failure to under- stand paralinguistic elements, for example, head nods. It has also been discovered that the meanings of these can be taught, by making the conventions governing them explicit.[19] This shows conclusively that for instance, head nodding does not *cause* someone to go on talking, but *encourages* them to, that is, has a similar status to the sentence 'Go on, that's very interesting' which might perfectly well serve to encourage someone to continue talking during a telephone conversation, in which only sentences (and their inflections) were exchanged. In these cases neither the mechanism nor the function is capable of explication in causal terms, but they are disturbingly like the routine of animals in which the mechanisms are indeed causal, but the functions are not. There is a great temptation to slip into treating them as if they were just another case of an ethological routine. Any residual doubts that anyone might have as to the status of human head-noddings, smiling, floor apportionment and the like, can be dispelled by reference to Argyle's distinguished work in teaching paralinguistics to certain classes of mentally disturbed patient.[20] In this we have a perfect example of the use of the concepts proper to formal episodes in the construction of an account of an enigmatic episode. And the propriety of treating head-nodding in conversation as paralinguistic and subject to convention is checked out by the existence of episodes such as those engineered by Argyle, in which by following explicit rules, head-nodding can be used to produce the required result in the encouragement and maintenance of conversation.

There are other ways in which intermediate cases can be identified. A formal episode has an explicit script. Much that is clearly formal in character may be bound only by quasi-rules or conventions which could be written down but have been learnt not by reading and following the rule book, but perhaps by scrutiny of earlier perform-ances and imitation of them, and so on. When one considers cases where the imitation seems not to be based upon deliberate scrutiny and conscious effort to conform, one begins to enter once again the area of what we call 'enigmatic episodes'. It is our contention that most of the episodes of social life are, with respect *either* to well-founded knowledge of causal mechanisms, *or* with respect to explicit rules or well-established conventions, enigmatic. They constitute an empirical problem field. What are the principles of order which are to be found at work in them? It is relatively easy to identify their Act-action structure, but what then? What binds together the actions into a sequence? One can proceed according to either of two para-digms. One can attempt to penetrate the area of the enigmatic from that pole which we have called causal episodes, and adopt that kind of episode as the model for the understanding of those whose etho-geny is unknown. Or one can try the other tack, and look upon formal episodes as the general form of the model for the exploration of the enigmatic. In many episodes, adequate understanding may be reached only by an exploitation of both models. We shall tackle the problem of their consistency later. We believe that the causal model has been relatively dominant in social psychology and related areas of sociology. But we believe that in recent years the scientific instinct of some distinguished investigators has led them to proceed from the other pole, and to try the formal model, a technique which has never quite died out in sociology. In philosophy, both Wittgenstein[21] and Shwayder[22] have shown this tendency. In sociology, the methodology of both Goffman[23] and Garfinkel[24] can be looked at as an example of this switch. We wish to advocate an explicit methodology for the understanding of social phenomena based upon an explicit recognition of this Copernican Revolution in the social sciences. The detailed development of the formal episode model for social psychological studies will occupy us in the next chapter. In this matter, as indeed in practically everything else we advocate, we are conscious not so much of innovation but of saying systematically and clearly what a good many people have been muttering by way of reaction against the dominant model.

The ethnomethodology of H. Garfinkel, to which we referred above, has a good deal in common with the kind of study we would call ethogeny. But we would be inclined to dissociate ourselves from what we take to be a fundamental assumption of Garfinkel's way. It seems to us that he takes it for granted that all the episodes of social interaction between people can be analysed as cases of rule or convention following, and that the only methodological question is not whether? but which? He offers two main techniques for discovering what the rules are. One is the technique that has come to bear his name. 'Garfinkelling' is the process of deliberately creating a hiatus in the social fabric so that, in the efforts which are made to restore that fabric, the rules and conventions which were the un-considered substance of the fabric before the garfinkel become explicit and observable. There are various orders of garfinkel, a second order garfinkel, for instance, being created by so acting as to force a person to evince a belief about a matter on which they have already avowed an opinion, and the like. The second technique, which we believe to be of very much greater scientific value, is the close study of a person who is 'passing' in a role which he or she has deliberately chosen to adopt. Garfinkel's classical analysis[25] of the rules related to the presentation of self by adolescent girls derives from his long interrogation of a person 'Agnes', who, though originally a boy, chose to pass as a girl, and had to learn as explicit principles the conventions and rules which operate in the lives of the girls whose society he wished to join, and to follow those rules deliberately. Agnes knew, in a way which no girl could possibly know, what were the conventions of girlish life. Obvious further applications of this technique would be to study indicators of social class by interrogating 'con men', who pass in a class which is not that which they learned to occupy by the usual route. This technique is a special form of one of the main methodological tools of the ethogenic approach, which we shall discuss extensively in the next chapter, namely taking the dramaturgical standpoint.

The argument of this chapter leads to a distinction between acts and actions which will play an essential role in the further analysis of the structure of episodes. We shall identify two levels of structure, or two degrees of analysis of episodes.

OVERT STRUCTURE: an episode is described in terms of the acts performed or attempted; or even parodied, mirrored or pretended, and the actions which have to be done in order to perform them. We have already seen that this involves taking notice of the accounts given by the people involved, either by way of anticipatory, contemporaneous or retrospective commentary. Once this description of the Act-action structure has been arrived at, we must try to identify the pattern within which the actions can be made intelligible as the performance of acts. Four models are available for this purpose, and there may be others. These models do not constrain the episodes into quasi-physical phenomena, but are chosen just so that the interplay of language, the mediation of the interaction symbolically as well as non-verbal interactions, can be given appropriate weight. The models are rituals, routines, games and entertainments. In short, each episode of human life has, in very varying degrees, something of the nature of a ritual, and something in the nature of a game and so on. And rituals and games have something of each others' nature. We shall lay out the structure of each of these models in turn, that is, we shall lay out the system of concepts, whose metaphorical employment of the episodes of human life serves to develop a view of the pattern of acts in an episode, under which they become intelligible. The way we discover which model to use is by taking the dramaturgical standpoint, that is, by supposing that life is a dramatic performance, and trying to reconstruct the script.

COVERT STRUCTURE: The course of an episode is influenced by two further factors; the permanent and transitory powers and states of readiness of the people concerned, the Powers structure of the episode, and the flux of emotions, its Arousal structure. We must notice that these are connected, in that amongst the necessary conditions for certain powers and states of readiness are the existence of certain emotional states, while emotions are the meanings of states of arousal. These factors form the 'covert' structure of an episode, not because they cannot be known to an observer, but because there have been thought to be epistemological problems involved in their attribution to people other than one's self. There are also the problems involved in the epistemology of the concept of 'power', in contrast to the simpler concept of 'disposition', which does not seem to involve reference to a somewhat mysterious 'human nature'. These problems will be dealt with in Chapters Twelve and Thirteen. We can proceed in cheerful independence of them in identifying the covert structure of an episode by reference to its overt structure. Since we have treated intentions and similar concepts as having to do with the accounts people give of acts rather than the causes of the actions by which the acts are performed, we have no further level of structure for the empirical study of episodes. Any insertion of physiological knowledge into the analysis will come in the specification of the 'nature' component of a powers attribution, and we are quite confident that the powers concept works perfectly satisfactorily with quite unspecific 'natures' terms, i.e. we do not need to know what feature or which state of a person is responsible for his having the particular capacities, capabilities, tendencies, liabilities and readinesses that he has in order for us to be able correctly to attribute them to him.

REFERENCES

1. N. Tinbergen, 'Ethology', in R. Harré (editor), *Scientific Thought*, 1900–60, Oxford, 1969, Ch. 12.
2. K. Z. Lorenz, *Studies in Animal and Human Behaviour*, translated by R. Martin, Methuen, London, 1970.
3. J. Douglas, *The Social Meanings of Suicide*, Princeton University Press, 1967, 241–5 ff.

4. C. D. Spielberger, in S. Rosenberg (editor), *Directions in Psycholinguistics*, Macmillan, New York, 1965.
5. E. Berne, *Games People Play*, Penguin, London, 1970.
6. A. R. White (editor), *The Philosophy of Action*, Oxford, 1968.
7. J. L. Austin, 'A Plea for Excuses', *Philosophical Papers*, Oxford, 1961.
8. R. S. Peters, *The Concept of Motivation*, Routledge and Kegan Paul, London, 1958.
9. G. E. M. Anscombe, *Intentions*, Cornell, Ithaca, New York, 1966.
10. C. Taylor, *The Explanation of Behaviour*, Routledge and Kegan Paul, London, 1964.
11. J. L. Austin, *loc. cit.*
12. S. L. Lyman and M. B. Scott, 'Accounts', *Am. Soc. Rev.*, 33, (1968), 46–62.
13. T. M. Newcomb, *Am Psychologist*, 11, 535–86.
14. E. Aronson and D. Linder, *J. Exp. & Soc. Psych.*, 1, (1965), 156–71.
15. A. J. Lott and B. E. Lott, 'Group Cohesiveness as Interpersonal Attraction', *Psych. Bull.*, 64, (1965), 259–309.
16. P. F. Secord and C. W. Backman, 'Interpersonal Congruency, Perceived Similarity and Friendship', *Sociometry*, 27, (1964), 115–127.
17. R. E. Park and E. Burgess, *Introduction to the Science of Sociology*, Chicago University Press, Chicago, 1969; first published, 1921.
18. J. L. Simmons and G. J. McCall, *Identities and Interactions*, Free Press, New York, 1966.
19. M. Argyle, *Social Interaction*, Methuen, London, 1969, pp. 336–55.
20. M. Argyle, *Europea Pedagogica*, 5, (1969), p. 72 ff.
21. L. Wittgenstein, *Philosophical Investigations*, Blackwell, Oxford, 1953, Part I.
22. D. S. Shwayder, *The Stratification of Behaviour*, Routledge and Kegan Paul, London, 1965, Part Three.
23. E. Goffman, *The Presentation of Self in Everyday Life*, Allen Lane, The Penguin Press, London, 1969; Anchor Books, New York, 1959.
24. H. Garfinkel, *Studies in Ethnomethodology*, Prentice-Hall, Englewood Cliffs, New Jersey, 1967, Ch. 1 and Ch. 2.
25. H. Garfinkel, *op. cit.*, 116–85, 285–8.

CHAPTER NINE

The Structure of Formal Episodes

THE ARGUMENT

How Formal Episodes serve as Scientific Models for Enigmatic Episodes

1. The set of rules, following of which generates the Act-action structure of the formal episode, serves as a *paramorph* for the invention of a set of rules, which can be offered as a model for whatever is tacitly followed in the generation of the enigmatic episode. This is creative theory construction, and corresponds to the development of ideas of hypothetical causal mechanisms, which is the heart of natural science, and provides a theory for the explanation of enigmatic episodes.

2. The Act-action structure of formal episodes can serve as a *homoeomorph* for analysing the overt structure of an enigmatic episode. This provides a heuristic for the analysis of episodes.

3. The analysis of the accounts of the participants provides the analogue of the natural scientists' attempts, by the use of microscopes and the like, to check the authenticity of his theoretically developed models of real, but unknown, generative mechanisms.

Rules

1. Rules generate actions through the actor making reference to them in consciously monitoring and controlling his performance.

2. It is often necessary for understanding action to make reference to a second order system of rules used in selecting the rules for acting.

3. Rules can determine expectation for the same reason as they can guide action.

4. Being propositional, rules can appear in accounts, and appear among reasons.

5. Rules are general, and so distinguished from orders and commands.

6. The investigation of the sources of authority of rules involved in social action is an empirical matter.

7. Role is a derivative concept, based upon the conception of a set of rules obeyed by a particular participant.

8. Using formal episodes as the source of paramorphs for the sources of social action, we shall say generates the Role-rule system of models.

The Structure of Formal Episodes

The Classification of Formal Episodes:

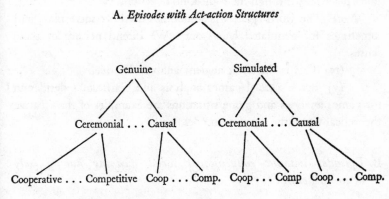

'...' indicates intermediate cases.

The Associated Ethogenic Models

a. The Liturgical Model:

(i) Rule-condition: each action or saying and its place in the Act-action structure is specified by rule or convention.

(ii) Role-condition: the actions of each participant are specified by rule or convention.

(iii) Role-restriction: the kind of individual who may be permitted to perform the role may be governed by rule.

Note. Ceremonies frequently commit the participants to future action which may only be explicable by reference back to the participation by the person in the ceremony. Only *failure* to fulfil the commitment is in need of additional explanation.

(iv) The rite is the set of movements, specified in the litany by which the actions (the ritual) appropriate to perform the act are performed.

(v) Ritual-like Act-action structures tend, for obvious reasons, to develop around entities having some degree of sanctity.

b. The Game or Agonistic Model:

(i) The fact that actions are specified only according to kind, allows individual differences, e.g. in skill, in specific performance.

(ii) Thus it is possible to have *competitive* performances.

(iii) This requires sanctions for misplay, so that competition takes place only through the right kind of actions.

Note. The word 'game' is sometimes used for mere play, and sometimes for simulated behaviours. We intend neither of these senses.

(iv) This is the most ancient analytical model.

(v) Berne's social games analysis and Garfinkel's desiderata for games analyses and game situations are examples of the creative theoretical use of the agonistic model.

B. *Episodes without conventional social meaning having only action-structures*

(i) Rules are followed in performing the actions, but not so as to achieve a conventionally defined upshot. The outcome is causally related to the actions performed. Such episodes are to be called 'routines'.

(ii) Often the rules form a system, which is to be explained through the exploitation of causal laws, e.g. the system of rules which must be followed in servicing a car.

(iii) Like ceremonials and games, routines may be genuine or simulated.

Plans can be defined with respect to anticipatory commentaries upon any of ritualistic, game-like or routine-like episodes.

C. *Episodes having only action-structures but no outcome.*

(i) There is neither upshot nor outcome from the actions performed. These are to be called 'entertainments'.

(ii) This category of episodes rounds out the analytic scheme and is required to account for certain social episodes, e.g. certain forms of conversation.

The general theory of this book is that we should draw upon our knowledge of the structure and genesis of formal episodes in developing a conceptual system for the analysis and study of many of those episodes which, because they are neither obviously formal nor in any obvious way generated by the actions of causal mechanisms known to the natural sciences, we have chosen to call enigmatic. In order to do this we must have already made a careful analysis of the structure and modes of genesis of formal episodes, that is episodes which are generated by the conscious following of explicit rules by the participants. Only then can we develop suitable models for the unknown structures and generative sources of enigmatic episodes. We must try to work out what kinds of formal episodes are possible in order to have to hand a system of concepts for the classification and systematization of the rules and conventions and formal plans that emerge from the analysis of accounts.

In the chapter on methodology we distinguished between two kinds of model used in natural science. Homoeomorphs are those for which source and subject are the same. Characteristic examples are simplified schematic representations, like wiring diagrams which enable us to grasp the structure of complex entities. Paramorphs are distinguished by having a different source from their subject. A fluid model for the unknown mechanisms of electrical conduction is a characteristic paramorph. The electrical fluid is modelled on real fluids, and is supposed to behave like them to some extent, and it is a model of the unknown mechanism of electrical 'conduction'. Both concepts of models are needed to enable us to understand how formal episodes can serve as the conceptual basis for the understanding of the enigmatic.

Understanding of some enigmatic episodes is gained by imagining a set of rules for them, as if they had been produced by explicit rule-following. The process of following the imagined rule-set is a paramorph of whatever did generate the Act-action structure of the episode, and may lead to its discovery. The paramorph may enable us, for instance, to identify a certain set of conventions which we can come to see are operative in the ethogeny of the episode. By imagining that a face-saving episode is a sort of ritual, Goffman[1] was able to identify the conventions which seem to operate in those episodes where a *gaffe* is covered up by face-saving moves among the people in a group. Here we see the essential creative function of the paramorph in suggesting the existence of some feature of the episode which escapes ordinary observation, or which may only come to light after an intensive interrogation of the participants, as to their states of mind and so on, when taking part in it.

However in order to pick out an Act-action structure in an enigmatic episode, to select those actions and sayings which hang together into a structure having an intelligible principle of unity, from all the phenomena present in the time-slice from which the episode is extracted, it is necessary to use the Act-action structure of formal episodes as homoeomorphs for the structure of the enigmatic episodes. For instance identifying those parts of a complex and many sided episode which make up the Act-action structure of a bit of ritual enables Goffman to isolate the face-saving actions within a slice of life, to the maintenance of which 'face-work' is directed. So the use of one type of formal episode to form the source of the paramorph of the mode of generation of an enigmatic episode may be consequent upon the use of the same kind of formal episode to provide the concepts needed to develop a homoeomorph of the Act-

action structure of the episode. Thus the Act-action structure of an enigmatic episode can be looked on as a homoeomorphic model of the episode developed by using the concepts appropriate to a particular type of formal episode. Of course it is possible that this Act-action structure might have been produced in a manner which can only be understood in terms of the concepts derived from the analysis of the kind of conscious rule following which generated a *different* type of formal episode. Some of Berne's 'life-games'[2] which we shall discuss below, show this feature. They have a ritualistic Act-action structure, but an examination of the kinds of rules that appear in the underlying rule-following seems to suggest their ethogeny is best understood by assimilating the rules to those found in game playing, since at a deeper level of analysis the episode seems to involve traps, competitions, strategy, winning, losing and so on, even though the game has been ritualized, and, at some level of understanding by the participants, the outcome is never in doubt. Many episodes are complex in another way too, in that they can be analysed to show an interweaving of Act-action structures whose understanding may demand concepts drawn from more than one type of formal episode. Nevertheless these complexities can be mastered by patient analysis, and careful deployment of the concepts involved.

We have made frequent reference to rules, rule-following, monitoring performances, and so on, all of which assume an intuitive understanding of the notion of 'rule', and of what it is to follow a rule. Clearly rules are propositions and they guide action. Both these features need further working out.

Rules guide action through the actor being aware of the rule and of what it prescribes, so that he can be said to know what to do in the appropriate circumstances by virtue of his knowledge of the rule, and the explanation of his knowing what to do lies in his knowing the rule and being able to recognize the occasions for its application. Though the concept of rule can be used to explain how an actor comes to know what to do, it still leaves open the question as to why he chose that rule to guide his conduct, nor does it explain why he actually acts on the rule, rather than doing nothing. In explaining action by reference to rule it is necessary to add some further account of wants, needs, or the expectations of others, the

awareness of which would prompt a man to action in accordance
with the rule. Thus instancing the rule answers the question 'How
did he know what to do?', but not the question, 'Why did he do
this thing then and there?'. This does not exhaust the matter. There
is also the problem of choice of rule. Again there are many situations where one can discern rules for selecting rules at work. At this
level, too, the distinction between the explanation of a man's knowing which rule to select and his actually selecting it, must be maintained. Further distinction among kinds of rules, such as the
distinction between rules of tactics and rules of strategy can be
developed in the context of the appropriate model.

The fact that a rule is, as it were 'future directed', means that it
can be thought of not only as guiding action but as determining
expectation. Knowing a rule is not only to know what one should
do, but also it gives one some ground for expectations one may
have of the behaviour of other people who accept the rule. Indeed
one way of ensuring that our expectations of the behaviour of others
is stable is to extract agreement to accept a rule. This feature of rules
is discussed in some detail by Shwayder.[3]

More important still, from our point of view, is the fact that the
propositional nature of rules fits them to appear in accounts of and
commentaries upon action. Indeed they are a common feature of
the accounts that are produced in a justificatory context, and commonly in the form particularly noticed by Shwayder, in which the
content of a rule is expressed in terms of the expectations of others.
It should be noticed that rules refer to actions and not to acts. Acts
are referred to when the rule itself comes under scrutiny and has to
be justified, because the justification of a rule must come from a
reference to the act which will be achieved by following the rule,
that is by performing the actions the carrying out of which are the
conventional means of doing the act. Thus, a rule may be offered as
a reason for an action, as Shwayder too points out,[4] and may be
justified in its turn by reference to an act and the rule or convention
by which those actions are the performance of that act. Thus a rule
has the general form:

[In order to achieve A (the act)] do $a_1 \ldots a_n$ (the actions)
when S (the occasion or situation) occurs. Thus the questions

'Why?', 'What?', and 'When?' are answered by the rule. 'Why?' because the rule is introduced just to ensure the doing of the actions appropriate to the performance of a certain act; 'What' because the explicit prescription of the rule is of an action; and 'When?' because a rule tells one what to do when certain circumstances obtain, or when certain other things have been done, and in this way differs from an injunction, order or command. Because of this situational feature, a rule is general, and can be followed again and again, while a command is usually specific and meant to be operative for one time only. A command has to be repeated to be operative on another occasion. 'Close the door' is a command. 'Always close the door when you leave' is a rule. Rules need not be confined to the prescription of actions of just one kind. They may prescribe quite complex sequences of different kinds of actions in a more or less strict order. The instructions for dismantling and reassembling a gun may be looked upon as a single rule prescribing a complex and ordered sequence of actions of different descriptions.

Finally there is the problem of the authority of a rule, and the origin of the sanctions which ensure that a person who adheres to it follows it on the appropriate occasions. We are concerned with the rules of social behaviour and so with the authority and sanctions that operate in that realm. In our view this field has not been much studied. It is clear that the discovery of the sources of authority operative in ordinary social behaviour by the identification of the real and operative sanctions is a matter of great practical as well as theoretical import. Much work remains to be done in this area, both philosophical analysis of the concepts involved and detailed empirical exploration, though social psychologists have made some progress on questions of authority and sanctions.

By considering rules in relation to the people who follow them we can generate the important concept of 'role'. We shall have much to say later in this book about roles but for the moment we shall simply introduce the concept as derived from a particular way of partitioning the rules followed in a kind of formal episode. Role can be defined as that part of the Act-action structure produced by the subset of the rules followed by some individual defined as belonging to a particular category of person. In this sense, the 'role of the bridegroom' is that sequence of actions and sayings that the individual who is filling the role of bridegroom performs by following the rules for the behaviour of bridegrooms. A role is what a person in a specific category does, but in a formal episode his actions and sayings are generated by his following the appropriate subset of rules. Role is not the only basis for partitioning the rules relevant to a particular kind of episode. They may be partitioned in a time dimension, as for instance the rules governing the Olympic Games can be partitioned into those which are followed in the opening ceremony, those referred to in the management of the athletic competitions, and those which determine the Act-action structure of the closing ceremony.

A role, then, is the set of actions a person of a particular type or category is expected to perform within the Act-action structure of a certain kind of episode. The bridegroom's role is to do certain kinds of things at the appropriate moment. Thus, role consists of a sequence of actions, and knowledge of role consists of knowing the rules which enjoin these kinds of actions in the proper order and in the appropriate circumstances. But, of course, much role filling is not a performance generated by conscious following of explicit rules. It may be explained by reference to conventions which are only dimly perceived as such by the role players, or it may be explained by reference to paradigms and be generated by imitation. In this and other ways we shade off into the enigmatic region in which analysis in terms of roles and rules can be seen as the application of a model. The formal episodes wherein the concepts of rule and role have literal application generate *Role-rule models*. We now turn to the analysis of the formal episodes upon which the Role-rule models are based, to find in their Act-action structure and ethogeny the material for developing a powerful set of models for the understanding of much that is neither obviously formal nor clearly biological in origin in human social life.

We have seen that the understanding of formal episodes involves the deployment of the concepts of role and rule. We propose now to develop an account of the structure of several possible conceptual systems based upon the ideas of role and rule, by which the sequences of actions of some important kinds of formal episodes can be explained. These will serve as preliminary sketches of sources for the creation of models for the understanding of certain classes of enigmatic episodes.

Among the many distinctions which can be used in the classification of formal episodes, there is that between episodes in which a certain sequence of actions are conventionally held to constitute the performance of an act, and those where this is not so. This criterion enables us to distinguish *ceremonial* episodes, such as marriages, coronations, baptisms, the delivering of verdicts, and the like from all other formal episodes. The distinguishing feature of these episodes can also usefully be put in terms of meaning. In them the meaning of the actions is the act performed in doing them. Indeed, ceremonies are partially identified by J. L. Austin as those actions *in* the doing of which an act is performed.[5] There are *no causal* relations between most of the actions which make up the ceremonial sequence, and none between the actions performed and the act achieved. We should notice in passing that the kinds of acts conventionally performed in the carrying out of certain sequences of actions may be enormously various.

Typically episodes of this ceremonial sort are distinguished from those in which it is *by* doing something that an act is performed. It is by firing the pistol that an act of murder is committed. Here the relationship between the action and the act is partly mediated by a *causal* relation between the firing of the pistol and the death of the victim, and partly by legal, that is, conventional devices, by which the death is given a particular meaning as a murder, by reference to certain rules and conventions of law and society. Notice that the explanation of why putting a bullet into someone leads to their death involves the natural sciences, while the explanation of why certain deaths are treated as homicide involves a structure of reasons and justifications.

Our first distinction then is between episodes whose Act-action structure is purely ceremonial, and those in which it is partly causal. Many episodes which we ordinarily mark off as *rituals* are of a purely ceremonial character.

Our second distinction is between those episodes in which every participant *cooperates* with the other participants, and those in

N

which there is some measure or degree of *competition* involved. A marriage ceremony is, in most cases, wholly a cooperative affair, while a boxing match, seems, on the face of it, to be wholly competitive. But the distinction is not absolute. The bride and groom, and the parents of each may compete for the attention of the guests, and in many societies the style of the marriage is part of an ongoing competitive relationship between families. On the other hand there is a high degree of cooperation between the contestants in a boxing match, at the very least in more or less abiding by the rules. An episode such as a boxing match, differs in this way from a mere brawl. It is for this reason that a boxing match has some title to be treated as a formal episode.

Many, though by no means all, of the episodes which we ordinarily mark off as *games* are of a competitive character. We notice here, and will develop later, the point that the rules of formal competitive episodes are usually such as to allow an element of uncertainty in the outcome of the competition, either through the intervention of chance, or through the demand for a skilled performance, at which in theory, all the participants can reach a similar but not identical level. Many games, such as card games, are so constructed as to introduce both forms of uncertainty. One of the ways in which uncertainty can be introduced into a formal, rule-governed sequence of actions is by restricting the degree of specificity of the actions enjoined by the rules. A player must play *some* shot at the ball if he is to score in cricket, but the specific form of the shot and its scoring power is a function of the skill of the player.

There may be ceremonial elements within a basically competitive structure, such as the ritual of glove-raising to mark the outcome of a boxing match, and there may be competitive elements within a basically ceremonial structure. There may be episodes which can be considered either as ceremonial competitions or competitive ceremonies, such as sacred games. These episodes were evidently a fairly widespread feature of ancient society, since they apparently occurred in the ball courts of Yucatan, as well as in the stadia of classical Greece. It is clear that ceremonial episodes can vary enormously in the degree to which they are cooperative or competitive.

For various purposes, which we will explore in the next chapter, human beings go through the motions of formal episodes, following the rules, but without really meaning the actions as the performance of the acts, and without really competing. The appropriate rules are followed but the actors do not mean their actions to be taken literally as what they seem. In doing this they generate episodes whose Act-action structures are *simulations* of the *genuine* forms of ceremonies, games and so on. It is easy to see that this phenomenon too is a function of the unique capacities of people, in that it is possible only because of a different attitude in the *second*-order monitoring of the simulated performance. At the first level of monitoring the performance must be controlled to be as like the real thing as is necessary to produce a convincing simulation. But at the level at which that monitoring is monitored, the participant knows that his performance is not genuine, and he does not intend his actions to be taken as the literal performance of the acts they would represent in a genuine episode. A dramatic performance is the archetype of a simulation of an Act-action structure, and we shall devote considerable space to the consideration of that type of episode.

In summary, then, our taxonomy can be expressed as follows:

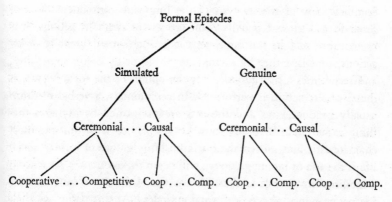

'...' indicates the existence of intermediate cases.

Ceremonials

A ceremonial as a formal episode is usually characterized by the existence of a fully formulated and wholly explicit set of rules, according to which the actions which each person who takes part must perform for the act intended to be successfully achieved. This is often taken a step further by the differentiation and definition of specific roles, that is, action patterns which are to be performed by one person, but different individuals may from time to time 'occupy' the role, i.e., be entrusted with the task of performing these patterns of action. The liturgy which sets out the rules for a ceremonial may be part of verbal tradition, or it may be in written form, for instance in a prayer-book.

The liturgical model is derived by imagining a liturgy as a para-morph for the unknown and unformulated conventions and rules the following of which generates the Act-action structure of some enigmatic episode. For this to be possible, the Act-action structure of the enigmatic episode must be susceptible of a description under which it appears to have something of the character of a ceremonial. To develop the model, we must begin with a thorough analysis of its source, the ceremonial as a formal episode.

We will develop the concepts of the liturgical model from the point of view of the analysis of the linguistic component of cere-monials, as well as from the point of view of symbolic actions. It is often the case that the same act can be performed verbally or by actions, that is, either by saying something or by doing something, and sometimes a liturgy will allow an option of the form by which the symbolic action is performed. In ceremonials, a verbal medium usually predominates and the acts are performed by saying some-thing rather than by doing something. It is our view that the most characteristic and indeed the distinguishing feature of human social life is the use of language, so we will begin this section by presenting a modified form of J. L. Austin's analysis of the use of language for the performance of acts in formal episodes.[6] At this point, we shall confine ourselves to the conditions under which the linguistic per-formance of acts are possible. We shall find that this analysis generates two very important concepts with which we are already familiar, which will form an essential part of our analytical scheme.

For any use of language by which an act is performed, conditions for the satisfactory performance of the act can be discerned. The two most general conditions are:

1. There must be a conventional procedure. This is most easily satisfied by a *rule-condition*, that there exists a set of rules for the performance of the sequence of actions, sayings of appropriate words or making of the proper gestures, adherence to which ensures that the words uttered are such that the act is performed. The rule-condition can be satisfied by anything from accepted conventions to written liturgies, provided they are explicitly formulated. Analysing an episode as a ceremonial requires as a first step the identification of the act which is being performed or attempted, and the discernment of the rules which must be followed for the appropriate actions to have been performed and verbal formulae to have been uttered.

2. The procedures must be carried out by the appropriate people. This is most easily satisfied by a *role-condition*, that is, there exists a set of prescriptions for the behaviour of the people and the choice and arrangement of the circumstances, adherence to which ensures that the act is performed in the course of the specified sequence of actions. Since it is characteristic of a ceremony that it can be performed by different individual people for different individual people, it is rare for the prescription of personnel to involve specific individuals. The rule-condition determines what each person must say and do in the ceremony, that is, each role is specified by a subset of the rules of the rule-convention, that is, the role-structure and the rule-structure are not independent. For instance, the role of the priest in a marriage ceremony is specified by a subset of the rules of the rule-convention defining the ceremony. The performance of certain roles in ceremonies may be more or less strictly confined to categories of people. In many religions, entry to the role of priest as defined by the appropriate subset of the rule convention is restricted to the members of one sex. This restriction can be conceived of as a rule, but it is not one of the rules of the rule-convention defining the ceremony, even though failure to observe it may render the ceremony void. Austin's example was the restriction which limits

the class of individuals who can fill the role of 'bride' in the marriage ceremony to human females, so that the marriage ceremony cannot be successfully performed when the putative bride is a monkey. Very few roles are wholly unrestricted. We shall distinguish role-prescriptions which are related to the rule-convention which governs the actions required for the performance of the acts from role-restrictions, which control entry to the role, i.e., which determine what kind of person can do these actions. The role-conventions for a ceremony consist, then, of role-prescriptions and role-restrictions.

Austin's other conditions concern the conditions under which the act in an episode can be said to have been done, that is, the conditions under which the rule and role conventions can be said to have been adhered to. He notices that this usually amounts to the requirement that the rules have been followed correctly and completely. These conditions are almost never invoked positively. They are usually used to identify one or other kind of failure.

The rule and role conditions determine not only what people actually say and do, but more importantly what they are ready to say and do. This may vary from episodes in which everyone is alert and paying attention, for instance a coronation, to episodes in which the ceremonial ritual is carried through inattentively and from habit. It follows from the fact that, in formal episodes the participants are obeying or following the rules of a role-convention, that any individual peculiarities outside those of the role-restriction are not relevant to the understanding of the episode. If the act performed is the crucial feature of an episode then, provided that the ceremony is performed according to the rule and role conventions, the thoughts and feelings of the individuals concerned and, indeed, their intentions, plans and the like, have no bearing upon the episode, though they may be vitally important to what happens subsequently. If the ceremony is not properly performed, it may then be pertinent to pay attention to individual peculiarities in attempting to account for the breakdown. The sudden refusal of the bride to say 'I will' may have to be accounted for outside the rule- and role-conventions which are the action-generating rules of marriage ceremonies, though her saying of it, however shyly and reluctantly does not have to be accounted for, other than by reference to those conventions, that is, it is enough to explain her saying 'I will' to instance the rule-convention under which persons in that role are required to say that sentence, in order to get married.

Austin lays down a third set of conventions which seem to lie outside the rule and role-conventions of the formal episode itself.[7] They become operative when that episode is seen as a sub-episode within a wider slice of life. They amount to the requirement that, in the course of the ritual or formal episode, the thoughts and feelings of the participants should be proper and appropriate, a convention that we have already noticed has nothing to do with the success of the episode. He also notices that the subsequent conduct of the participants should be appropriate for those who have taken part in those roles in that ceremony. These contingent conditions are features of those episodes participation in which leads to some kind of commitment. And they are themselves each of rather different character. Clearly, if a ceremony involves a committal to some further course of action, and that course of action is not pursued, some account of the failure must be given, if only by way of excuse, though, of course, no account or justification of the obedient pursuit of the proper action need be given. Only if a man fails to pay his gambling debts do we require an account which might involve his feelings and intentions on making a bet. If he does pay up, those feelings and intentions are irrelevant. It seems odd to treat either of the principles in this category as conventions, but they do have a great deal to do with the analysis of a formal episode, since they lay down the conditions under which the flux of emotions, the thoughts and feelings of the participants become relevant to the analysis of the episode. They are quite essential methodological principles, since many formal episodes go awry, and these principles lay down the method of accounting for the deviation or failure.

The concepts of role and rule are well-defined for formal episodes, and it is quite clear how a formal episode should be analysed using them. Their use, in accordance with the modified Austinian account of them that we have given, constitutes the application of the concepts of the liturgical model. It is also clear that the application of these concepts, and so of the liturgical model to informal episodes cannot be direct and unproblematic, since in this extended use these concepts begin to take on something of the air of metaphors. Informal episodes are *like* ceremonial rituals, but how like? Some informal episodes are *very* like rituals, e.g., a Swedish dinner party, some seem to be very unlike rituals, e.g., a picnic, some are not wholly ritualistic, but have elements of ceremony, e.g., a University class. According to this view, 'role theory' does not provide the means for a literal description of episodes, but is the working out of a model, and role theory itself is the presentation of the intuition that many informal episodes have something of the character of formal episodes. We shall show that the matter is actually very much more complicated than this.

In the application of the liturgical model, an episode is being treated as having something of the character of a ceremony. In formal episodes to which the liturgical conceptual system applies literally, it is important to distinguish between the *rite* and the *ritual*. And this distinction has application when the concepts are applied to informal episodes to create a generative rule system as a model for whatever produces the action of which it is constituted. A ceremony is a sequence of movements and utterances performed according to rule, or custom, having the force of rule, by (or in) the performance of which some act is done. The sequence of movements is the rite, the prescribed order of service or set of rules which are adhered to by those performing the rite gives these movements meanings as the ritual in which an act is performed. The rite could be described wholly in terms of movements, and sentences uttered, as, for instance, might be done by an eavesdropping anthropologist. But without the rule book, he would be unable to decide what was strictly part of the rite and what was not. Only by attending to the accounts of the episode could he be sure of picking out which movements were the rite, that is, had meaning as actions. A cough, for instance, might be part of the rite, and might not. It could be that a nervous priest *always* coughed at the elevation of the Host. A Chinese anthropologist might be uncertain whether the cough was part of the rite, and this could be settled only by discovering what the ritual was, that is, what actions were prescribed. Even that would not tell him what act was being performed. In short, the rite is the concrete realization of the Act-action structure of the episode, while the liturgy is the set of rules for performing the ritual.

A more general feature of the model and its application is the tendency for ceremonial to develop around the treatment of some entity which has sanctity. This point is made by Goffman, who notices that the effect of turning the actions taken with respect to a sacred object into a ceremonial is to prevent profanation. We cannot see that there is a conceptual connection between sanctity and ritual, but think it worth pointing out in passing that one important empirical condition which prompts the use of the liturgical model in the attempt to identify Act-action structures is that some entity has some claims to inviolability. The best way of ensuring this is to lay down quite specific rules as to the way people must behave with respect to that object. In Goffman's study, 'Face-work',[8] a person's 'face' is the sacred entity. The identification of such an entity in an episode would give good grounds for expecting the application of the liturgical model to be fruitful as an analytical tool, because it might reveal the way the participants actually understood the episode.

The Game or Agonistic Model

In the preliminary derivation of possible 'role/rule' structures of the acts of an episode, a game was identified as that kind of formal episode whose Act-action structure was such that there could be some form of competition between the participants. In that formal episode called a football game, the players are obliged to abide by the rules, in that once the rules have been infringed, the referee 'stops the game', and restarts it again with a penalty for the infringement. Play which is outside the framework of the rules is not part of the game. Thus, what is and what is not an element of the Act-action structure is determined by reference to a set of rules. Without a knowledge of the rules, it would be impossible to decide which movements and sayings are actions in the game. It follows that a description of the episode in terms of the movements of the players is incomplete. A football match is competitive, in that there is always the *possibility* for the formal requirements of victory to be met by either side. Finally, the specific end-state, victory for whom and by what margin, is not determined by the rules, but by the course of play. This feature makes possible the employment of strategies, the analysis of which will occupy us below. This analysis, while sufficient to distinguish games from cooperative episodes, is capable of greater definition.

It follows from the fact that there are rules which determine which actions are part of the game and which are not, that the rules of any game partition all possible actions in the situation and by the people involved into three sets, those permitted, those not permitted, and those which are not part of the game in either sense, that is, not all possible actions are ways of performing the acts of the game episode. This is further complicated by the fact that the rules deal only with types of action. For instance, in soccer the player who wishes to play the ball must do so with his foot or head, but the specific action by which the act of playing the ball is performed is not enjoined. It is clear that this feature of the rules is a necessary condition for the result of the game to be problematic. The uncertainty is introduced via variations in the particular forms of actions by which the various acts of the game are performed. In most games, the issue would not be problematic were the rules not adhered to. Twenty-two men could easily put a ball into a net were they to cooperate in passing it along, and even the most spirited bulls could be safely disposed of with a burst of sub-machine-gun fire.

The fact that failure to adhere to the rules makes the issue less problematic, and that games involve competition to win requires that there be means for ensuring that the rules are obeyed. And this allows us to make the obvious distinction between those games which are under the control of a referee, with the power of discipline, that is, with the power to identify an action as not in accordance with the rules or specifically forbidden by them, and consequently to decide and pronounce sentence, and those games in which the adherence to rule is self-imposed. There are important intermediate cases. Playing patience is a performance which is self-disciplined, playing soccer is notoriously a performance in which much of the adherence to rule is maintained by the disciplinary powers of the referee. But in many children's games there are several players and no referee, and yet there may be quite strict adherence to rule. It is also clear that *each* child does not discipline himself, as a patience player would. Adherence to the rules is maintained by 'the force of public opinion' as we might say, which amounts in fact to the disciplinary effect of the criticisms by the members of the play group of the one whose actions infringe the rules.[9] In the vast majority of informal episodes of real life which are not games, there are usually no referees, so that the basis of the analogy upon which the use of the game model must rest must be the kind of maintenance of rule which children's games exemplify. It is worthwhile noticing that many activities which are commonly called 'games' that are played by children, are not games in the sense of our Role-rule model group. Dressing up may be part of playing a game, as we commonly say, but with respect to our Role-rule group of models, is an element in the preparation of a drama, a kind of formal episode outside the categories we have elaborated so far, involving a different attitude to the rules which are being followed. This misleading common usage can lead even the most sensitive ethogenists astray, as for instance Scott and Lyman in their discussion of the case of R.R.[10] R.R.'s play-acting, that is, his presentation of an artifactual and carefully monitored self, is assimilated to 'playing a game', i.e., pretending, a concept from the dramaturgical model, but where the main burden of the paper is that the life of stigmatized individuals may contain elements of games in the sense of this section, i.e., rule or convention bound contests.

The obvious criteria by which games might be classified as, for instance, by whether the rules are explicit (a code), or customary (a tradition), stated or unstated, and by whether there is a referee or whether adherence to the rules is ensured by less formal devices, must be supplemented when the game model is applied to the analysis of informal and enigmatic episodes by reference to the kind of upshot or result which ends the game. This follows from the fact that the point of using the game model is to provide a conceptual system for analysing the action of an episode. What we identify as elements of the Act-action structure will be crucially dependent upon what the final outcome of the 'game' is supposed to be. Lyman and

Scott identify face-games (following Goffman), relationship-games in which the upshot is a new status distance equilibrium, and exploitation-games in which the upshot may be the agreement by the victim to some course of action, or perhaps the performance of the course of action itself. This last distinction is important in applying the agonistic model. Is the upshot of a seduction the surrender of the victim or the subsequent act? Many commentators have taken the surrender to be the upshot, that is, to be what the game is aimed at, in that some players would regard the game as successfully concluded by the surrender, and perhaps wish to proceed no further. It is clear that just which actions are seen as forming elements of the Act-action structure depends upon identifying the outcome, that is, what is to count as the achievement of victory.

The use of an agonistic model for the analysis of the Act-action structure of an enigmatic episode, and in explanation of the form that structure takes, is of great antiquity. Both courting and seduction have been treated in this way, one of the most elaborate treatments being found in Ovid's *The Art of Love*.[11] It is also the basis of much eighteenth-century drama. A play is a simulated Act-action structure, and in a great many plays of the period the structure is glossed as the playing out of an elaborate game, with strategies, ploys, and the possibility of ultimate victory in the surrender of one or other of the players. It would not be too fanciful to see some of the plays of the period as social psychological analyses of the dynamics of the social order, using the agonistic model. This is particularly true of *The Man of Mode*, by Vanburgh, which has been carefully analysed by Harriet Hawkins in this spirit.[12]

The most detailed and sophisticated modern work in this style is Berne's *Games People Play*. It must be remembered that the function of these models in a scientific exploration of social behaviour is two-fold:

i. By treating an enigmatic episode as if it were a game a certain Act-action structure will be discerned in that episode. It is worth emphasizing that to understand an episode fully it may be necessary to apply more than one model to it, and that more than one Act-action structure may be discerned within it.

ii. The application of the model also serves to create a paramorph of the means by which the behaviour is produced by the participants, for instance, it may allow us to formulate a set of 'rules' and 'strategies' which we can imagine were being adhered to by the participants. And in the accounts that we get from the participants we can look for items which correspond to the elements in the theoretical model of the ethogeny of the episode.

Thus, a Role-rule model has both a descriptive and an explanatory role, the former related to the way the episode is described from the social point of view, and the latter to how participation in it is accounted for from an individual point of view. The use of a Role-rule model, then, actively creates a *social-cum-psychological* analysis.

As we saw in the general analysis of games and the game model, there are three main defining features of game and game-like episodes:

1. There are rules and conventions which specify the type of action which is part of the game. These could perhaps be called specifications of the play.

2. There is a specified form of outcome, in which one or more of the participants are winners and others losers. There may be a third category of people involved, exemplified by linesmen, umpires and ball-boys in tennis tournaments.

3. Conditions (1) and (2) ensure both that there is an outcome and that the exact form of it is uncertain. This leaves room for skilful play, which includes efficiency in the performance of permitted actions, and strategies. Goffman, in his paper 'Where the Action Is',[13] has pointed out that there may be game-like interactions with the forces of nature, as in mountaineering and roulette, where an extended notion of strategy may have application. In games where the opponents are human or animal, this third condition requires that the intentions of one or more of the participants should be concealed from the others. Thus, a game involves an element of dissimulation or dishonesty as a function of its competitive nature. It is a feature of a game that this element is explicitly or tacitly recognized as legitimate, and an accepted part of game episode structures. Thus, in game analysis one looks for rules, outcomes and strategies in the accounts given by the participants. This is nicely

summed up by Garfinkel in setting out the conditions under which
a game analysis of an episode fails. He points out that if an episode
cannot be construed as issuing in some form of victory for one or
other of competing participants then it is not game-like in our sense.
In analysing the accounts his subject 'Agnes' gave of various episodes in her life, he notes that 'there were many occasions whose
structure was such as not to contain any criteria whereby a goal
could be said to have been achieved, a feature intrinsic to game
activities'.[14] This is our condition (2) above.

Berne's development of the game concept as an analytical tool is
in the context of therapy, but the structure of his analysis is applicable in many other contexts.[15] This is much the same as that we
have outlined above: there are rules or conventions governing per-
missible plays, there are rules defining roles in the game, and finally
there are the rules which specify what the outcome is and what
counts as winning. In the therapeutic environment game-playing is
assumed to be destructive, and the aim of the therapist is to gain an
admission by the players that they *are* playing a game. Thus, he
manoeuvres them into what we have called more generally a context of justification in which accounts are called for, and then he
shows the players that their accounts are susceptible of analysis as
descriptions of games and their explanations of what they have said
and done are explanations typical of people engaged in game-
playing. For instance, there is more or less awareness of the aim,
there is more or less awareness of the development and use of
strategies, and there is more or less awareness of the delights of
victory implied in the content of the accounts. A very full classification of life games, ordered by content, can be found in Berne.[16]
The reader should however beware that quite a number of the Act-
action structures included among Berne's 'games' lack competitive
form, and are probably best construed as ceremonies by which one
participant ritualistically humiliates the other.

We shall sum up this section with a *précis* of Garfinkel's excellent
set of nine desiderata,[17] characterizing genuine game-like situations
in a very general way.

The following five desiderata are common to both formal game
episodes and to game-like episodes, and their application both to

some formal and some enigmatic episodes is what constitutes the basis of the game model.

A1. The Act-action structure of the episode analysed is a function of the rules.

A2. Characteristically, success and failure are clearly decidable and one or the other outcome is ordinarily very little subject to reinterpretation.

A3. The basic rules define the action, as well as such concepts as 'fair play' and so on which characterize action commentaries, and refereeing.

A4. Within the rules, the player may be more or less efficient and still be in the game. This is a condition for the possibility of the competitive use of strategies, working out to a victory rather than stalemate. The outcome of very few games or game-like episodes really turns on chance.

A5. Games have a time limit within which success or failure must be achieved.

The following four desiderata are applicable only to enigmatic episodes, on the hypothesis that they are game-like.

B1. It is possible for a player to leave the game, or in certain circumstances to change it, if it is going badly. In this respect, game-like episodes differ from most formal game episodes, though even in these, many rule-books allow for the resignation of one of the players. However, if a player in a formal game resigns just because the game is going badly, he is a 'bad sport'. There are various degrees to which a similar opprobrium may attach to someone who 'resigns' in a game-like episode.

B2. Being in a game (game-like episode) involves suspending some of the procedures of 'serious' life.

B3. Mutual biographies established by players as a function of their actual play are specific to that game-episode, as, for instance, precedents upon which to base expectations of behaviour.

B4. 'Although strategies may be highly improvised and although the conditions of success and failure may, over the course of the play, be unclear to the players, the basic rules of play are known and are independent of the changing present state of the game and of the selection of strategies.'

A most important kind of episode which appears frequently in the fine structure of everyday life is the *triumph*. Triumphs are ritualistic sequences in which the outcome of competitive episodes are marked formally. Within strictly formal episodes they are exemplified by the procession of the matador and his assistants around the ring at the end of the bull-fight, by the victory lap at Le Mans, and by the playing of the national anthems of the winning athletes at the Olympic games, while they stand on a specially prepared rostrum, with the winner at the highest point. There are complementary rituals of abnegation, in which ceremonial humiliation is heaped upon the losers, as in the presentation of the wooden spoon at the end of a rugby competition. Triumphs (and the complementary ceremonies) seem to have several important functions. Not only are they used to celebrate current victories, but they may be repeated again and again in the apparent celebration of the outcome of old battles. It is clear that, in certain cases, the repetition of the triumph has the actual function of confirming the status of victor and vanquished. The ceremony in which the Mayor of the City of Oxford presented the Vice-Chancellor of the University with a shilling every Friday, in perpetual payment of a fine once incurred by the City, could be regarded as a device for reaffirming the relative status of the two corporations.

Berne has made clear the important role that triumph-like rituals have in everyday life, particularly within close groups like families, where fierce competition for status may occur. Victory in any one of these battles is insufficient to maintain positions unless it is confirmed by little rituals of triumph and abasement. Berne has pointed out that what may look, to an outsider, like a genuine competitive struggle between man and wife, may in fact be a ritual ceremonially reaffirming their status, since the episode proceeds through its various stages in a standard and formal way.[18] It is clear that in the understanding of episodes such as a family quarrel it may be necessary to draw upon concepts from the formal episodes which form the model for much of human social life. A family quarrel may become intelligible only when it is seen as a ceremonial performance of a simulated competition, or game.

In this chapter we have attempted no more than a sketch of

the structure of formal episodes. If we are right in our belief in the importance of the structure and ethogeny of formal episodes as the source of models for the understanding of more enigmatic episodes which may become intelligible only after careful investigation, then an important field of research in any future social psychology must be the more detailed analysis of formal episodes of all kinds.

Finally, we should notice a category of formal episode which is distinguished by the fact that, though the actions which occur in such episodes are generated by the following of relatively specific rules, they cannot be construed as the performance of acts. We shall call these 'routines'. They are sequences of actions which are generated by the actors following rules, but in which the outcome is not related to the Act-action structure by a meaning-convention. A routine is performed simply by the faithful carrying out of the required sequence of actions. The outcomes of routines are causally, not conventionally related to the sequence of actions. For instance, servicing a car is a routine, a sequence of actions generated by following a set of rules, and the outcome, better running say, is causally related to the actions performed according to rule by the mechanic. Notice that in this sort of case the actions and rules can be justified by reference to empirical knowledge of the effect of the actions performed. We shall recommend that the term 'routine' be retained even for those sequences of actions which have become habitual, provided that the habit is engrained in a series of perform-ances which were cases of conscious rule following. Thus the actions performed by a person driving a car can be treated as a routine since they were once performed consciously according to rule.

Within the general category of routines it is possible to distinguish what we shall call 'authentic routines' from 'simulation routines'. Washing the machines after milking the cows is, on most farms, a routine. Since it is done for the purposes of getting the cow-shed clean, it is an authentic routine. But if the same actions are gone through in the course of a play about country life, then, even though there may be real cows and real detergent on the stage, the routine is a simulation in various degrees of the authentic routine. The conceptual boundary between authentic and simulation routines has been perceptively discussed by J. L. Austin.[19] The upshot of his analysis is the principle that authentic and simulation routines generally differ in that in the simulation routine the actions are not being properly performed but only imitated to give the impression that they are genuine, but there are cases in which authentic routines can be distinguished from simulations only by our knowledge of the intentions of the people involved. At a stage play we are seldom in doubt because the whole ambience of the theatre decides the status of the performance in advance, but there may be cases, such as those involved in children's play where only intention can distinguish. Austin's famous case of the spy who really cleans windows in order to pretend to be a window-cleaner is such an intermediate case. This analysis has some relevance to the widespread use of deception in psychological experiments, particularly with respect to the question of intention.

We can find a place within each of the Role-rule models we have distinguished so far, for actions performed according to *plan*. This is the most characteristic form of activity for an organism whose major style of behaviour is the conscious self-monitoring of its own performances. A plan generally aims at some specific outcome, and it has the force of a rule, in that behaviour will be monitored and modified to be in accord with it. Unlike a rule, a plan may have only one application, but, like a rule, it only exists if a person is capable of including it in an anticipatory commentary upon whatever he is going to do. On this construal, plans include intentions as a special case, an intention being a very simple plan including only one act, and perhaps involving only one action. Plans relate to the actions required to perform the appropriate acts. The colloquial usage of the words 'plan' and 'planning' are such that they are used both for simple intentions and for more complex anticipations of action. For instance, if one says one is planning to sell one's car, this may mean no more than that one is intending to, and would not normally be taken to mean that one is putting in a lot of thought as to be best sequence of actions to bring off the act. However 'marriage plans', for instance, are intended sequences of actions, related to specific times and places, such as particular dates and particular churches and the like. In this form they could figure in anticipatory commentaries upon action. The most general definition of 'plan' might then be the intended sequence of actions described in an anticipatory commentary.

Generally speaking, plans are built around specific actions. There is an air of paradox about stating that one is planning to win a game, unless perhaps it is a bout of professional wrestling in which there can be 'plans to lose'. In a game context a plan is usually concerned with a specific sequence of intended actions by the players aimed at a specific outcome within the set of rules which detail the general conditions of play. In fact a plan can appear in the accounts appropriate to each Role-rule model context. But generally the following out of a plan generates a sub-episode which fits our category of routine. So following a plan, within a game say, introduces a routine within the game context.

We do not intend to go further into the analysis of plans in this book in view of the fact that there already exists in the work of Miller, Galanter and Pribram[20] an excellent, sadly neglected study, in considerable depth and detail, of the ways plans function in self-guided behaviour, together with a very subtle analysis of the variety of kinds of plans that there can be.

Our last category of formal episodes upon which to base Role-rule models are 'entertainments'. Like routines, they are the result of following rules, but they are not performed for the sake of any outcome, either conventional as in a game or ritual, or causal as in routines. Many sequences of actions which are colloquially included amongst games would fall into our category of entertainments. For instance, a child playing pat ball, according to rule, but with no intention in mind other than of performing according to the rule is engaged in an episode which we would distinguish as an entertainment. An entertainment is an episode in the accounting for which rules figure, but there is no superstructure of intentions, aims, plans and the like. Some enigmatic episodes are undoubtedly intelligible on the model of the entertainment, when a person can be brought to see that their actions are in a sequence which follows a convention which they accept, but for which there is no intended outcome or conventional upshot. Humming a tune is often such an episode. It does nothing, and it is producing neither pleasure nor pain. But it is a particular tune, so is in some sense a performance under self-monitoring and connected to rule.

REFERENCES

1. E. Goffman, *Where the Action Is*, Allen Lane, The Penguin Press, London, 1969, Ch. I, originally in *Interaction Ritual*, Doubleday, New York, 1967.
2. E. Berne, *Games People Play*, Penguin Books, London, 1970.
3. D. S. Shwayder, *The Stratification of Behaviour*, Routledge and Kegan Paul, London, 1965, Part Three, Section 9.
4. D. S. Shwayder, *op. cit.*, Part III, Section 8.
5. J. L. Austin, *How to do things with words*, Oxford, 1965, Lectures VIII, IX, X.
6. J. L. Austin, *op. cit.*, Lecture III.
7. J. L. Austin, *op. cit.*, Lecture IV.
8. E. Goffman, *op. cit.*, pp. 25–6.
9. P. M. Opie and I. Opie, *Children's Games in Street and Playground*, London, 1969.
10. S. J. Lyman and M. B. Scott, *J. Health and Social Behaviour*, 9, 3, 183.
11. Ovid, *The Art of Love*, translated by J. H. Mozley, Loeb, London, 1929.
12. H. Hawkins, *Likeness of Truth in Elizabethan and Restoration Drama*, Clarendon Press, Oxford, forthcoming, Chapter IV.
13. E. Goffman, *op. cit.*, pp. 125, 127–8.
14. H. Garfinkel, *Studies in Ethnomethodology*, Prentice-Hall, Englewood Cliffs, N.J., 1967, p. 148.
15. E. Berne, *op. cit.*, p. 44.
16. E. Berne, *op. cit.*, pp. 65–147.
17. H. Garfinkel, *op. cit.*, pp. 140–1.
18. E. Berne, *op. cit.*
19. J. L. Austin, 'Pretending', *Philosophical Papers*, Clarendon Press, Oxford, 1961, pp. 201–18.
20. G. A. Miller, E. A. Galanter and K. H. Pribram, *Plans and the Structure of Behavior*, Holt-Dryden, New York, 1960.

CHAPTER TEN

The Dramaturgical Standpoint

THE ARGUMENT

I

Performance

If accounts are to social psychology what microscopes are to natural science, we must look into the general conditions under which accounts are generated.

Role Distance

1. Performances can *always* be consciously self-monitored, though not all performances actually are. This is a basic human power, and not further explicable in psychological terms. Its basis lies in the system character of human neurophysiology.

2. A specific utilization of this power has been studied by Goffman under the concept 'role distance'. We consider a general form of the utilization of this power, which we shall call 'taking the dramaturgical standpoint'.

The General Form of the Dramaturgical Standpoint

1. Treat the episode one is engaged in, whether as actor or audience, as a dramatic performance.

2. Reconstruct the script, the stage directions, etc., which can

be analysed according to the Role-rule model scheme, as if it were a play script in which rituals, games, routines and entertainments were simulated.

The Historical Origins of the Dramaturgical Standpoint

1. Erasmus (1549) used it as an analytical tool in his discussion of society in *In Praise of Folly*.

2. Jonson (1629) treated it not only as an analytical tool but as constitutive of much of the structure of social episodes, in a Goffman-esque manner.

3. De Laclos (1782) used it both analytically and exploratorily in his didactic novel *Les Liaisons Dangereuses*.

The Development of the Dramaturgical Standpoint

1. Naïve role-theory uses only the bare outlines, e.g. script, performances, actors, etc. It does not draw upon dramatic criticism for deeper or more refined analyses.

2. More subtle analyses can be developed by exploiting analogies with dramatic categories.

    a. In plot structure, dramatic category, etc., as tragedy/comedy distinction for instance.

    b. In character analysis, e.g. major and minor (types) etc.

II
Style

3. Goffman develops the Jonson-Duclos duality.

    a. GI: *The Constitutive Principle*: People monitor their performances according to dramatic principles.

    b. GII: *The Explanatory Principle*: In order to understand certain sequences of social behaviour these should be analysed for Act-action structure by reference to dramatic principles, and the accounts analysed for explanatory purposes as if they described the work and mode of performance of actors.

    c. Goffman's analytical concepts.

        (i) impression management (performance).

        (ii) cooperation and mutual support in impression management (team).

        (iii) place of performance and place of preparation of performance (back and front regions).

        (iv) discrepant roles are those played by people who put on countervailing performances or send up the performance being staged.

        (v) The proof that these are performances is found in the fact that certain facts about the performers would discredit the performance and must be concealed.

    d. Other analytical frameworks can be fitted within the generalized dramaturgical standpoint by exploiting the full range of R-r models.

I *Performance*

We have laid great stress on the discovery of the rules and conventions being followed by the participants in an episode through the analysis of the accounts they are ready to give of what is being done or attempted in that episode. It is now time to consider the conditions under which monitoring commentaries can be produced. The general condition which makes them possible at all is the *fact* that human beings are characterized by their power to be aware of what they are doing and to control and modify their performance in accordance with specific rules and plans. In order to become aware of what rules, plans and so on are being followed it becomes necessary to monitor the monitoring so to speak. We must step back not only from the performance, but from the control of the performance. And this too we can do. A very specific form of this 'stepping back' has been discussed by Goffman, under the title of 'role distance'.[1] In taking role-distance a person shows that he is aware that he is putting on a performance by giving little signs that subtly mock that performance. In order for this to be possible he must be aware of his monitoring control over his actions, in particular those actions that constitute the performance. The most generalized form of role-distance we shall call 'the dramaturgical standpoint'.

In taking the dramaturgical standpoint we ask ourselves how we would perceive what we are doing were we acting deliberately, and following a script as in a play. By taking the dramaturgical standpoint we are in a position to discover not only the general nature of what we are doing, that is, which of the general types of Role-rule model is appropriate to the analysis of the episode, but under the guidance of that discovery to produce a commentary detailing the rules, plans and conventions we are following and the meanings which the several parts of the performance have for us. Thus adopting the dramaturgical standpoint is a way of attaining the general position from which it becomes possible to discover the ethogeny of an episode, that is the rules, meanings and so on which are responsible for the structure of an episode, by being the rules and conventions which are followed by a conscious agent in doing and saying the things that make up the overt structure of the episode. Thinking of the performance as if it were a play demands that we pay attention to just those features we have drawn attention to in earlier chapters as the system of reasons for the actions which constitute the monitoring, anticipatory or retrospective commentary in a justificatory context. This standpoint can be taken vicariously by an onlooker as well as actually by a performer.

Seeing oneself and others as actors draws attention not only to the 'script' but also to the roles being played, that is to the *personae* under which the various people involved are presenting themselves. We have already drawn attention to the distinction between the biological individual and the social one, and to the very important fact that dimensions of variability are very different for each. One and the same biological individual may present a variety of internally consistent personae in different social situations, no one of which is more authentically *him* than the others. We have noticed that this feature of human beings has been fixed into a social system in Japan, while for Western society the structuring of these personae in each biological individual is a more contingent matter.[2] From the dramaturgical point of view an episode is treated primarily as an interaction of personae, of social individuals, and only secondarily as an interaction of biological individuals. This is exactly like the play itself, in which the roles of Hamlet and Ophelia and their interaction constitute the drama and any number of different biological individuals can play them, while it is also true that those very same biological individuals may play quite different roles in a different play. In this chapter we shall explore the consequences of drawing a thorough-going analogy between human life perceived from the dramaturgical standpoint, and the performances of stage plays.

The Origins of the Dramaturgical Standpoint

The idea that the episodes of human life can be viewed as if they were dramatic performances is of considerable antiquity. The idea was a commonplace of social analysis from the sixteenth to eighteenth centuries. Throughout that period the dramaturgical model was seen both as a determinant of social behaviour and as an analytical tool by the help of which the actions of an episode can be given a plausible Act-action structure. The force of the dramaturgical model was well understood by Erasmus. 'If one at a solemn stage play,' he says in *The Praise of Folly*,[3] 'would take upon him to pluck off the players' garments, while they were saying their parts, and so decipher unto the lookers-on the true and native faces of each of the players, should he not, trow ye, mar all the matter? And well deserve for a madman to be pelted out of the place with stones? Ye should see yet straight ways a new transmutation in things, that who before played the woman should then appear to be a man, who seemed youth should show his hoar hairs, who counterfeited the king should turn to a rascal, and who played God Almighty should become a cobbler as he was before. Yet take away this error, and as soon take away all togethers, in as much as the feigning and counterfeiting is it that so delighteth the beholders. So likewise, all this life of mortal men, what is it else but a certain kind of stage play? Whereas men come forth disguised one in one array, another in another, each playing his part, till at last the maker of the play, or book-bearer, causeth them to avoid the scaffold, and yet sometimes maketh one man come in two or three times, with sundry parts and apparel, as who before represented a king, being clothed all in purple, having no more but shifted himself a little, should show himself again like a woebegone miser. And all this is done under a certain veil or shadow, which taken away once, the play can no more be played.' Erasmus goes on to develop this theme, that if the affectation is wholly taken away then nothing man-like remains. The Stoics aim of stripping away appearance leaves nothing but a stone god. In short the task of the social psychologists is to identify the parts, not to look for a common entity behind the parts.

Most of those who used the dramaturgical model in this period used it just as an analytical tool, and reserve their fiercest moral condemnation for those people who adopt the dramaturgical standpoint as a way of organizing their lives.[4] Both Erasmus and Goffman would have seen that very condemnation as itself the acting out of a part. In Jonson's *The New Inn*[5] the model is shown both as a determinant of action, and as an analytical tool. By the eighteenth century the deliberate adoption of the dramaturgical model as a determinant of one's social behaviour had become the central fact of social life amongst the leisured class. Moralists found this a cause for condemnation. Perhaps the sense we give to 'dramatization' in episodes of ordinary life, of giving a heightened and false significance to features of episodes is a reflection of this moralistic attitude to the use of the model as a determinant of Act-action structure. However, in order to condemn they had first to describe the kind of life-style upon which they wished to moralize, and in the course of doing so, one author at least, gave a classical account of the adoption of the dramaturgical ideal for the organization of all the episodes of life. This account is to be found in Letter 81 of *Les Liaisons Dangereuses* by C. de Laclos.[17] In this letter the Marquise de Mertreuil describes how she trained herself as a social actress, and then, as she says 'I saw that to feign love successfully one had only to join the talent of a comedian to the mind of an author. I practised myself in both arts and perhaps with some success; but instead of seeking the vain applause of the theatre, I resolved to employ for my happiness what others sacrificed to vanity.'[6] Not surprisingly the decline of the dramaturgical model as an explicit social determinant in the nineteenth century was accompanied by a decline in its use as an analytical tool. The social sciences in the nineteenth century were early condemned to the sterility of the 'mechanical' model. Comte's philosophy of positivism was among the influences leading to this disaster from which the human sciences still suffer, but it was not the only one. It is perhaps more just to say that his philosophy of social science reflects the general currents of thought as much as it determined them. It is part of our purpose in this book to show the way towards a non-trivial and fruitful methodology for the scientific study of human life by developing a full-scale alternative to the futile and trivial mechanical model.

The development of the dramaturgical model can be taken in two stages. The first stage is represented by naïve role theory, as developed for instance by Biddle and Thomas.[7] Here the bare outline of the components and structure of a dramatic performance forms the source of the model. They sketch the source in the following analysis of a stage performance: 'When actors portray a character in a play, their performance is determined by the script, the director's instructions, the performance of fellow actors, and the reactions of the audience as well as by the acting talents of the players. Apart from differences between actors in the interpretation of their parts, the performance of each actor is programmed by all these external factors; consequently there are significant similarities in the performance of actors taking the same part, no matter who the actors are.'

At this stage of analysis, the kinds of plays that can be performed, and the kind of characters that can be portrayed, and the manner in which they are to be portrayed form no part of the source of the model, and therefore they are not reflected in it. The model is set out as follows: 'Individuals in society occupy positions, and their role performance in these positions is determined by social norms, demands and rules; by the role performance of others in their respective positions; by those who observe and react to the performance; and by the individual's particular capabilities and personality.

The social 'script' may be as constraining as that of a play, but it frequently allows more options; the 'director' is often present in real life as a supervisor, parent, teacher or coach; the 'audience' in life consists of all those who observe the position members' behaviour; the position members' 'performance' in life, as in the play, is attributable to his familiarity with the 'part', his personality and personal history in general, and more significantly to the 'script' which others define in so many ways. In essence, the role perspective assumes, as does the theatre, that performance results from the social prescriptions and behaviour of others, and that individual variations in performance, to the extent that they do occur, are expressed within the framework created by these factors.'

It is easy to see that the model contains just those features for which analogues have been identified in the source, that is in the analysis of the drama and its staging. The model can be more adequately developed only by undertaking a deeper analysis of its source, dramatic performances, in the course of which the analogical basis for more subtle concepts to be introduced into the model can be found. The dramaturgical model as employed by naïve role theory simply introduces the idea that there are roles, performances, and so on. It makes no attempt to provide a classification of these roles and performances. To develop the model further, such a classification can be attempted, and can be based upon the classifications of the theatrical sources of the model. A certain strand of everyday commentary upon episodes reveals some of the language of this more advanced view, as when people are said to be putting on a tragic act, to be the victims of tragedy, and the like.

Act-action structures can be classified by a taxonomical system analogous to the classification of plots. The components of plot, as analysed by Bentley,[8] are:

i. the arrangement of incidents in chronological order,

ii. the selection of incidents to create suspense.

Suspense is introduced by so selecting the items portrayed that the outcome cannot be anticipated with certainty, from the information given, though it is assumed that the outcome is 'predestined', i.e. will be seen in the end to be inevitable, and is, of course, actually determined by the script. In this it differs from the suspense of a game, where the following of the rules is not itself sufficient to determine the outcome.

iii. the incidents are arranged according to some principle in terms of which they have meaning, i.e. the actions portrayed have meaning as appropriate for the performance of the acts simulated. The complex of causes and reasons, which might be offered as an account of the actions, makes the outcome intelligible with respect to the acts performed.

A similar point has been made by E. M. Forster.[9] A plot exists, he says, when a structure of causality or reason is imposed upon a chronological sequence, i.e., when the presence of each element in the sequence can be accounted for with respect to the simulated outcome. As in the case of the lower order Role-rule group of models, the model may function analytically, enabling an investigator to pick out the significant incidents in an episode; or determinatively, controlling the actions performed by actors by the need they feel to do all of those things that would accomplish the acts attempted.

It follows from this that Act-action structures should be classifiable not only as routines, games, rituals or entertainments, but also in accordance with the same variety of principles that are involved in the corresponding kinds of plots. For instance Kitto's broad distinction between dramas of principle and dramas of character,[10] should find an analogue in the analysis of episodes. Similarly the traditional distinctions between comedy, tragedy, melodrama should also find employment as the sources of concepts for the detailed analysis of simulated routines, rituals, games and so on. The corresponding Act-action structures will be defined by identifying the principles involved in the plotting of these distinct kinds of plays. It is clear that a play does not include everything that would be said and done by the people involved in the incidents portrayed, and consequently the function of the corresponding analytical concepts in the analysis of real life episodes would be to pick out only some of the things that happened, those which could be given meaning with respect to the acts of the episode, i.e., as the actions by which the acts are performed.

A play is not just a plot but involves characters, and from the analysis of character the notion of role can be further developed from another point of view. It is crucial to see that a character in a play corresponds to a *role* in life, not to a person. This is because the actions of the character are *all* meaningful with respect to the acts of which the plot consists; and correspondingly, defining a role *selects* those actions of the people involved in an episode which satisfy the rule-conventions for bringing about the acts of the Act-action structure. Thus the analysis of character should provide a source for a model for the analysis of roles. There is a valuable analysis by Eric Bentley,[11] in which he analyses character by function in representation of the plot, that is the presentation of the Act-action structure of the simulated episode. The traditional distinction between 'flat' and 'round' characters is shown by Bentley to amount to a distinction between consistent and inconsistent ensembles of actions performed by the character. In the ethogenic spirit this can be seen as a distinction derivative from consistent and inconsistent ensembles of powers and liabilities. It is not insignificant for social psychology that 'flat' characters, i.e., those which simulate people with consistent ensembles of powers and liabilities are typically minor characters, and are almost universally taken by dramatic critics to be exemplifications of *types*, rather than portraits of putative individuals. Cattell was not the first to look for standard ensembles of powers and liabilities, since the identification of these was a feature of the *commedia del arte*, and of the *caractères* of seventeenth- and eighteenth-century France. The popularity of these ensembles transformed them into myths, that is real people adapted their behaviour to them, and standardized their reactions around the types. The dramatic critics' almost universal relegation of these characters to types is further evidence for our distinction between the unitary biological individual and his multiple set of social personae.

The nearer a major character is to matching a real human being the less is he of use as the basis for a concept to be used in a role analysis, but the more his actions are valuable in the identification of Act-action structures. The point is that interaction cannot be understood in terms of roles alone, because it is *people* who interact and they act out an episode with a structure. Major characters perform a different role in the drama from the minor, 'flat' characters, in that they serve to magnify the simulated Act-action structure. Othello is an *ordinary* man in a typified situation, where the episode is purified of extraneous elements. The study of major characters in the drama has value for the development of the dramaturgical model only indirectly, as a heightening of the subtlety of the plot structure, which serves as a model for the Act-action structures of episodes. Shakespeare's 'art is shown in the way he displaces the accent, carrying us from the static idea "a jealous man" to an experience of jealousy. Being an experience it does not consist of abstract qualities, nor can it be defined by them. It is defined by dialogue (poetry) and action (including the inner action or struggle, as mentioned by Coleridge). The impression given is less that of a typical character being tagged, than that of a man having a typical experience.'[11, 12]

II *Style*

The capacity for the higher order control of performance that derives from the specifically human power of monitoring the monitoring of performance allows the introduction of *style* into the execution of actions. By this means a social actor can control the presentation of himself to others. Human beings use style to present a certain appearance. The use of the dramaturgical standpoint to explore this important aspect of social life was begun, in our time, by E. Goffman. We propose to use his book, *The Presentation of Self in Everyday Life*,[13] to illustrate this.

The dramaturgical standpoint has a double role, in that it is both explanatory of, and constitutive of the stylistic features of performances in real episodes. It can both be applied to and derived from the observation of actual episodes. We express this point in two principles:

GI: *The Constitutive Principle*: For certain purposes people control the style of their actions, sometimes consciously and sometimes not, and superimpose this upon other activities.

For instance work may be done in a manner in accordance with the principles of a dramatic performance in order to project a certain impression of the people working to an inspector or manager. In some of Berne's 'games' the game may be played out through the style of the performance, rather than in its content. In the game 'Poor Little Me', for instance, perfectly ordinary tasks may be being performed in a self-pitying way.

The principle GI means, in effect, that in the accounts people give of their *own* activities, dramaturgical concepts *do*, as a matter of fact, figure.

GII: *The Explanatory Principle*: In order to understand, that is to provide a plausible account for the details of what people are doing, one must see their activities in terms of deliberate followings out of one or more rules or conventions of style. In fact what people are doing is rarely properly described as *just* eating, or *just* working, but has stylistic features which have certain conventional meanings associated with recognized types of personae.

This principle means, in effect, that in the accounts people (including social psychologists) give of the activities of *others*, stylistic concepts *should* figure. In contrast to GI, which is an empirical hypothesis, GII is a methodological principle.

The necessity for the adoption of GII follows from the generality of the application of GI. Even in those cases where we can hardly claim that the actors are tacitly *imposing* a stylistic form upon their actions it may be illuminating to apply and to imagine how role-rule concepts might account for the way they perform their actions.

We think it worth while at this point to lay out Goffman's ethogenic methodology in five points or principles, supported for the sake of exposition from the *Presentation of Self in Everyday Life*. We will also note how utterly different this methodology is from that derived from the mechanistic model of man which, so often, forms the conceptual basis of laboratory experiments.

1. People impose conventional stylistic forms upon their activities, that is upon the episodes of their lives. This is described by Goffman as follows: 'activity oriented towards worktasks tends to be converted into activity oriented towards communications . . . sufficient self-control is exerted so as to maintain a working consensus (as to the impression being conveyed); an idealized impression is offered

by accentuating certain facts and concealing others; expressive coherence is maintained by the performer taking more care to guard
against minor disharmonies than the stated purpose (e.g. some worktask) of the performance might lead the audience to think was
warranted. All of these general characteristics of performances can
be seen as interaction constraints which play upon the individual
and transform his activities into performances. Instead of merely
doing his task and giving vent to his feelings, he will express the
doing of his task and acceptably convey his feelings'.[14]

In contrast, in the experimental situation, the person is thought of
as an organism or subject exposed to certain treatments or conditions, and expected to respond in predictable ways. What if, instead,
we think of persons serving in an experiment as imposing a role
and rule structure on the situation? Then, instead of a passive
subject, we have an active participant who might try to fathom
what the experimenter is up to and accordingly manage the impression he presents to the experimenter so as to fit one of several
possible roles that relate to the role in which he has cast the experimenter. The work of Friedman and others is a partial recognition of
the role-rule model, but the full implications are not spelled out by
them. Certainly, if we adopt the role-rule model, laboratory experiments in social psychology become very different from what we
traditionally conceive. We noted in Chapter Three that in many
experiments the role-rule model for interaction between strangers is
adopted by the participants, with important consequences for the
outcomes and the interpretation of the experiments.

2. Next to 'Performances', 'Team' is Goffman's most important
concept, for with it he expresses the mode of organization of the
people involved in an episode so far as they co-operate in stylistic
matters. The team are those who put on the performance, and are
distinguished both from the audience, those for whom the performance is staged, and the outsiders, those who are neither team
nor audience. It is clear that the 'team' is a grouping of people
produced by the need for co-operation in the presentation and of a
certain style, consonant with one or more of the role-rule models.
This is clear in Goffman's definition of 'team'.[15] 'A team, then, may
be defined as a set of individuals whose intimate co-operation is

P

required if a given projected definition of the situation is to be maintained. A team is a grouping, but it is a grouping not in relation to a social structure or social organization but rather in relation to an interaction or series of interactions in which the relative definition of the situation is maintained'. The identification of those groupings which are teams in this sense, is as germane to the understanding of the episodes of human life as such concepts as social class. The fact that a young man and the waiters in a restaurant may form a team for which the audience may be the one young girl to whom the man is giving dinner is at least as important a feature of *that* dinner episode as the identification of the members of the team and audience as being of this or that social class.

For the episode in the restaurant to succeed, the girl must not become aware that her host and the waiters *are* a team, putting on a performance for her benefit. They may not fully realize it themselves. The fact that in everyday life we are not at the play, in church or on the sportsfield requires that much of the inner structure of episodes must not be acknowledged. 'Thus,' says Goffman,[16] 'a team . . . is the kind of secret society whose members may be known by non-members to constitute a society, even an exclusive one, but the society these individuals are known to constitute is not the one they constitute by virtue of acting as a team.'

Again, thinking of the laboratory experiment, we may ask whether or not in fact the participants in an experiment, together with the experimenter, do not in fact form a kind of team. How that team defines the situation and how that definition relates to the interaction which occurs has everything to do with the 'results' obtained from the experiment, and how these results are to be interpreted.

3. Specific features of Goffman's conceptual system derive from certain specific features of each of the role-rule set of models, seen from the dramaturgical standpoint as the carrying out of a performance. From that standpoint comes the idea of two regions, front and back, contrasted as the place where the performance is carried out and the place where it is prepared. This feature, though prominent in simulated routines such as real stage plays, is found in episodes conforming to the liturgical and game models too. The

vestry is the back region with respect to which the chancel is the front, and the field of play is front region with respect to the changing rooms, practice pitches and the like. Applying the three models together Goffman produces the following analytical scheme from the dramaturgical standpoint:

'The performance of an individual in a front region may be seen as an effort to give the appearance that his activity in the region maintains and embodies certain standards.'[17] Thus, in a number of different ways performances can be seen to have succeeded or failed. Of course in the discussion from which we are quoting Goffman is concerned only with impression management, and there are very many other things that might be aimed at in a performance. These standards fall into two groups, those to which verbal or other interchange with the audience must conform, called by Goffman, 'politeness' and those to which ancillary activities in view of the audience, but not specifically addressed to them must conform, called by Goffman 'decorum'. This corresponds to the different conventions for the performance of actors, and the crowd, on the stage. For instance, specific remarks made by one member of the crowd to another should not be audible, and the like.

The principles, rules or conventions of decorum can be subdivided into those which are moral (ends in themselves, e.g. 'rules regarding non-interference and non-molestation of others') or instrumental (not ends in themselves, e.g. 'duties such as an employer might demand of his employees—care of property . . .').[18]

4. One of Goffman's most important innovations is the concept of *discrepant role*.[19] A discrepant role is made possible by the fact that the structuring of, say, a worktask, as a performance in a certain style, is achieved by the imposition of certain conventions derived from some or all of the role-rule set of models upon the manner of an activity. Thus one who will not accept that imposition, and so refuses to join the team, may adopt one of two major kinds of discrepant role. He may go on doing the primary task in the ordinary way, say working his machine in a lackadaisical and bored way when the rest are putting on a show of keenness in the course of developing, say, a strategy for putting something over on the management. He may instead put on his own show in opposition to

that of the team. He may do this either by giving away the team, making subtle mockery of their performance in several ways identified by Goffman, or by maintaining a countervailing performance with his own team, which might consist of just himself. At a committee meeting one member may put on an elaborate show of boredom in opposition to a performance of keenness and interest in an item, put on by the other members. In that way he denies the validity of their performance.

Many experimenters have encountered participants in their studies who play discrepant roles. They foul up their performance by not following instructions, they engage in clowning if there is an audience composed of other participants, they perform the task in a lackadaisical and bored way. Typically, such participants are eliminated from the data analysis. But what is not generally recognized is that the participants who are not playing discrepant roles are actively taking roles which in their case fits in with the experimenter's purposes.

5. It follows from the Principle GI, that people do monitor their performances in real life, that there should be some phenomena of human life that are intelligible only when seen as consequences of the adoptions of the dramaturgical standpoint. Since Principle GI is an empirical principle, whether there are such phenomena or not would be a test of its correctness. With respect to his limited aims and limited exploitation of the dramaturgical standpoint, Goffman finds certain kinds of embarrassment intelligible only under the assumption that the real life episode is controlled in accordance with certain stylistic convents and structured by reference to a role-rule model, only explicable from the dramaturgical standpoint. 'The past life and current round of activity of a given performer typically contain at least a few facts which, if introduced during the performance, would discredit or at least weaken the claims about self that the performer was attempting to project as part of the definition of the situation. . . . When such facts are introduced embarrassment is the usual result'.[20] This is rather misleadingly expressed in the language of causality, that is the introduction of the discordant facts has embarrassment as a *result*. We need make no tacit claims about causes. All that is required is that in the explanation of, and in the

accounting for someone's embarrassment, the discordant fact be cited and be regarded as a convincing sort of explanation. The cause of the embarrassment may be much more complex, in that it could be that the discordant fact was not brought fully to the person's attention, but it was what led the other participants to change their behaviour subtly, which affected the one who felt embarrassment; and many other possible complexities. Nevertheless, the most important fact to be mentioned in accounting for the embarrassment is the escape of the discordant fact.

The laboratory parallel is to be found largely in those trial runs and pilot projects where the experimenter slipped up in his management of the experiment, and thereby affected the behaviour of the participants in unwanted ways, forcing him to discard the results.

What is an inspired and intuitive technique for Goffman becomes a methodology for ethogeny, that is a rationally grounded systematic set of techniques designed to answer and solve problems of a certain kind. From an ethogenic point of view some perspectives for the analysis of episodes that Goffman thinks are different from his own, can be shown to have a place within the role-rule set of models.

The other frameworks he notices are the following:

1. 'An establishment may be viewed "technically", in terms of its efficiency and inefficiency as an intentionally organized system of activity for the achievement of predefined objectives.'[21] This is clearly a mode of the liturgical model, in that the question of achievement is raised. The ritual of a marriage ceremony could be criticized as 'over-elaborate', and e.g. on that basis some people might prefer a marriage according to a simpler rite.

2. 'An establishment may be viewed "politically", in terms of the actions which each participant . . . can demand of other participants . . . and the use of sanctions.'[22] From the ethogenic point of view the 'political perspective' is achieved by laying emphasis on the origin and maintenance of the rule-conventions of the Role-rule models.

3. Viewing an establishment 'structurally' is how Goffman describes the identification of the status and roles of participants in the activities of the establishment. The ethogenist looks upon this as

the emphasis on the role-conventions of the Role-rule models.

4. 'Finally', says Goffman, 'an establishment may be viewed "culturally", in terms of the moral values which influence activity in the establishment—values pertaining to fashions, customs, and matters of taste, to politeness and decorum, to ultimate ends and normative restrictions on means.'[23] In ethogeny this perspective is nothing but the study of the kinds of accounts that people give in justification of the dramatic scenarios, and conventions, the rites and rituals, and the rules of the games in accordance with which they live out the episodes that make up their lives as social beings.

We have already glimpsed the fact that the method employed by Goffman involves the use of the Role-rule models in making sense of the episodes whose intelligibility is disclosed by adopting the dramaturgical perspective. In *Where The Action Is*, particularly in the first and last chapters, explicit liturgical and game models come to the fore. The bulk of the essay 'On Face Work' is the exploitation of the liturgical model, under which the various means by which 'face' is maintained and saved is treated as if they were rituals. The general structure of 'face' rituals is expressed in the sequence, 'challenge, offering, acceptance and thanks'.[24] In this sequence of acts we have an Act-action structure, in terms of which all 'face' episodes can be analysed and understood to have meaning as actions. A great many particular sequences of the actions of rituals, i.e. rites, will be found to be expressive of this structure. Though unlike real rituals, the initiation of a specific rite will not necessarily be followed by the proper, subsequent steps. Goffman notices,[25] that the emotional flux which we have called the Arousal structure of an episode, may interpenetrate the Act-actions structure, in that, at certain points in a rite, it may be proper to express a particular emotion. This expression may be realistic or it may be quite conventional, or any degree between. That is the Arousal structure, the real emotional flux in an episode, is not necessarily related to those expressions of emotion which appear as part of the Act-action structure, in speech, acts, gestures, facial expressions and the like. That someone properly says 'I'm sorry' certainly does not entail that he feels any degree of sorrow. We generally *express* grief when we are *supposed* to express it, i.e. when it is proper, and not when we actually feel it. Indeed among Anglo-Americans it may be improper to express grief when we feel it, and proper to express it when we do not. There is a complex Anglo-American style of behaviour at funerals, in which the overt expression of grief is a means of concealing whatever real grief is felt, and must be seen to be so.

Goffman's use of the full spectrum of Role-rule models can be seen in his development of a game model for understanding certain episodes that involve face-work. He notices that sometimes the conditions that are necessary for the fruitful application of a game model are satisfied. As he says 'Every face-saving practice which is allowed to neutralize a particular threat opens up the possibility that the threat will be wilfully introduced for what can be gained by it.'[26] The awareness of this step as a ploy by the putative victim initiates the 'game' sequence, so that an episode whose Act-action structure is at the beginning ritualistic, liturgical, can be transformed so that the latter parts of its Act-action structure must be seen in the light of a game model. As Goffman says, explicitly introducing the game-model concepts,[27] 'The purpose of the game is to preserve everyone's line from an inexcusable contradiction, while scoring as many points as possible against one's adversaries and making as many gains as possible for oneself.' Finally Goffman offers, as the deepest and subtlest level of analysis of the Act-action structure of 'face' episodes, an explicitly *joint* liturgical and game model. There is nothing odd about this jointure. There were semi-formal episodes in human life which were literally *sacred games*, having both a liturgical and a sporting element. The actions performed were the means by which certain acts were done, but the Act-action structure was not determinate as to outcome for any particular individual, though of course, it was fully determinate as to the kind of outcome. Thus what is from the point of view of an individual a game, albeit a deadly one, becomes from the point of view of the judges, players, spectators and others involved a rite, since there will be a victory, and a victor, and in that victory, by whosoever hand, the act will be achieved. The ball courts of Yucatan, and the *stadia* of Greece were equally the scenes of episodes whose Act-action structure can only be understood by the application of the joint liturgical-game model.

This jointure is possible only if the actions are so arranged that it is possible to distinguish the fact that there will be an outcome from the fact as to which person is the actor in that outcome. In the sacred games as in the everyday saving of face the ritual is employed competitively by the individuals involved, but whoever is the victor, the fact that his victory has been achieved within the rite ensures that face has in fact been saved. This is beautifully set out by Goffman in *Where The Action Is*.[28]

Finally, in the eponymous essay of *Where The Action Is*, Goffman makes explicit use of a specific game model, namely employing concepts appropriate to episodes which are games of chance, in the analysis of episodes which, at first sight, are not games at all. For instance, mental health is what is hazarded by those who take psychedelic drugs in the bravado spirit of gambling, and so on. Just as in his *Presentation of Self*, he employs the principle we called GI, to show that people do themselves construe certain episodes as having the Act-action structure of a game of chance. 'Given the practical necessity,' he says,[29] 'of following a course of action whose success is problematic and passively awaiting the outcome thereof, one can discover an alternative howsoever costly, and then define oneself as having freely chosen between this undesirable certainty and the uncertainty at hand.' Thus one represents oneself to oneself, and perhaps to others, as a 'gamblin' man'. Another interesting use of an explicit game model from the dramaturgical standpoint is in M. B. Scott and S. M. Lyman's analysis of the state of mind of those stigmatized people who seem paranoid.[30]

In short, Goffman's method is the explicit and subtle exploitation of the Role-rule models, for the development of a conceptual system for making an analysis of the Act-action structure of episodes from the dramaturgical standpoint. The justification of the method is made out both by exhibiting the force of the analyses, and by showing that some episodes are structured the way they are because the people involved are bending the course of events so as to present the episode as a dramatic or practical routine, a ritual, a game or some blend of all three. Finally one should add that there are those for whom only the fourth in our group of models can provide a life structuring, namely those for whom every episode is but an entertainment. For an example of this, refer to the account by Wilfred Sheed[31] of the former style of life of the English upper middle class, where one hid effort, feeling, commitment and the like under a style of effortless superiority.[32, 33]

REFERENCES

1. E. Goffman, *Where the Action Is*, Allen Lane, The Penguin Press, London, 1969, Ch. 2, originally in *Encounters*, Bobbs-Merrill, Indiana, 1961.
2. J. L. Simmons and G. J. McCall, *Identities and Interactions*, Free Press, New York, 1966.
3. Taken, with modern spelling, from Sir Thomas Challoner's translation, 1549 edition.
4. For instance, Ben Jonson in 'Discoveries', *Works*, VII, lines 1093–6.
5. H. Hawkins, 'The Idea of a Theatre in Jonson's *New Inn*', *Renaissance Drama*, 1967, pp. 205–26.
6. C. de Laclos, *Les Liaisons Dangereuses*, Paris, 1782, translated by R. Aldington, Folio Society, London, 1962, p. 206.
7. B. J. Biddle and E. J. Thomas, *Role Theory*, Wiley, New York, 1961, p. 4.
8. E. Bentley, *The Life of the Drama*, Methuen, London, 1965.
9. E. M. Forster, *Aspects of the Novel*, Penguin Books, London, A557, 1963.
10. H. F. D. Kitto, *Form and Meaning in Drama*, Methuen, London, 1956, pp. 199–245.
11. E. Bentley, *op. cit.*, p. 48.
12. For a general exposition of the dramaturgical standpoint see S. L. Messenger, *Sociometry*, XXV, 1962.
13. E. Goffman, *The Presentation of Self in Everyday Life*, Anchor Books, New York, 1959; Allen Lane, The Penguin Press, London, 1969.
14. *Ibid*. pp. 56–7.
15. *Ibid*. pp. 90–1.
16. *Ibid*. p. 91.
17. *Ibid*. p. 93.
18. *Loc. cit.*
19. *Ibid*. pp. 123–46.

20. *Ibid.* p. 184.
21. *Ibid.* p. 211.
22. *Loc. cit.*
23. *Ibid.* p. 212.
24. E. Goffman, 'On Face Work', *Interaction Ritual*, Doubleday, New York, 1967, reprinted: E. Goffman, *Where the Action Is*, Allen Lane, The Penguin Press, London, 1969, Ch. 1.
25. *Ibid.* p. 18.
26. *Loc. cit.*
27. *Ibid.* p. 19.
28. *Ibid.* p. 25.
29. *Ibid.* p. 125.
30. M. B. Scott and S. L. Lyman, 'Paranoia, Homosexuality and Game-Theory', *J. Health and Social Behavior*, 9 (1968), 179–87.
31. W. Sheed, *A Middle Class Education*, Sphere, London, 1967.
32. For a thorough analysis of the concepts used to describe the springs of human action, seen from the dramaturgical standpoint, see K. Burke, *A Grammar of Motives*, California University Press, 1969; Prentice-Hall, New York, 1945.
33. For a sociological perspective on the presentation of self see A. Strauss, *Mirrors and Masks*, Free Press, New York, 1959.

CHAPTER ELEVEN

The Empirical Checking of Role-rule models

THE ARGUMENT

Checking the Authenticity of an Account

1. From the dramaturgical point of view the social psychologist is in the role of audience.

2. An account must be expected to show shifts from model to model, and the psychologist must be prepared to take up different auditing roles in consequence.

3. In formal episodes the accounts of actors and audience *must* be concordant, or the episode has failed in its intended purpose.

4. Enigmatic episodes:

   a. In participant observation the social psychologist is both actor and audience, and both perspectives must be made concordant; either

     (i) because they really are concordant, or

     (ii) apparent discordance leads to a reappraisal of either or both perspectives.

Here there is self-negotiation as to the best account.

   b. When the social psychologist is an engaged observer, but not a primary participant, he must negotiate his account with the accounts of the actors.

5. The authenticity of the Role-rule group of models has a partial check in the fact that there are some episodes, namely the formal, where they have literal employment.

It is impossible to arrange for comparable testing of mechanistic models, since the behaviour of language-using, consciously self-monitoring, rule-following organisms is generated in ways wholly different from the genesis of the behaviour of e.g. gases, to which the mechanistic model has literal application.

6. a. The mechanistic models used in physics have their authenticity preserved by adversion to further parameters, whose variations account for apparent disparities in behaviour. Thus mechanistic theories are strongly deterministic.

b. The corresponding preservatory moves in the use of anthropomorphic models involve the use of 'back-stop' concepts, such as 'just wanting to'.

(i) But these do not introduce further parameters, their function is to preserve the absolute status of the person as agent.

(ii) They are such as can appear arbitrarily at any point in an account, so we are not entitled to assume the same manifested behaviour has been generated similarly.

The Negotiation of Accounts

1. Negotiated accounts may lack authenticity through two kinds of *post hoc* modification.

a. A reason which was not considered at the time of the decision to perform the actions under scrutiny is provided in retrospective commentary.

b. Even monitoring commentaries may be subject to correction in the light of later considerations, particularly in the reidentification of emotions, since these are the meanings given to states of arousal, and their true meaning may emerge only under later negotiation.

c. There is no application in ethogeny for the concept of 'absolute truth', since all accounts are revisable in principle.

d. The physical sciences also work within an open context. One cannot negotiate with atoms in the strict sense, but there is something epistemologically similar in the fact that indefinitely more information may become available about them, so that any state of 'knowledge' is revisable in principle.

e. Perfect truth is not even viable as an *ideal* in psychology.

It does not follow that we are left with no viable concepts of right and wrong theories, mistakes and their correction and so on.

2. a. The Standard Form of Negotiation can be defined around a three-person interaction, the primary participants and the 'third man'. This itself constitutes an irreduceable social interaction, so that the primary participants with the third man constitute a set of secondary participants. This is not the beginning of an infinite regress because the possibility of the dramaturgical standpoint intervenes.

b. A model for negotiation of accounts could be found in family therapy or marriage counselling, etc.

c. Empirical research is needed on the movement of opinion within a secondary social interaction.

d. Initial discordance may be resolved by

(i) inward resolution; in which the third man modifies his account to accord with those of the primary participants,

(ii) outward resolution; in which the primary participants modify their accounts to accord with that of the third man.

(iii) Usually some degree of both inward and outward resolution will occur we suspect.

e. The initial plausibility of inwardly negotiated accounts may be illusory. The dangers of lack of authenticity are more difficult to guard against than those involved in outward negotiation. No final arbitration of truth is possible. This fact does not make the social sciences less objective than the physical sciences. It corresponds exactly to the irreduceably inductive character of general hypotheses in the physical sciences, and the impossibility of the final and absolute confirmation of theories.

The Epistemology of the Role-rule Group of Models

How do we know when it is appropriate to apply one of these models to an episode, or to use a conceptual system in the description of an Act-action structure that may be some suitable combination of concepts derived from the group as a whole? And how do we know when this has been done well or ill, correctly or incorrectly? How do we know what roles are being filled in the course of an episode, and what the litany, script or rule book is? Or indeed whether there is one? Of course for formal episodes which are literally ceremonials, routines, and games, there is no problem. The roles and rules are quite explicit and known to many. And for episodes centred upon a single person, how do we know what plan that person is pursuing?

In the application of the Role-rule group of models to enigmatic episodes it should be clear by now that from an explanatory point of view it is not what is done that matters, that is what actions or movements are performed, but what is supposed or thought to be achieved by them, that is what acts are meant to be performed or, more generally, what the aims and intentions of the actors are. To get a clue as to this we have to know how those involved are 'taking it'. This can best be gleaned by eavesdropping on the anticipatory, retrospective or monitoring commentary if one is being given. The problem for the social psychologist is when to apply the models to cases where the actual commentary does not report an Act-action structure that is of this sort, or where there is no commentary at all. With the help of the Role-rule group of models a social psychologist is equipped with a conceptual system for providing that sort of commentary when commentary is lacking, or when it seems to provide an alternative commentary to that being thought or spoken which gives a better insight into what is going on. How do we know when we have got a better insight? How are commentaries checked out?

It is an important preliminary to answering these questions to realize that the Role-rule group of models together with the drama-turgical standpoint, not only enable the actions of the performers to be construed within an Act-action structure, but they also involve the idea of spectators, congregations, audiences, that is people before whom the performance takes place, and in many cases for whose benefit it is all done. A social psychologist, by adopting one or more of these models, automatically creates an audience by becoming an engaged spectator rather than a detached observer, and therefore automatically achieves the appropriate degree and mode of distance from the episode, that is puts himself in the position to give a meaningful account for that slice of life. It is very important to notice that the audience and one or more of the players may be the same people. A play-reading in a private house, where everyone present reads a part is *not* a performance without an audience, though players and audience are the same people. The most profound discoveries of social psychology will be made by those who, while playing a part, filling a role and so on, can be their own audience.

In the study of informal episodes the whole array of Role-rule models may need to be complementarily deployed to understand the place of the engaged spectator as an episode modulates through different forms. That is there may not only be a shifting from priest to player, that is a transformation of role, there may be a change from member of congregation to spectator to audience, i.e. a corresponding shift from one dramaturgical standpoint to another. In the flux of models it is not only the actors and those participating in the action who are seen in different lights, there is also differential relations between those who look on and the performers, because the relation between the spectators of a game and the players is not the same as that between the congregation and a priest, nor are either identical with the relation between the audience and the actors at a play. Indeed that last relation is itself a complex of different possible relations from participation through to alienation. As Eric Bentley put it 'The mirror on the wall is only one, the mirrors in the mind are many.'[1]

A clue as to how checking-out can be achieved is to be found in the case of formal episodes. When an episode is really a ritual, or a drama or a game the account given by the participants is definitive, because they are performing just in accordance with the rules, and the acts of the episode are performed by just the actions laid down in the liturgy, script, or rule book. For formal episodes it is a necessary truth that the account given by the audience, congregation or spectators must coincide with that given by the actors by way of commentary, because in a formal episode the actors must know what act they are performing, and the audience must know what acts are being performed or they are just not the audience, spectators or congregation at that performance.

Checking an account of an enigmatic episode in terms of one or more elements of the Role-rule group of models can take two forms. In the case where the social scientist is himself an actor, a player or acolyte, or could be considered to be such in accordance with the model, then his account as a member of the audience must square with his perception of his role and the rule-convention which defines it. But the squaring may be a squaring off as it were. That is it may be that disparity between account and perception of the situation as actor is removed by a realization that the performance is itself not what it seems. An admirable fictional account of this manner of resolution of an ambiguity can be found in *The Magus*, in the gradual discovery by the hero that what he takes to be a drama is actually (that is, is most usefully perceived as) a rite.[2] And in the course of the book there are brief shifts into the game perspective as well. For enigmatic episodes the very same actions can be seen as the performances of different acts, and so the very same episode can be seen as possessing different Act-action structures. All this allows for a *negotiation* between actor and audience as to what the Act-action structure of an enigmatic episode is. The most that we can make of the question 'What is the *real* Act-action structure?' is what description of the Act-action structure can be negotiated most widely between audience and actor. When the social scientist stands right outside the episode, empirical checking of accounts will be reduced to a negotiation between himself and the participants as to what the Act-action structure is, and perhaps whether there is any Act-action structure present at all. The only possible sense that can be given to the concept of 'the rightness of an account by an ethogenist' is that his account should be the most stable element in a negotiation of accounts, that is the actors will be ready to modify their accounts in the direction of his, when discrepancies exist.

We have already seen that the Powers and Arousal structures of episodes are not like this, since they have physiological connections of various modes and degree, that, with respect to these models they contain a non-negotiable component, though, of course, physiological elements enter social reality only as they are giving meaning by those who experience them.

The mode of analysis of episodes which reveals their Act-action structure through the application of the Role-rule group of models is not without implications as to the nature of those individuals whose interactions are episodes, that is people. In the first part of this study the inability of the 'mechanical' model of man to cope with essential features of people such as their linguistic powers, which endow them with the capacity for commenting upon their actions and so making the formulating of plans and following of rules possible, with all that this implies, became clear. In using the Role-rule group of models an ethogenist is treating people on occasion as like priests, or like actors, or like players. In important ways neither actors, priests nor players are like the kind of entities which fit the 'mechanical' model. The notion that the attributes of entities can be treated as parameters, that some can be maintained constant while a chosen one is deliberately varied, is an essential feature of that model. At the heart of it is the idea of logically independent properties, which covary in a regular way. From this derives the idea of experimental design in which there are dependent and independent variables. The attempt to treat social phenomena as the interaction of entities which are essentially fitted to the mechanical model has been characteristic of the mistaken attempt to model psychology on a positivist view of physics, as has often been pointed out. It stands in great contrast to the method of analysis of accounts by the use of the Role-rule group of models. If they are adopted an ethogenist looks for something like scripts, liturgies, books of rules, *as well as* correlations, statistics and significance measures and he seeks the explanations of the *phenomena* he *observes* in the *account* he *elicits*. He proceeds always at two levels, the descriptive and the explanatory. He behaves like a real scientist. The advantages of the ethogenic approach can be summed up in the advantages of the Role-rule group of models in the analysis of explanatory accounts.

Since there are episodes in human life which really are the performance of plays, the carrying out of ceremonies and the playing of games, the Role-rule group of concepts does have *literal* employment in some episodes. This is an important point which is overlooked in elementary role theory, c.f. its absence from Table 6 in B. J. Biddle and E. J. Thomas, *Role Theory*.[3] The analogies that justify the metaphorical employment of the conceptual system are

Q

based upon likenesses and differences between entities of the same kind, namely episodes in human life, and between people acting and 'acting'. The mechanical model has *no* literal employment in human social life. The analogies that would justify its employment would have to be made out between highly incomparable entities, namely between language-using, act-performing self-monitoring organisms, and such entities as do fit the 'mechanical' model, such as confined samples of gas, or short lengths of electrical conductor.

The 'mechanical' model is strongly deterministic, that is it depends upon a strict application of the principle that a particular change in a parameter leads to an identical consequential change in another parameter, *always*. 'Always' here means that should there be a change in parameter not followed by the expected change in some other parameter then a third parameter has broken loose, as it were, and is varying. The use of the Role-rule system of models does not lead to a science which is deterministic in this way. It allows, however, for the introduction of some very important back-stop concepts, such as decisions and wants, by the help of which differential individual responses can be incorporated in a scientific psychology. We may choose to act out this or that episode in a dramatic way, or we may not. Of course these choices are subject to accounting, but we have already noticed that the giving of accounts itself must terminate, and the final step in a sequence of reasons may be the final back-stop of the bloody-minded, that of 'I just don't want to'. On the Role-rule group of models similarities in people's behaviour does not necessarily derive from similarities in external manipulation or change of a parameter, or from internal modifications, but from shared meanings and commonly accepted conventions, rules and paradigms. Rules of behaviour do not have the status of laws of nature since they can be ignored, defied or changed,[4] and because adherence to them is not necessarily a reflection of the presence of identical or even very similar physiological states and mechanisms in the entities involved. A hydrogen atom always emits light of just such and such wavelengths because it has just such and such a structure, and that structure is the causal mechanism *always* responsible for that behaviour. Similar behaviour does *not* necessarily imply similarity of reasons for that behaviour. The system of reasons has to be looked into independently. And this must be done through the collection and negotiation of accounts.

Negotiation

Explaining human actions by giving reasons, discovering meanings, beliefs and so on differs in two important respects from explaining physical phenomena by describing causal mechanisms. To discover the meanings, reasons, rules, beliefs and so on, the participants in a social episode must be asked to tell their thoughts and feelings, and to take the dramaturgical standpoint with respect to their self-monitored performances. Frequently the accounts which contain this kind of information will be retrospective commentaries. When they are, they are open to two kinds of *post hoc* modification.

1. In the course of reflection upon his own actions a person may come to form the opinion that some action which at first consideration seemed not to be done for a reason could be explained and a reason for it given. In this situation the participant is in danger of creating an explanation which is not true of the actual genesis of the action or sequence of actions under investigation. This sort of case is commonly associated with an extended discussion of the background of an action, and has been much discussed in the context of Freudian accounts of action.[5] It is well known that Freud himself was deeply concerned with the problem of the authenticity of an account which supplied the reasons for a hitherto inexplicable action and was generated in a dialogue between analyst and patient. Freud's discussion of this[6] shows how the difficulty is resolved for therapeutic purposes and can serve as a guide to an ethogenist.

2. A person may also come to be persuaded that his account should be changed even if derived from a monitoring commentary. For instance it is common to want to reidentify emotions. A little reflection may lead one to reconstrue an emotion originally identified as righteous indignation, as jealousy instead. It would be tempting to think that the reconsideration is right and the original identification wrong. One might be tempted to say this because it might be

felt that there can be greater honesty and less self-deception in 'emotion recollected in tranquillity'. And yet it might equally well be argued that in both the cases we have cited it could be claimed with equal justice that reflection had falsified the original psychic state.

Clearly there is no possibility of an objective, neutral account by which these and similar ambiguities could be finally resolved. The solution must be found within this situation. We believe that an adequate solution can be found by admitting the possibility of ambiguity while encouraging a negotiation of accounts in the attempt to resolve it. The physical sciences work within a similar open context. It is not possible finally to ratify all theoretical explanations in physics, and whatever theoretical explanations are widely accepted are always open to revision in one or more directions. Obviously one cannot negotiate with atoms and the dimensions of possible revision are of a very different nature, but both physics and ethogeny share an *essential* revisability, however different it may be. The demand for final, absolute unrevisable *truth* cannot be met in either field. In ethogeny it is not even viable as a theoretical ideal. The possibility of endless reinterpretation must always remain and it must always be admitted that each interpretation has some explanatory power.

The context of negotiation can be defined schematically around a minimal three person interaction. There are the two people who are the primary interactants, whose relationship and actions constitute the social phenomenon under investigation. The third person looks on, and negotiates accounts with the primary pair. Each person will be in a position to observe features of the interaction not available to the other two. A negotiation consists in the pooling of viewpoints, and the subsequent correction of accounts. As we have made clear in other contexts the 'third man' may be one of the primary interactors who has adopted the dramaturgical standpoint. There may even be a negotiation of accounts in a highly collapsed interaction where only one biological individual is involved. Imagine a person observing his own self-exhortation or self-deception, and commenting critically upon it. The standard situation of negotiation is typified by a 'family therapy session',[1] such as a man and wife discussing their relationship with the help of a marriage guidance counsellor. The counsellor's job is not just to act as referee but to enter into the relationship as negotiator of accounts. We suggest as part of the programme of empirical studies of a reformed social psychology a very careful and detailed analysis of the movements of opinion in the course of these and other negotiations. Some work has already been done,[8] but there is a rich field of study available particularly if attention is paid to how opinion *moves* in the course of the negotiation. Of course psychotherapy depends upon the possibility of such movement and much practical ethogenic epistemology must exist in clinical practice. Indeed one of our aims as ethogenists is to bring together the realm of clinical and social psychology in a systematic way, and the business of the negotiation of accounts makes the most natural point of contact.

In the course of a negotiation various situations may occur. It may be that there is immediate agreement between all three parties, and there is no conflict between accounts. This does not mean that all three accounts must be identical, but that they must form a coherent whole, so that no item in one contradicts or discounts an item in another. In such a situation we shall speak of the accounts as being 'authentic'.

Should there be disparities between accounts then movement may occur in several directions. It may be that the participants may come to agree amongst themselves, but differ from the engaged observer. If in the course of a negotiation the observer modifies his account to accord more with that of the actors we shall call this an 'inward resolution', while if the actors modify their accounts in the direction of the observer's account we shall speak of an 'outward resolution'. The degree of concordance achieved in either inward or outward resolution will be the measure of the authenticity of the account.

There is some difference, we are inclined to think, in the confidence we have in the final outcome, depending upon whether the negotiation is inward or outward. If inward resolution occurs one is more inclined, at least at first sight, to suppose that the result is an account with greater authenticity. After all, one might argue, the participants are the best authority as to the ethogeny of an episode. If they agree, for instance, in their explanation of why one accords greater status to the other, and the observer is persuaded to modify his account to conform with theirs, the matter would seem to be settled. However a great deal may hang in actual cases on the expertise and experience of the observer, his wit, insight and the like. Just as in physics, one observer may be better than another, so that the mere fact that there has been an inward resolution, in the absence of information about the observer, leaves room for a degree of scepticism as to the authenticity of the account.

But in clinical situations, and indeed in much ordinary life there is outward resolution. Here the dangers are more obvious and so are more readily guarded against. The most obvious is that the observer by sheer force of personality, or superior expertise or for a host of other possible reasons, forces the concordance in his direction, either falsifying the ethogeny or introducing artifacts in the form of false memories and so on in the primary participants. We will be drawing attention in the last chapter to a case where this danger is of some importance. In discussing how a reformed social psychology would go about the study of attitudes we will notice that there comes a point in the eliciting of accounts from those holding the attitude, at which further pressure to create a justificatory context, by the investigator, may lead to a change of attitude, for instance by emphasizing a manifest contradiction that actually exists in the cognitive structures of the person involved. In our view only the experience and sensitivity of the ethogenist can guard against this kind of thing. *It cannot be guarded against by replacing the investigator by a machine*, since a context of justification can only be created by questioning carried out by a human investigator. The social psychological investigation is itself a social episode, as several psychologists have recently forcibly remarked.[9]

REFERENCES

1. E. Bentley, *The Life of the Drama*, Methuen, London, 1965, p. 150.
2. J. Fowles, *The Magus*, Jonathan Cape, London, 1966.
3. B. J. Biddle and E. J. Thomas, *Role Theory*, Wiles, New York, 1966, pp. 41–4.

4. E. Goffman, *Where the Action Is*, Allen Lane, The Penguin Press, London, 1969, p. 35.

5. P. Ricoeur, *Freud and Philosophy*, Yale University Press, New Haven and London, 1970, Book III, Chs. 1, 2.

6. S. Freud, 'Construction in Analysis', *The Complete Works of Sigmund Freud*, Hogarth, London, 1964, Vol. XXIII, pp. 261–5.

7. J. G. Howells, *Theory and Practice of Family Psychiatry*, Oliver and Boyd, Edinburgh and London, 1968, pp. 97–110, 843–910.

8. R. E. Pettinger, C. F. Hockett and J. J. Danehy, *The First Five Minutes*, Martineau, Ithaca, N.Y., 1960.

9. H. Tajfel, 'Experiments in a Vacuum', in J. Israel and H. Tajfel (editors), *The Context of Social Psychology, a critical investigation*, Academic Press, London, 1971.

CHAPTER TWELVE

Human Powers

THE ARGUMENT

Psychology and Physiology

1. Common knowledge of the springs of human action, psychological discoveries and neurophysiological knowledge must be capable of some sort of synthesis.

2. No conceptual system yet presented has achieved this without some degree of unacceptable reductionism.

3. The conceptual system of ordinary discourse, elucidated by linguistic philosophers, must be preserved, but must also be elaborated so that genuine additions to knowledge, made by psychologists, can be identified and preserved.

4. These desiderata are met by a system built upon the concept of human powers. This is another way in which the social sciences can be made to match the physical sciences, in that the modern physical sciences too depend upon a conceptual system based upon the concept of powers.

Powers

1. Contemporary Usage
   a. For general capacities, associated with concept of agency. In this sense the concept of 'power' is related to a field of possibilities, ordered in space and in time. The characteristic generic powers of human beings are associated with the handling of symbols.
   b. For specific states of readiness.

c. Both usages involve the individual who has the power, being in a certain state in virtue of which he does have that power even when not exercising it.

2. Enabling Conditions

a. Being in these states is satisfying the enabling conditions.

b. (i) Intrinsic enabling conditions: these are related to the identity and individuality of the thing having the power.

(ii) Extrinsic enabling conditions: these are more or less temporary modifications of state, not affecting the preservation of individuality, or identity, even transitorily.

The Analysis of Powers Ascriptions

1. The general form is that of the ascription of a likelihood to behave in a certain way in virtue of the nature or state of a thing.

2. Likelihoods to behaviour as ascribed to human beings can be analysed into

a. the conditions for the power to be manifested, which form a set of incompletely specified alternatives,

b. a description of the expected behaviour.

3. To ascribe a power it is not necessary that the state or nature in virtue of which the person is likely to behave in the given way be explicitly known.

4. A power-ascription can be analysed into

a. a D-component, which is generally of conditional form, having as consequent a specific form of behaviour, the B-element, and, as antecedent, an open set of relatively specific alternative conditions for the manifestation of the behaviour. This is the C-element.

b. an N-component, in categorical form, which will not in general be specific, in which the intrinsic enabling conditions for the possession of the power will be stated. The N-component described the nature of the possessor of the power, in virtue of which he has the power, so far as that nature is known.

The Vocabulary Appropriate to Each Component

1. Ordinary language contains a vast repertoire of terms for human behaviour, capable of being used to make very fine distinctions indeed. We call these, and neologisms with a similar logic, O-terms.

2. Psychologists have introduced several galaxies of technical terms, mutually incompatible, and conforming neither to the logic of ordinary language, nor to that of the advanced sciences like physiology or physics. We shall call these P-terms.

3. Physiologists, and other genuine natural scientists, have a technical vocabulary conforming to the logic of the advanced sciences.

4. a. The behavioural or B-element, in power ascriptions must use O-terms, so as to remain within the province of phenomena of interest to psychology, as we have emphasized in earlier chapters.

b. P-terms can figure in the ascription of powers, as part of the specification of the N-component, of the states and natures of the people who have the powers; or, in some cases, of the conditions under which the power is manifested.

Conditions

1. Following the line of argument of Chapter Five, we can distinguish between extrinsic and intrinsic enabling conditions, e.g. a man lacks the power of speech if there is a defect in his nature as a human being, and we call him aphasic. But it may be that he cannot exercise a power because, though he has the right nature, there may be a failure of an extrinsic enabling condition with respect to the power of speech. For instance, some children do not manifest the power of speech only because they are deaf.

2. For scientific purposes we need to consider both physiological and psychological intrinsic enabling conditions, i.e. the nature of a person in virtue of which he has his powers will be, for practical scientific purposes, a psycho-physical mix.

The Explanation of Inabilities

1. 'Not wanting' is the back-stop which preserves our status as an agent when we fail to act when the enabling conditions have been fulfilled.

2. 'Not being able to bring oneself to' claims the complementary status of a patient, but preserves the conceptual system.

3. All those items, the non-obtaining of which prevents the exercise of powers in action, but which lie outside the person, we lump together as circumstances. This is an extremely variable and loose category.

Stimuli

1. Stimuli are the changes which lead to the actual exercise of powers in action.

2. The preservation of the concept of agency requires that we distinguish

   a. external stimuli (the person reverts to the status of an ordinary thing),

   b. internal stimuli (the person preserves his status as an agent),

   c. spontaneity of action.

Note. The application of this distinction to particular actions is not affected by the ultimate referral of internal stimuli to historically prior external ones, since the genesis of action on an internal stimulus, say a sudden springing to mind of a memory, is consciously self-monitored and, in social matters at least, subject to control by rule.

3. a. This leads to the distinction between resistible and irresistible stimuli. The line between them is drawn differently in different cultures.

Note. The conditions analysis and the powers analysis must mesh, in that intrinsic enabling conditions are identical with the existence of the states and natures of people in virtue of which they have their powers, while extrinsic enabling conditions, circumstances and stimuli mesh together as the C-element of the D-component of a powers ascription.

b. In our view the investigation of the natures and inner states of people by the technique of analysing accounts is as vital a part of psychological science as is the study of overt behaviour and the conditions of its manifestation, and must be the basis of any psychological explanation that pretends to be scientific.

c. In practice we cannot easily examine the conditions, particularly those we have identified with the natures of people, so we ascribe the fulfilment of these conditions on the basis of our recognition of the existence of states of readiness to exercise powers. Our detailed knowledge of these natures is acquired by the assembly of an appropriate ensemble of models.

'The readiness is all'. W. Shakespeare, *Hamlet*, V. ii

Psychologists must be in command of a conceptual system with which they can present a unified account of human behaviour and its genesis. The products of psychological research must be accounts of human life in which three apparently disparate kinds of information are fully fused. An adequate conceptual system must be such that common knowledge of human thought and action can be integrated with the discoveries that psychologists have made about the sources of certain kinds of behaviour, and the origins of certain kinds of thoughts and feelings. It must be possible to express knowledge culled from both these sources in a way that can be integrated with the rapidly increasing understanding of the human nervous system. A unified account is impossible without a system of concepts which allows the concepts of each area of knowledge to be used together in an acceptable way while preserving their capacity for autonomous employment. To achieve conceptual unity by reducing the concepts of any two of these areas of knowledge to those used in one favoured area requires distortions and falsifications that even the most optimistic positivists now find unacceptable.

The descriptive and explanatory concepts of ordinary language, and those derived therefrom belong in a system which has lately been greatly illuminated by the philosophical study of mental concepts initiated by Ryle's *Concept of Mind*.[1] We have argued in earlier chapters that the structure of this system must be preserved for an authentic account of human thought and action. The valuable discoveries of professional psychologists, however muddled and superficial some of them may appear to be, can be integrated within this system and much dross eliminated by paying strict attention to the modelling of new concepts upon those of ordinary language. The concepts with which physiological knowledge is expressed, however, do not belong within this system of concepts. Such terms have much in common with the concepts of other sciences. New insights into the structure of the natural sciences have shown that they are not, and could not be, the deductively ordered systems of generalizations that positivists supposed them to be. Their logic is much more complex. The purpose of this chapter is to show how the concept of a 'power' which was introduced earlier in the description of modern physical science, and concepts like it can provide a system capable of being used to bring a unity of an acceptable sort into the whole field of disparate kinds of knowledge of human beings. In this way, knowledge expressed in the conceptual system derived from ordinary language descriptions, explanations of behaviour and their extensions (including what psychologists have added), and the discoveries of physiologists can be brought together into a total view of people. Ethogeny demands a conceptual system in which all sources of knowledge of human life can generate information which can be integrated into a single, though elaborate system, through which we can understand the genesis of behaviour.

The Array of concepts under the generic term 'power'

We propose to use the term 'power' as a generic term for a wide variety of concepts, which have an important structural element in common, though they show considerable differences in detail. The common element is the structure of the sentences which are naturally used to explicate the ascription of a power, liability or tendency to some thing or person. We choose 'power' as the term for the generic concept, since it is already in use for two out of the four main species of concept we have in mind.

There are two contemporary uses of the word 'power'.[2, 3, 4] It is sometimes used for very general capacities, in such expressions as 'the power of speech', 'the power of locomotion'. In this sense, an individual who has the power of speech

i. is one who can speak, i.e., is capable of a certain kind of performance;

ii. in accounting for particular exercises of this capability we look within the individual who has the power of speech, or the power of locomotion, or whatever generic power we are considering. One who has a generic power is an agent; he is one who initiates his own performances, that is explanations of their genesis terminates with such items as the wants, needs or intentions of that individual.

By our choice of the power concept we bring the concepts of possibility and agency to the fore. The account of possibility which we advocate depends upon connecting it with the ideas of plan and intention. The possible will be defined, for ethogenic purposes as (a) that course of action which is conceived in advance of the actual performance, and (b) that course of action which could be conceived as an alternative to whatever was actually done. Possibility exists because human beings have the power to make anticipatory and retrospective commentaries, and to imagine what is going to happen or what might have been. And to be an agent is to control one's monitored performances by reference to one's plans or intentions, or to social rules.

Thus possibility in the ethogenic context is related to such concepts as 'plan', 'foresight' and the like. These in their turn can be referred to that very general linguistic capacity or power to handle symbols. Such powers endow their possessors not only with the capacity to conceive plans and to discuss what might or could be done, but also endow them with the powers of symbolic interaction, which were seen by G. H. Mead[5] as the basis of all social phenomena, among men and social animals. This entails the existence of capacities to understand symbols as well as to emit them, and is what enables us to use symbols reflexively, i.e., to understand what

we are saying as well as to give ourselves orders. Non-verbal interaction is not reflexive since it need contain no element of awareness.[6]

'Having the power to do so and so' can also be construed as
meaning something like being sufficiently prepared, being in an
adequate state of readiness. We shall treat states of readiness as being
those states which endow an individual with short-term capacities,
on the model of the military conception of a state of readiness which
hinges on having all the available soldiers in the right place properly
armed at the right time. This is not the usual permanent disposition
of the nation's manpower. It endows that nation with a short-term
capacity to defeat its enemy. It endows it with transitory military
power.

In both these main cases 'having the power' involves being in a
certain state, and in the case of human individuals, being an agent.
There is nothing mysterious about being an agent. It has to do with
the balance between and changes in external and internal, intrinsic
and extrinsic conditions in the accounts that are given of the genesis
of action. The further refinement of the distinctions between these
various kinds of conditions will be made later on in this book. Thus
agent concepts or powers are distinguished by whether they involve
long-term capacities, or short-term capacities, and whether they are
related to permanent features of an entity or are the products of
transitory states of readiness.

In addition to agent concepts, the description of human life
requires a full complement of patient concepts. These we shall call
generically 'liabilities'. There are long-term liabilities (like being
liable to catch colds) and short-term liabilities (like being irritable
when just woken up). In both cases, the liabilities exist because of
permanent and temporary intrinsic *states* of the person respectively.
Like powers, liabilities may be reflexive. We need to distinguish
those liabilities where we are patients to our own impulses, which
one might call 'weaknesses', from those where we are patients to
impulses or pressures of various sorts whose source is not in ourselves, which one might call 'pronenesses'. This scheme does not
correspond exactly with ordinary usage. Unlike powers, liabilities
may manifest themselves either because of internal changes or
because of external influences. One who exercises a power and is an

agent must figure as the source of his action in his or our account of it, while he who succumbs to a liability may either have 'only himself to blame' as we say, or it may be that in accounting for the manifestation of the liability, we look for the source in circumstances external to himself. In either case there is the suggestion that reflexive action on his part might overcome the liability.

Much of human social life can be seen as the exercise and the circumvention and blocking of the exercise of powers, as the succumbing to and the mastery of liabilities. The terms 'exercise', 'circumvention', 'succumbing to', 'mastery of', 'manifesting' and 'overcoming' seem to have very precise relation with the different species of power-concepts, and they must be used precisely since they catch, very exactly, the nuances of meaning which differentiate the three species of powers.

Analysis of Power Ascriptions

The ascription of a power to a human being can be explicated in a statement having a similar structure to the ascription of a power to an inanimate substance or thing. We shall begin the peculiarly human application of this concept by describing, first of all, the common structure of the explication of all power ascriptions. To ascribe a power to an individual or substance is to ascribe to it a certain likelihood towards some specific behaviour, in virtue of being the particular thing or specific kind of thing it is. The exegesis or explication of a power ascription will consist of two main components, one concerning the behaviour, which is the exercise of the power, the other concerned with the nature or kind to which the thing or substance belongs. We shall examine each component in turn.

Sometimes the word 'disposition' has been used to express the likelihood that something will behave in a certain way in appropriate circumstances, and the fact that dispositions are ascribed to things which are not then behaving in the appropriate way, or not then having the appropriate effect is explained by the idea that inherent in the dispositional mode of talking is the implication that these behaviours or effects occur only when certain conditions are fulfilled. To say that a man is of a benevolent disposition is to say that he will be very likely to behave in a kindly and generous manner, and that he will be very likely to entertain certain opinions, and feel certain kinds of emotions and so on in the appropriate circumstances, i.e., if certain conditions are fulfilled. It is worth noticing that in ordinary language the term 'disposition' is used for a man's style or manner of acting, rather than for his readiness to perform specific actions. We prefer to use the expression 'likely behaviour' for what a man is ready to do.

The powers and readinesses of human beings usually involve the existence of very much more complex states and forms of behaviour than do those of simple chemicals or things. However, their logic is sufficiently similar to allow us to use the simpler notions of the powers of things and materials as models for our understanding of the powers of human beings. Saying that something is poisonous is usually understood to mean that if it is consumed it will have certain bad effects upon a person. We do not need to know exactly what are the conditions under which the behaviour is likely to occur or the effect be brought about, but since the substance is not always behaving in the way implied by the ascription of the power we do know that that behaviour is conditional upon certain conditions being fulfilled. We certainly do not need to know exactly and exhaustively under which conditions the specific behaviour *will* occur. Indeed, in human contexts, we have good reason to think that the very idea of exact and exhaustive prior knowledge of conditions is incoherent. It should also be remembered that there are often several different sets of conditions, the obtaining of any one of which would be sufficient for a certain, specific behaviour being likely to be manifested. The D-component of a power ascription is conditional, and the conditions form an open disjunction. Thus the D-component has the form:

'If either C_1 or C_2 or C_3 or . . . obtain then B is likely to occur' and each of C_1, C_2, etc. may be specified in more or less detail.

To say that something has the power (or liability) to behave B-wise is to say that this mode of behaviour is possible *in virtue of* the nature of the thing in question. The expression 'in virtue of' will be

R

elucidated later. The first point to notice about a power ascription is that it is not necessary for the proper ascription of a power that the nature in virtue of which the power is possessed be known in detail. The force of the 'nature' clause would perhaps be more clearly expressed by 'in virtue of the nature of the thing, *whatever that is*'. A powers ascription thus opens up a line of investigation other than the study of the behaviour of things and materials. The 'nature' component, originally unspecific, can be more and more precisely specified as the nature of the person or substance having the power or liability is more fully understood. The discovery of the behaviour of penicillin was the result of a different kind of investigation from the discovery of its chemical nature, in virtue of which it had its power to halt disease. Knowledge of the natures of things and materials can be, to a first approximation, treated as a conjunction though the conjuncts are not simply additive since later entries in the list of characteristics which together make up the nature of a thing or person may profoundly modify our understanding of earlier entries. Thus the 'natures' component can be represented, at least superficially, by an open conjunction. This we shall call the N-component, and represent it by (N_1 and N_2 . . .), an open conjunction of categorical assertions as to the nature of the thing or material involved. Notice that the conditions which have to obtain for something to be ready to act will be part of the N-component of an explicated powers-ascription.

A power ascription then has

I. A D-component, which is conditional. The conditional has a B-element, describing the expected behaviour, which must be specific, within the limits of which the descriptive vocabulary is capable. The conditional has a C-element in which the conditions are described which must obtain for the behaviour to ensue when the entity is in a given state of readiness. These conditions may not be known even in part, nor may all possible alternative conditions under which the behaviour is evoked be known.

II. An N-component, which is categorical. At any time the exact nature of N may not be known. The conjuncts of the N-component may refer either to permanent or temporary states of the individual.

Empirical investigation may yield more *disjuncts* for the *C*-element, that is, it may be possible to discover more about the conditions under which *B* occurs. Empirical investigation of the natures of things and people may lead to more *conjuncts* for the *N*-component, expressing more detailed knowledge of the nature of the thing or material involved, in particular what is involved in the entity being in its various permanent and transitory states of readiness. This logical structure is common to all power ascriptions, whether to human beings, rats or humbler inorganic substances and things. The ethogenic approach conceives of psychology as the study of human powers, that is, the joint study of human behaviour and human nature.

Restrictions on the Vocabulary of each Component

'Ordinary' language is rich in terms for the description, evaluation and explanation of human thoughts, actions and feelings. The complex logical structure of this vocabulary has recently been illuminated by the studies of philosophers in philosophical psychology. Terms drawn from this vocabulary and neologisms modelled upon terms in it have been called *O*-terms.

'When he saw the bull, he blanched and ran, because he is a coward.' This statement is couched wholly in *O*-terms. At this point we wish to insist, following linguistic intuition, that to ascribe a cowardly nature to the man is to say more of him than to assert some open set of hypothetical or conditional statements, detailing what he is liable to do in various circumstances. It is also to describe an *N*-component. It is to say something about what that man *is*, i.e., to specify one member of the set of his possible personae, whether or not he is blanching as he usually does when he sees a wasp, whether or not there are any threatening animals to run from, whether he is sweating before an interview, or boasting of his cleverness afterwards. The vocabulary of *O*-terms is well supplied with terms with which to describe the conditions under which actions might be performed, to describe those actions themselves, to ascribe a wide variety of states of readiness to people, and to detail the natures of the human performers. We *can* specify the *D*-component and the *N*-component of power and liability statements entirely within the *O*-term vocabulary. From an ethogenic point of view, laymen must be considered capable of a protopsychology.

In addition to coining neologisms within the same system of terms as the *O*-term vocabulary, such as R. W. White's conception of 'competence', psychologists have introduced terms which exist within fragmentary conceptual systems of a quasi-technical kind. Such terms as 'ego-strength', 'cognitive dissonance' and the like, cannot all be explained wholly in terms drawn from the *O*-vocabulary, nor do they all obey the syntactical and logical rules of that vocabulary. Some can be understood only within the fragmentary conceptual system of which they form an essential part. Their meaning cannot be grasped otherwise. Freud's conceptual system, featuring terms such as 'id', 'super-ego' and the like has a more highly developed structure than most and its vocabulary is certainly not a simple extension of the *O*-term vocabulary for describing human beings and accounting for what they do and say. For instance, it contains terms for states of mind that are supposed to exist when people are not aware of having them. We shall call the vocabulary of relatively independent psychological conceptual systems *P*-terms. We know that the *P*-term vocabulary does not form a single conceptual system, though items from various fragments tend to shake down together in the *N*-component of much professional psychological talk. It is also important to notice the variety of *interplay* between the systems of *O*- and *P*-terms. Many *P*-terms can be explicated with the help of the *O*-vocabulary while some *P*-terms have been absorbed into it. These are facts of crucial importance for understanding how a science of psychology is possible, and we will return to it.

Physiologists have their own vocabulary, which conforms to the requirements that any system of concepts must meet to form the conceptual basis of an explanatory natural science. They formulate hypotheses, create and discard models, conceive of hypothetical mechanisms, prove and disprove the existence of such mechanisms, and so on. The vocabulary which they deploy is a scientific vocabulary and we will call it the vocabulary of *S*-terms. *S*-terms make their way into power ascriptions both in the N-component, and in the D-component, but only in the C-element of the latter. We may describe the nature of the person involved in some piece of behaviour in physiological terms, e.g., the use of the term 'schizophrenic' by a biochemically-oriented psychiatrist. We may detail the conditions which obtained for him to behave, or to be capable of behaving or liable to behave in that manner in a similar way, *but we must restrict ourselves to O-terms and neologisms whose principles of use conform to those of the O-vocabulary to describe what he did*. Only thus do we remain within the science of social psychology. Sometimes the changes in the *natures* of people which affect their behaviour can be described in physiological terms, and it is a legitimate ambition of that science to discover as many as possible of the physiological conditions of behaviour.[8] But the B-element of the D-component must be expressed in O-terms. Psychology is concerned with the study of the actions and interactions of human life, and in the O-term vocabulary we already have a system of terms to describe that life. If new modes of behaviour develop they can be described by the addition of neologisms to that vocabulary. The ethology of Konrad Lorenz[9] is an example of the development of a B-system for creatures which do not already have their own, i.e., dumb animals. Lorenz's discoveries pose questions for solution by physiologists at the N-level, either by neurophysiological discoveries or by the development of models, as in the systems-theory approach of D. Macfarland,[10] which help to generate hypotheses about the N-component for the powers and liabilities of animals. The vocabularies of P-terms which function in 'island galaxies' of concepts, however, have considerable importance. They can become relevant to human life through coming to be connected with the O-term vocabulary by incorporation in the N-component of a powers-ascription. Their use for recognized forms of behaviour may throw that behaviour into quite new lights. Psychologists contribute to our understanding of people both through an extension and reappraisal of common knowledge, and through new models of human nature. Later we shall see in more detail how P-terms fit into the N-component with examples from Freud, Festinger and Cattell.

From the ethogenic point of view, human life is conceived of as a flux of states of readiness, only some of which issue in actions which appear as the exercise of powers. To have a power is to be in a state of readiness to exercise it. Liabilities are similarly related to the state of individual organisms. We believe that only by viewing human life in this way can actual episodes be understood. From this point of view the centre of the metaphysical stage comes to be occupied by that which can have and exercise powers, that is, by individual things and persons, and particular pieces of material. But an individual, whose powers are exercised or held in abeyance, exists in an environment, the state of which is partly responsible for what can, might and actually does happen, that is, both for the existence of states of readiness and for their occasional translation into action. The traditional distinctions in terms of which the causes of action are discussed, namely, between conditions and stimuli (or efficient cause) need to be refined and radically overhauled when they are looked at from the powers point of view.

CONDITIONS: the conditions which have to obtain before action is possible can be broadly divided into those the obtaining of which must be predicated of the individual or material which has the power of action, and those, the obtaining of which is predicated of the environment. We put the matter in this rather roundabout way to avoid having to speak of properties. We have followed current practice in speaking of what is predicated of the individual which has or lacks the powers in question, as 'enabling conditions', i.e., they are those whose obtaining will lead to the existence of a state of readiness in the individual. Those conditions which obtain in the environment we shall call 'circumstances'. We shall return to a separate study of them.

The most important distinction amongst enabling conditions marks off those which account for the possession of a power by a person and those which make possible the exercise of powers already possessed. If we conceive of the nature of a human being as what is responsible for his being in all the permanent and transitory states of readiness which endow him with his characteristic cluster of powers, then the conditions which must obtain for him to possess those powers will be that he be in or capable of being in those states of readiness. These states will be *intrinsic* to his very being as an individual. Their obtaining we shall call, following our general account in Chapter Five, the satisfaction of the intrinsic enabling conditions. The conditions necessary for the exercise of a power are not intrinsic to the very being of a man, since they may obtain quite independently of his characteristic capacities and liabilities. We shall call them extrinsic enabling conditions.

The most illuminating examples in philosophical psychology often come from explanations which are given for failures and inabilities. We do not usually have to bother ourselves about giving an account when things go smoothly. This is a fact of central importance to the philosophy of mind and the methodology of psychology, but we will not dwell on it here, other than as an explanation of our choice of examples. We shall exemplify the above distinctions among conditions, by the example of a man who, when spoken to in a challenging way, fails to respond. If we think that the failure is due to the set of intrinsic enabling conditions not obtaining, then we say he is aphasic, that is, lacks the power of speech. We cannot anticipate in advance all the extrinsic enabling conditions which must obtain for him to be able to exercise his powers of speech, but we can recognize the explanation that he cannot answer because he is deaf and did not hear the question as the assertion that an enabling condition, extrinsic with respect to the power of speech, is not fulfilled. It is often difficult to determine the exact boundary between intrinsic and extrinsic enabling conditions. Is a man's being deaf a failure of an intrinsic or an extrinsic enabling condition? With respect to his powers of speech, it is extrinsic, but with respect to his powers of observation, say, as an ornithologist, it might be held to be intrinsic. We believe that our knowledge of what conditions must be *fulfilled* for a man to have and to exercise a power is best derived from the open set of accounts by which we explain his *failure* to exercise a power, when we would normally expect him to do so. Both intrinsic and extrinsic enabling conditions contrast with external conditions, having nothing to do with his nature as a man. A gag or ear-plugs are external conditions leading to a failure to exercise the power of speech.

Further consideration of the intrinsic enabling conditions whose obtaining ensures the possession of a power, liability or tendency, leads to a rather more complicated set of distinctions. There is clearly a great difference between those intrinsic features of a person, which are permanent and those which are transitory. There is a difference between accounting for the failure to respond to the challenging proposition by reference to a man's stupidity, and accounting for his failure to respond by explaining that he is too tired. Amongst transitory intrinsic enabling conditions are a person's store of information, his current biochemical make-up and the like. Accounting for failure to respond may involve the fact that the man does not have the relevant information upon which a response should be based (though he could get it), that he is too drunk to think coherently (though he can sober up), and the like. *It is very important to see that the intrinsic enabling conditions may include both physiological and psychic items. A man's nature is a psychophysiological mix.* So far as we can see, there is, in practice, no conflict between nor priority amongst items drawn from the psychic states of a person and items from his physiological states when cited in this kind of context.[11] Ignorance and drunkenness seem to us to be accorded equal status in accounting for failure to exercise a power, and may certainly be conjointly ascribed to the same man at the same time with respect to the same failure.

The distinction between the permanent and the transitory intrinsic enabling conditions must be taken as marking the poles of a spectrum of states of a person, rather than a clear, hard and fast division.[12] For instance, though anxiety is usually a transitory state of mind, and being anxious can be offered as a transitory intrinsic enabling condition for a person's current powers and liabilities, it is well known that it may become, as the doctors say, chronic, that is, a permanent feature of the person, *who is then assigned to a certain category of human being, namely, the neurotic.* One way of making the distinction between the permanent and the transitory intrinsic enabling conditions is by seeing whether a condition (or its consequent power or liability) figures in the criteria for the classification of a person into one of the recognized categories of human being.

A final point about the explanation of inabilities is important here. Suppose the accounting for failure is countered at each stage by a rebuttal, i.e., evidence is offered rebutting the claim to stupidity, to fatigue, ignorance or insobriety, then *must* the person now respond? Indeed not. In the interactions of real human beings a final move is found, which is perhaps socially condemned but logically interesting. It is what we call the 'back-stop' move. In order to demarcate the kinds of back-stop moves that occur, we shall use the traditional distinction between patient and agent.

i. By saying 'I just don't want to' or perhaps by frowning and shaking his head, the person preserves his status as an *agent*, while conceding the existence of all intrinsic enabling conditions. A notional state, usually called 'perversity' or 'obstinacy' or, in British usage, 'bloody-mindedness', is ascribed and preserves the logical structure of the powers conceptual system.

ii. But by saying 'I just couldn't bring myself to . . .' or by looking down shyly, the person admits the obtaining of all the usual intrinsic enabling conditions, but claims the status of a patient. Again a notional concept, 'weak-mindedness', may be offered to preserve the powers conceptual system as an alleged state of a person in virtue of which he suffers certain liabilities.

Circumstances are those conditions in the environment which are necessary for the exercise of a power. The circumstances may be related to the powers of individuals in very diverse ways. There are those circumstances which we could call 'opportunities' which are related to the possibility of the immediate exercise of powers, that is, to the possibility of action, and there are those which are 'background' and which are related to the possibility of the act which is performed through the action. A man capable of stealing (intrinsic enabling conditions met), may be unable to steal because he has injured his hand (failure of an extrinsic enabling condition), that is, a picking-up action cannot be performed because there is something amiss with him.

There is no clear boundary between short-term intrinsic enabling conditions and extrinsic enabling conditions. For instance, we might want to say an injured hand changed him radically, even if only briefly. He may also be unable to steal because there is nothing around that is not screwed down, i.e., he lacks the opportunity. To *be* a thief is to be ready to steal and a man may properly be called a thief even when there are no unguarded objects which he could make off with. For a particular set-up to constitute an opportunity for theft there must be people with the readiness to steal. Amongst the background circumstances for theft we would list the existence of private property. 'Theft' is a concept logically related to the concept of private property, i.e., it is an action of picking something up deliberately that is not one's own private property that can be classified as an act of theft. But whether there are thefts, i.e., deliberate takings away of moveable things known not to be one's own, depends upon there being human beings (or jackdaws) ready to act in a certain way. And of course were there people and birds ready to act in this way, there would still be no thefts in the absence of the private property institution. There *could* be no theft were there no institution of private property, but there *can* be no theft when everything is securely locked up. Institutions are background, unlocked doors provide opportunities. It is not possible to draw a hard and fast line between background and opportunity, and the distinction is drawn differently depending on the particular interests of the investigator. For a policeman, opportunity includes such things as unlocked shops, but the socio-economic system is only a background factor; while for the political reformer, both unlocked shops and socio-economic factors may be classed under opportunity. This has to do with what each is prepared to consider might have been otherwise. But wherever the line is drawn, circumstances providing opportunities are a wholly different matter from the conditions which make people ready to steal, that is, which make them, in their very nature, dishonest. The environment is operative both in its effects upon the *natures* of people, and in providing opportunities and background for the display of those natures. Our conceptual system *must* preserve this distinction.

STIMULI. One of the most striking characteristics of human beings and other organisms is the fact that readiness and preparation does not by itself lead to action. Our conceptual system must allow for the formulation of the question of what stimulus occurred to bring about an action, given a state of readiness *whether or not the person doing the action is being considered as an agent*. Stimuli are usually identified as those *changes* in conditions, which lead to the exercise of powers or the falling into liabilities. To get clear about stimuli to action we need to introduce some further distinctions. The most important distinction is that between changes which occur *within* an entity, and those which happen *outside* it. This is a commonplace distinction much used in discussing the behaviour of things and materials. For instance, there are the stable explosives which must be detonated externally, and there are unstable ones which can be detonated by changes within the explosive material itself. An unstable explosive is detonated by an internal stimulus, and a stable explosive by external stimulus. This distinction has the most obvious and commonplace of applications to human behaviour. Often without any apparent change in the external conditions a man begins to do something. Cases such as these are clearly distinguishable from those situations in which it is clear that he has received some external prompting. Despite the fact that there are myriads of intermediate cases, our conceptual system is such that we ascribe some inner change to explain the inception or inhibition of action when outer conditions seem to be unchanged. This conceptual pressure towards a simple dichotomy may be part of the origin of 'back-stop' moves. Empirical studies have shown that the boundary drawn by common observation between the inner and the outer stimulus is not always correct, and much study has recently been devoted to the apparently insignificant changes in the environment, particularly the human social environment, that prompt people to action in various ways.[13] Nevertheless, the invasion by the external of the area of the apparently internal leaves the distinction unimpaired. The distinction is also preserved in the Freudian referral of the internal stimuli to historically prior external situations. The rationale of historical referral will be an important issue in the discussion of the question of the origins of human powers and liabilities. Traditionally, the dichotomy between innate and learned capacities was used. After the development of Lorenz's theory of imprinting, as the basis for a theory of the origin of some powers of organisms, and particularly the most characteristic human power, the power to use languages, our conceptual system must operate with the trichotomy between the innate, the imprinted and the learnt. It is a blemish on

Chomsky's theory of language that it seems to rely on the pre-Lorenzian traditional dichotomy.[14]

Human beings are sometimes called to account for what they do. The structure and variety of accounts has been expounded earlier. We now distinguish between those changes in internal states and conditions which could be drawn upon in giving an account, such as the thoughts we had, or the impulses we felt and those which we do not *normally* incorporate in an account, such as changes in the output of the pineal gland. Notice that one way of drawing a distinction between the psychic and the non-psychic states of a person is by testing whether the existence of, or changes in these states normally figure in accounts. There is no necessity that we should be able to specify in any precise way the internal changes and states of affairs reference to which can figure in an account. What makes a good account is not whether the terms used in it refer to events whose nature we can specify because we are fully conscious of them, but whether the account is acceptable. That involves such criteria as whether it is the sort of account that a person of that type should give, whether it is an account of a form acceptable to others, as well as those features which make it acceptable to oneself.

Cutting right across the distinction between internal and external stimuli is the distinction between resistible and irresistible stimuli. There is a strong tendency in Anglo-Saxon culture to treat all internal stimuli as potentially resistible, and to confine the irresistible to a sub-class of kinds of external stimuli. Anglo-Saxons tend to confine the concept 'acting under duress' to external influences stimulating a man to action, such as overpersuasion, force, threats and the like. However, in some cultures the line is drawn differently, as for instance when in Latin cultures certain internal phenomena such as impulses to violence or unrestrained joy or grief are acceptable in an account of an action. No internal prompting of such impulses can be presented as irresistible in an Anglo-Saxon explanation of an action, while for a Latin man it is a commonplace and accepted feature of accounts.[15]

The classification of conditions must mesh with the analysis of powers, and in this meshing the place for empirical investigations and the means for the assessment of the results of such investigations can be found. The analysis of a power attribution yields a *D*-component and an *N*-component. The *D*-component has a *C*- or conditions element which is open to further specification, being as one might say a 'knowledge node'. The *D*-component contains a *B*-element, in which what the person does or suffers is described, and this must conform to the logic of the *O*-system of concepts. The *C*-element of the *D*-component will contain all those conditions whose obtaining is relevant to the performance of an action but which do not affect or are not involved in the nature of the person involved either temporarily (like alcohol) or permanently (like the acquisition of a new skill), that is all those which are circumstances or stimuli. This element will also contain the extrinsic enabling conditions, that is, those conditions the obtaining of which is necessary for the exercise of the power, but not for its possession.

The really radical departure proposed by ethogenists, as against dispositionalists, is to separate the intrinsic enabling conditions into a separate analytical component, and not to include them in with all the other conditions for action as dispositionalism does. The *N*-component comprises the description of whatever features of a person are pertinent to accounting for his readinesses and powers, and which endure throughout an episode in which he is involved, and some of these might be permanent and characterize the person in many or all the episodes of his life. Some are more transitory and may characterize him only in one or few episodes. A person may get into a state in which he is capable of murder only once in his life. That state, though enduring through the homicidal episode in which, of course, no murder may actually occur, and hence properly figuring in the *N*-component, may never characterize him again. We are rightly suspicious of him ever after, since he has demonstrated that he is liable to become capable of murder, and that liability must be regarded, *prima facie*, as indicative of his nature. We have already seen that the total set of intrinsic enabling conditions will usually make up a psycho-physical mix. Just as a chemist studies both the behaviour and the chemical composition of a substance, and tries to explain the behaviour by reference to the composition, so ethogenically oriented psychologists will study both the behaviour and the nature of human beings, and try to discover what features of a person's nature are responsible for the powers, liabilities and tendencies that are manifested in his behaviour, as well as those which, for one reason or another, do not appear in overt action.

Finally, we can say that a state of readiness exists when *all* the conditions except the circumstances and the stimulus conditions are satisfied. But one should notice that this is a metaphysical remark, and not an epistemological hint. We do not come to know that a state of readiness exists by coming to know that all the conditions for its existence have been satisfied. We are very far from being able to satisfy ourselves as to what are the relevant conditions, let alone whether they are satisfied on a particular occasion. But it is fairly easy to recognize when people are in states of readiness, some of the time. The players in the football lineup who are ready and alert, can be distinguished, even from fifty yards, from the ones who are not. Most people can tell when a kitten is about to spring. And we are very often aware of our own readinesses, and suffer the frustration of missing our chance, and the like. *We know that the conditions have been satisfied from our recognition that an animal is in a state of readiness, alert and so on.* Indeed, this sort of case could be taken as paradigmatic of the direction of the epistemology of much of the province of psychology. (cf. Schachter's studies of the emotions referred to on p. 15.)

In the next Chapter, we will consider in more detail, the *N*- or nature component of a powers ascription.

REFERENCES

1. Milestones in the elucidation of this conceptual system are S. Hampshire, *Thought and Action*, Chatto and Windus, London, 1965, C. Taylor, *The Explanation of Behaviour*, Routledge and Kegan Paul, London, 1964, E. Anscombe, *Intention*, Blackwells, Oxford, 1957, Cornell University Press, Ithaca, New York, 1966, D. S. Shwayder, *The Stratification of Behaviour*, Routledge and Kegan Paul, London, 1965, H. L. A. Hart and A. M. Honore, *Causation in the Law*, Oxford, 1959, P. F. Strawson, *Individuals*, Methuen, London, 1959, A. R. White, *The Philosophy of Action*, Oxford,

1968, particularly the Introduction, J. L. Austin, *How to do things with words*, Oxford, 1965.

2. W. Joske, *Material Objects*, Macmillan, London, 1967.
3. M. Ayers, *The Refutation of Determinism*, Methuen, London, 1968.
4. R. Harré, 'Powers', *BJPS*, 21, (1970), 81–101.
5. G. H. Mead, *Mind, Self and Society*, Chicago, 1934.
6. M. Argyle, *Social Interaction*, Methuen, London, 1969, 92–114.
7. *Nebraska Symposium on Motivation*, University of Nebraska Press, 1960, pp. 97–141, reprinted in *Personality*, edited R. S. Lazarus and E. M. Opton, London, 1967, Ch. 7.
8. cf. L. Weizkrantz, *The Explanation of Behavioral Change*, New York and London, 1967.
9. K. Lorenz, *Evolution and Modification of Behaviour*, Chicago, 1969.
10. D. Macfarland, 'Behavioural Aspects of Homeostasis', *Advances in the Study of Behaviour*, Vol. III, edited D. Lehrman, R. A. Hinde, E. Shaw, 1970.
11. S. Schachter and J. E. Singer, 'Cognitive, social and physiological determinants of emotional state', *Psychol. Rev.*, 69, 379–99.
12. P. Secord and P. W. Backman, 'Personality Theory and the Problem of Stability and Change in Individual Behavior; an Interpersonal Approach', *Psych. Rev.*, 68, 21–32.
13. M. Argyle, *loc. cit.*
14. N. Chomsky, *Language and Mind*, Harcourt, Brace, New York, 1968.
15. cf. 'Accounts', by S. M. Lyman and M. B. Scott, *American Sociological Review*, 33, 46–62, particularly in this context, p. 50.

CHAPTER THIRTEEN

Human Natures

THE ARGUMENT

Terms for Types of People

1. Terms like 'coward' are not used just as summaries of powers and liabilities, but are meant to have explanatory force, and to explain why a person displays this or that pattern of behaviour.

2. Sometimes the differential application of a pair of these terms may hinge only on differing accounts of similar patterns of action. It does not follow that the terms are being used merely to ascribe readiness to give this or that kind of account.

The Psycho-Physical Mix as the Form of Human Nature

1. There is a practical irreducibility of the psychic to the physiological in that physiological knowledge is very incomplete.

2. There is a theoretical irreducibility in that it seems that physiologically identifiable states of a human being affect human social action only in so far as they are given meaning with respect to what a person knows or believes about the situation.

3. Thus type terms, identifying kinds of man, will be analysed into a mix of psychic and physiological components, the former having an irreducible meaning component.

Note. These 'types of men' are social identities, and more than one may be associated with a given biological individual. Why a given biological individual has his unique complement of possible social selves must also be susceptible of explanation in terms of a higher order psycho-physiological mix.

4. The mix, at whatever explanatory level, constitutes the 'nature' term of successive powers attributions.

The Relations between Natures and Patterns of Behaviour

1. There are two such relations in natural science:

   a. Powers to produce certain patterns of behaviour are explained by reference to a structure amongst the elementary parts of substances and things, and the relevant structure is the nature of that substance or thing. Here the pattern of phenomena and the changing inner states of the entity are identical, but are manifested differently in two different modes of exploration.

   b. Powers are explained by the existence of inner states, of which the manifested phenomena are effects. These will be causal mechanisms responsible for producing these effects.

The Place of Classical Psychological Theories in a 'Powers' Conceptual System

1. The Nature of Man is unknown, and so the whole explanatory process consists of the assembly of paramorphic models, according to well-tried methodological principles, derived from the advanced sciences.

2. Freudian theory, for instance, describes such a model.

3. As a paramorphic model it is not a competitor of other models, or of physiological analyses, but can be one element in an ensemble, whose principles of concordance are as yet unsettled.

4. The total set of such models of his nature is each man's N-ensemble. It is *mediately* related to his social behaviour through his set of possible social selves.

5. Only the 'powers' conceptual system can accommodate these disparate elements.

   a. The behavioural element in the ascription of a power must be in O-terms.

S

b. The *C*-element which refers to the conditions under which the power is exercised and the behaviour manifested may contain *S*-terms, as well as *O* and *P*-terms.

c. The *N*-component may contain *P*- or psychological terms as well as *O* and *S*-terms, and these must be understood as describing psychologists' models for the structures at the basis of those relations of behaviour and action into which meaning enters centrally.

Explanation of the Complexity of Ethogenic Psychology

1. The particular cluster of powers and liabilities a man has at a particular time is highly variable, cf. the phenomenon of mood.
2. This requires the introduction of powers and liabilities to acquire powers and liabilities.

The Clustering of Powers

1. Each social self is manifested as a cluster of powers and liabilities. Personality studies should be concerned with the attempt to discover what clusters exist. Some combinations of powers and liabilities may never appear as personas actually manifested by human beings.
2. Each biological individual manifests a set of clusters, but it may be that the clusters are only of certain specific types.

Identity of Powers

1. We should notice that there are powers which can be manifested via different mechanisms, e.g. linguistic powers through speech or writing. These are related to intrinsic enabling conditions.
2. The same power may be manifested through different means, e.g. the use of different languages. These are related to extrinsic enabling conditions.

In these cases we shall speak of *generic* v. *specific* powers. In each of these categories a biological individual has fairly permanent powers.

3. There are also different kinds of uses to which a power can be put, e.g. linguistic powers can be used to communicate, or to insult. These are usually related to transitory effects upon the person by circumstances.

Examples of the use of the Powers conceptual system by psychologists

Cattell's 'Ego-strength'

1. This is offered as a 'source-trait', that is as a *long-term* fundamental generic power.

2. It is supposed to determine a cluster of specific powers.

3. Ego-strength is itself a power, so cannot characterize a kind of human nature. A higher order nature description is needed for that. This is dimly perceived by Cattell himself, who sometimes makes an attempt to provide it by reference to the Freudian model. A further component of the necessary psycho-physical mix might be forthcoming by reference to physiological matters, such as the effect on the nervous system of prolonged high adrenalin levels.

Festinger's 'Cognitive Dissonance'

1. The concept was introduced for the state of mind in virtue of which a person acquires the *short-term* power or liability to change an attitude.

2. Though this is theoretically a sound move the concept was not well thought out, and not embedded in an appropriate methodology, i.e. no analysis of accounts was undertaken.

    a. If it is based upon inconsistencies between cognitive items

        (i) it is unclear which of many possible inconsistencies is to be picked out as the operative one,

        (ii) whether a person must be aware of the inconsistency is not clearly laid down.

    b. If it is treated as a feeling of discomfort in virtue of which a person is ready to change an attitude, then this is subject to the test of whether reports of this feeling and its disappearance after the attitude change figure in accounts.

    c. When accounting has been attempted neither a feeling of discomfort, nor an awareness of logical inconsistency have been reported.

    d. At best the theory is a contribution to the ensemble of models, at worst it is false.

Readinesses

    1. In contrast to long-term powers, it is sometimes possible to tell, by observation, when an animal or a person is in a certain state of readiness.

    2. 'State of readiness' is a teleological concept.

    a. Each state of readiness is defined with respect to what the organism is ready to do.

    b. But the definition is related to the conditions of its application inductively.

    c. The apparent logical connection between a readiness and the action which the organism is ready to perform arises because of the generality of the inductive experience of the performance of the action on the fulfilment of the conditions necessary for the manifestation of the state of readiness in action.

Three routes to the Knowledge of Natures

    1. a. There are undoubtedly physiological states in virtue of which an animal or person is ready to perform certain actions, but because physiological states enter social reality only through the mediation of meanings, this route cannot form the basis of a practical psychological methodology.

    b. The identification of physiological entities relevant to psychological phenomena is dependent upon independent identification of the psychological phenomena, so cannot be substituted for them.

2. The ordinary route to knowledge of human nature uses terms like 'coward', which are clearly intended to be explanatory, but add little or nothing of empirical content to a mere cluster of powers and liabilities. Their function is to-stand-in for an explicit description of a kind of human nature. We believe that such terms do not adequately characterize a biological individual in *all* his social settings.

3. The psychological route involves assembling an ensemble of models, and physiological fact and theory as an explicit description of a theoretical human nature. It is the most promising, *but*

a. Its principles of internal concordance remain to be worked out.

b. At the heart of it lies the problem of an adequate account of the emotions.

'because he is a . . .'

When a man's liability to run from threatening situations is explained by describing him as a coward, what is the force of the clause 'because he is a coward'? Does this make his liability intelligible because the use of the word 'coward' tells what *sort of behaviour* he is likely to show, or is it because it tells us what *kind of man* he is? The dispositionalist theory of philosophical psychology treats it in the former way, while in the ethogenic approach the type of man can be referred to in an explanation of behaviour. In the Freudian and neo-Freudian theories of the development of personality and in physiological investigations a picture of the nature of a person is built up. In explaining readinesses to behave in various ways and his longer term powers this picture of the man's nature enters essentially. To say that he runs because he is a coward is not an empty tautology from the ethogenic point of view. A prudent man may also run. However alike the behaviour of the prudent man and the coward may be we will want to say that they are men of different nature. This difference may be manifested somewhere in their behaviour and styles of life. The prudent man may manifest his prudence in the kind of account he gives of his actions. But we must beware of falling into thinking that because differences·in nature are manifested in differences in what people do and say, those differences can be treated as reduceable further liabilities, for example, to talk in different ways and be disposed to give different kinds of accounts. We are also inclined to think that there are clusters of behaviour patterns, and to mark this by the use of terms like 'coward'. That a coward is boastful, and a prudent man circumspect are not accidental concomitances from this point of view. The association of different ways of talking and behaving with similar postures in the face of danger is explained by reference to differences in type of man. Terms like 'coward' stand in for explicit descriptions of human natures.

While the physiological basis of many powers and liabilities remains unknown, we must be content with a psycho-physiological mix as the structure of the nature of a man. And we must be prepared for the possibility that an adequate physiological basis may elude us for ever. That its discovery will be very much more difficult than has hitherto been supposed, and perhaps even impossible in principle, has been shown by the experiments of Schachter,[1] and the survey of the effects of psychedelic drugs by H. S. Becker[2] and many other similar effects. It may be necessary to characterize a man both by the state of his glands *and* by his social nature in order to account for his behaviour. The extent of a man's knowledge may be the relevant feature of his nature for the explanation of certain of his liabilities and powers, while the kind of brain-structure and biochemistry he has may figure in the explanation of others. More often, both psychic and physical characteristics may be needed for a full specification. There may be several levels of analysis before we pass from powers to natures. For example . . . the kinds of thoughts a man has may be referred to a further level of his nature by seeing them as the thoughts he is liable or likely to have. We may seek the explanation of this in his history. But that is to seek for an explanation as to why he is that kind of man, the kind of man likely to have that kind of thought. It is here that Freudian models of human nature fit in. The explanation of his having or currently being liable to have that kind of thought must be referred to his present state and not his history. Reference to his history explains how he became the sort of man he is. To say a man is a coward is *not* to speak in summary form of his liabilities, for if it were it would add nothing of substance to our account of him. It is to ascribe to him a certain nature, to say that he is a certain kind of psycho-physical mix. It is thenceforward an empirical question what it is for a man to be a coward, and not all such questions are exclusively physiological. All this is said under the caveat that more than one social identity may be manifested by each biological individual.

The system of concepts we have been advocating has a very similar look to the general explanatory schema which one finds exemplified in much of natural science outlined in Chapter Four. There we find that the occurrence of non-random patterns in nature under certain conditions can be described in conditional statements, and that these are explained by reference to the causal mechanisms responsible for producing them, as for instance, chemical reactions are explained by reference to ionic interchanges, syndromes of disease by the invasion of the body by micro-organisms and their behaviour therein, and so on. When the causal mechanism has not been identified, or perhaps is very difficult to observe for one reason or another, the paradigm of method is preserved by our imagining plausible mechanisms which might be responsible for the phenomena, and are, formally speaking, models of the unknown true mechanism. Our account of a man's nature in virtue of which he has the powers and liabilities he manifests in what he does and fails to do, or says and keeps quiet about, bears a similar relation to his manifest behaviour as the natural scientist's account of causal mechanisms does to non-random patterns among phenomena. There are two different ways in which causal mechanisms are related to the phenomena they explain in ordinary natural science. It is imperative, if psychology is to be preserved from another flirtation with an inappropriate paradigm of method from physical science, to be clear about these different relations and how they can help us to understand the connections between human powers and natures, and the social behaviour they explain, since both seem to be exemplified in ethogenic psychology.

In the one case the changing states of the causal mechanism are actually identical with the changing features of the manifest pattern of behaviour, of the thing or substance being studied. But they do not appear to the observer in the form they are considered to have in reality, that is as considered with respect to the nature of the causal mechanism. When we feel a thing becoming warmer physics tells us that what is happening to it is an increase in the mean speeds of its constituent parts. But we feel the warmth of the sun-drenched stone, and we do not feel a vibration. Yet we do not want to say that the stone has two physical properties, warmth and vibration. It has only one. This is an example somewhat similar to the form of relationship that exists between physiological and psychic phenomena. When a man feels a certain emotion and it is found that he is in a certain physiological state of arousal, this does not show that he is concurrently in two states, the psychic and the physiological. There is in reality only one state, which is manifested in one guise to physiological probing, and in another guise to the attentive consciousness of the person experiencing it. As far as most of our means of identifying and recognizing these states go there seem to be two different states, but as far as what we believe there really is in the world, there is only one state. This relationship is actually more complex and difficult to grasp even than we have so far shown, because the kind of the connections we make between these states and other states depends upon the guise under which they are being experienced. An emotion is roughly the meaning we give to our felt states of arousal. And emotions are connected with other emotions, with knowledge and beliefs, and so on in a network whose connections have a form suitable to connection between propositional items. But the state of arousal is causally connected with physiological and environmental changes by mechanisms known to the natural sciences and appropriate to explain chemical and physical changes. In just the same way successive sentences in a book can be understood as connected by logical relationships in so far as they are given meaning by a reader, and he can explain why they succeed each other by reference to their meanings in the context. But their succession can also be explained by reference to the physical processes by which ink and type metal impress those shapes on paper.

In the other case there is a distinct and separate process by which the states of the causal mechanism produce the manifest pattern of phenomena. Consider the pattern of phenomena that results from studying the distribution of blue and brown eyes in a family. To a good approximation these characteristics seem to obey Mendel's Laws. It makes perfectly good sense to say that the reason that someone has brown eyes is that his mother or father had eyes of that colour. But the mechanism responsible has two logically separable components. There is that by which the gene for eye colour is passed on from generation to generation, and that by which an individual with that gene comes to have eyes of that colour. The molecule DNA is involved in the transmission mechanism and the molecule RNA in the developmental mechanism. The state of the DNA causes the person to have blue eyes. It is not the blue-eye-state identified from a different point of view. The pattern of relationships among colours is a statistical regularity, and is not a causal relation. But the pattern of relationship between successive states of DNA molecules and between one of those states and the structure of a cell in a person's eye are causal relationships.

This paradigm is exemplified, for example, in what we have called 'conscious rule-following'. That a man thinks of a certain rule at a certain time may have one kind of explanation, while we explain the actual generation of his behaviour as due to his knowingly following that rule.

In the Freudian account of man, there is an imaginary apparatus of id, super-ego, repression and so on which is clearly a hypothetical mechanism offered as an account of the nature of man in explanation of his social behaviour. The powers and liabilities of people are seen as being possessed in virtue of the particular structure and content of Freudian entities that is unique to them. From a logical point of view, this structure is a model of the unknown nature of the man. To be a Freudian is to view the structure, not just as a plausible model, but as reality. But that step need not be taken for it still to be a valuable way of thinking about human nature. Viewed as a model of that nature, it is not a competitor with the physiology of the brain and nervous system, but forms one element in the psycho-physical mix. It is just because it is a model of the real nature of man that it can be held together with the physiological account as an element in a picture, 'total' enough to provide explanations of the genesis and maintenance of the specifically human powers and liabilities. For instance, in the work of psychologists like E. H. Erikson, we can see the picture animating and guiding research into the development of personality, and it may serve as an explanation of the particular set of personality-types each biological individual is capable of manifesting in various social circumstances. Each episode in the life of a person is given significance and forms part of a connected history if it is seen as playing some role that is significant or insignificant, in the development of the Freudian structure of mind.[3] The crises that count are those which can be seen to contribute, according to this model, to the development of particularly important features of the whole Freudian structure. The set of such models both Freudian and non-Freudian, together with the known physiological peculiarities that characterize a man, we shall call his 'N-ensemble'. The principles of internal coherence for N-ensembles are unknown at present.

It should now be clear why only the powers way of talking could possibly provide an adequate conceptual system for unifying all that can be known about human beings. There is no necessity whatever that the D-component and the N-component should be couched in terms drawn from the same vocabulary. We know that the D-component must contain O-terms in its B-element, that is, human behaviour must be described either in ordinary language or in terms conforming to its logical canons. We are under no necessity to try to perform the impossible task of translating O-term descriptions of human behaviour into S-terms in order to incorporate the discoveries of physiology in a science of psychology. There is no reason whatever why elements of the N-component should not be in S-terms, while the D-component is in O-terms, nor is there any need for the C-element of the D-component to be exclusively in O-terms. The conditions under which a man behaves in a certain way may be found to be specifiable completely in physiological or S-terms. A man may be found to behave recklessly (O-term) if his blood contains more than 80 mg. per ml. of alcohol (S-term), while the changes that occur in him which explain his recklessness may also be described wholly in S-terms, as changes in the state and perhaps in the structure of his nervous system. But 'reckless behaviour' is, of course, an O-term.

Psychology is or should be the study of human powers and liabilities, their origins, sources, conditions and the features of human natures upon which their existence depends. Just as a chemist looks for the chemical composition that is responsible for some substance having the power to arrest a disease, or at the structure of an entity liable to explode when detonated, so psychologists and physiologists must look for those features of human beings which are responsible for their having the powers and liabilities that they do.

Permanent and Transitory Powers and Liabilities

Much of the day-to-day life of human beings is a flux of states endowing the person with a variety of transitory powers and liabilities, some of which are exercised in doing things. A man normally friendly in his relationships with other people may, quite literally, be made 'angry enough to commit murder'. The phenomenon of mood is an example of the sort of conditions associated with the waxing and waning of powers and liabilities. It is one of the most commonplace psychological facts that one is not always capable of things that one can sometimes do, if one's mood is right. The total cluster of power and liabilities that a man has at any one time are highly contingent and depend upon the obtaining of very particular internal and external conditions, and these conditions are highly variable, making each life idiosyncratic. This fact offers one of the sources of the uniqueness of the episodes of human life. It also necessitates the introduction of higher order power and liability concepts, by which proneness to moods and the like can be ascribed, in the same way as having the power of speech is related to one's readiness on a certain occasion to shout insults. People differ in their liability to certain liabilities, in their power to acquire certain powers. Many of the powers which we wish to ascribe permanently to people are of this kind. And these permanent powers are possessed by people in virtue of their having certain fairly permanent natures.

We shall refer this to permanent and transitory changes in human natures later.

The Clustering of Powers

People have a wide variety of powers and liabilities. There are powers of action and refraining from action, powers of mind of various kinds, liabilities to feel certain kinds of feelings, to fall into certain moods, powers to affect other people and liabilities to be affected by them, and so on. We do not intend to go into any detail on the problem of the variety of powers, but wish to recommend it as a promising field for conceptual analysis, valuable to psychology. We are interested here only in noticing two distinct ways in which powers and liabilities can be found to *cluster*. There is the kind of clustering which puts together a character trait like 'trusting' with such a trait as 'adaptable'. These we shall call *contingent clusterings*. They are known by common observation, they are depended upon by novelists and playwrights, and they are the subject matter of the studies of personality psychology. We do not believe that such clusters are *accidental* ensembles, and look to psychology for the eventual explanation of their persistence. Personalities are distinguished by the kind of clusters of personality traits that are found to be manifested on particular kinds of occasions. The *same* personality cluster may be manifested by *different* people. A personality is not a nature, but the way the nature is manifested. We have emphasized in several places, that for each biological individual there is a group of possible personalities, which form a hierarchy ordered by the probability of their manifestation. A personality is a cluster of traits, that is, powers and liabilities of a certain sort that are generally found together, in one of the manifested personae. Despite the fact that some traits are usually found to cluster only with certain other traits, that is some clusters are rather standard, there is a strong body of opinion, led by G. W. Allport,[4] that the full set of powers and liabilities characteristic of any particular human being is a unique hierarchy of standard clusters. One must concede, at the present time, that we have reason to think that human beings, when their lives are examined in great detail, may each manifest a different set of clusters. It will follow from this that though there are enough similarities between kinds of people to make meaningful the use of particular common nouns for specific manifestation of human natures as personalities, the application of such a noun, on however good evidence, is not sufficient for cast-iron expectations as to the powers and liabilities that a person will manifest in every life situation. 'Even a worm can turn', that is the states of readiness he will take up in response to different conditions and circumstances may suddenly conform to a different pattern. There may be a very improbable persona whose manifestation on a particular occasion is the central fact of a biological individual's life.

Even the idiosyncratic natures of individuals have a certain stability. Their uniqueness may derive as much from the complexity of possible characters, as from the instability of any given cluster. And, in so far as there are stable clusters, these are found to have a certain structure. More likely than not, one sort of personality trait goes along with another of a very definite kind. For example, Gardner and others speak of 'people who were inclined to use the cognitive style termed "levelling" were the ones who, most typically, used the defence of repression'.[5] We should not wish to speak of 'people' in this context, but rather of personality-types elicited by the social circumstances of Gardner's 'experiments'.

It would be useful to investigate a number of different sources of ideas of 'structure', including the literary character and the astrological character. Taken at a fairly general level, we expect to find that power and liability clusters are repeated from person to person, particularly clusters of higher order powers and liabilities, but taken in detail we expect to find that there is very considerable degree of variation.

It is clear that 'structure' and 'nature' are closely related. Each distinguishable structure of powers and liabilities must reflect a distinguishable nature, though it is not, of course, identical with it, or identifiable with it. To suppose that they were identical was one of the mistakes of behaviourism.

From a wider, philosophical, indeed metaphysical point of view, the whole enterprise of this book can be seen as the attempt to replace a conceptual system, inherited from the seventeenth century and based upon the conception of substance and quality, with a system based upon the conception of an individual with powers. This 'dynamic' point of view had its origins in the eighteenth century, and was developed primarily as a theory of physics, by Kant and Boscovich. The expansion of the dynamic point of view into a full-scale theory of natural science is possible;[6] here, we are concerned only with the application of the dynamic point of view to the understanding of human life. But the successful application of the powers notion will depend upon our being very clear about some of the deeper metaphysical issues. The problems of identity are of the greatest importance for psychology, that is, the problems associated with providing a clear and, hopefully, a consistent set of criteria for deciding when there is one power being exercised or many; and whether in successive actions the same power is being activated or whether another power has come into operation. Unfortunately there are a variety of criteria evidently at work, even in the most mundane applications of the power concepts.

The first question to which we must address ourselves is the problem of deciding when two or more capacities may be referred back to the one embracing power. Are signalling with a flag, and shouting a message, exercises of the same power? Is the whistling 'language' of the Madeirans yet another exercise of that same power? To distinguish two important criteria, we must first distinguish between the mechanisms of action and the means. The mechanism of speech is a complex of structures, partly in the nervous system, partly muscular, and associated with a certain kind of knowledge and skill. The same mechanism is used in speaking French as is involved in speaking Spanish. Having the mechanism endows each human being with the power of speech, and it is evidently Washoe's lack of that mechanism which is responsible for her not having this power, so that her communication must be through the 'language of gesture'.[7] It may be that we share with Washoe some yet more general capacity, for instance, G. H. Mead's 'capacity for symbolic inter-action', which itself might be referred to the degree to which certain mechanisms (probably specifiable only in a psychophysical mix), are common to all or some of the mammals. However we may ultimately decide to answer that question its conceptual distinction is clear. Thus, a man's power to speak Spanish and his power to speak French are specific exercises *of the same power*, because the same mechanism is involved in the exercise of each power. We shall speak of the power to use language as a *generic* power, and the power to speak French as a *specific* power. The mechanism may be present without the 'means'. I may wish to insult someone in Spanish, be sufficiently roused, have good general linguistic capacities, but without a knowledge of Spanish I am totally incapable of the act I contemplate.

But the power to speak a particular language can be exercised for a variety of social functions. These, however, may be conditional on the flux of enabling conditions we have referred to several times, such as the emotions a person is experiencing. Suppose a person can speak English fluently and well. We would naturally regard this power as fairly permanent. But that man may be able to deliver insults in English only when he is sufficiently roused. That is, his readiness to abuse someone may be a very transitory affair. Not all the possible uses of English may be open to a man at all times. There may be some uses of which a particular man may never become capable. There are some men who are quite incapable of ever using English to insult someone to their face.

If we have a generic power then we generally regard any failure to acquire specific powers under it as a matter of extrinsic conditions. If an individual is known to have the usual linguistic capabilities of a normal human being, then the fact that he cannot speak a given language, say Spanish, is explained by his never having learnt it, that is, by the failure of an extrinsic condition. There are borderline cases. Some people seem to be able to acquire their native tongue without difficulty but have immense difficulty learning any second language. In such cases, where we know the person has tried, we are satisfied that the circumstances for fulfilling the extrinsic conditions have been satisfied, and are forced to explain the failure as due to an intrinsic linguistic weakness. The explanation of the failure will then be sought in the mechanism of language acquisition and language use.

However, if a man knows a language well, and does not exercise his power in insulting someone in what seems to be an appropriate social situation, we are more inclined to put this failure down to his emotional state (calm), or even his nature (phlegmatic), that is to intrinsic conditions. The importance of these distinctions lies in their relationship to the kind of explanation appropriate to a particular case. We seek an explanation in the nature, *or* transitory states of a person, *or* in his circumstances. Which direction we take will be determined by our view of the nature of the power or readiness involved.

When are successive performances exercises of the same power? When are successive states of readiness the activation of the same power? In short, how do we decide when *a* power is manifested *over again*, and when a new power comes into being? Suppose, on two different occasions, I am so aggravated as properly to be said to be capable of murder, and suppose that I am aware, probably retrospectively, of the quality and degree of my irritation. In retrospective commentary, I may well describe myself as having felt murderous, or even that I was murderous, on each occasion. When I am worked up in that way, I have the power to kill, though, of course, being me, I do not choose to exercise this power. There seem to be two criteria at work in this area. It might be argued that if, on each occasion, a different person is the target of my wrath, my state of readiness to kill differs, in that in the first instance I am ready to kill A, but in the second I am ready to kill B. It may also be psychologically true that I do not have the power to kill A when I have the power to kill B. By attending to the intrinsic conditions necessary to the obtaining of the state of readiness that gives me the power to kill, I may become aware that very different emotional tones diffuse each occasion. For instance, hot rage to smash may be a feature of one occasion, while cold hatred and enduring wish to poison slyly may be a feature of the other. We might be inclined to say that difference in emotional quality of the states of readiness entails a difference in the identity of the murderousness. To avoid the cumbersomeness of the multiplicity of powers that would be forced on us, if we followed this suggestion through, we prefer to identify the power with the common *act* of which a person in any of these states may be capable. Thus in each case he has the power to kill. Admitting any reference to the actions by which the act might be performed would also be cumbersome since that would introduce the further complication of the differing means appropriate to the differing states of readiness, a complication inherent in all attributions of powers to perform the specifications of an act, to real people.

We have already noticed the distinction between permanently possessed powers and liabilities, and those of more transitory duration. The theory of powers requires that since powers and liabilities must be referred to features of human nature in virtue of which they are possessed, the distinction between permanent and transitory powers must be referred to a distinction between permanent and transitory features of human natures. Psychologists have offered concepts both for permanent and for transitory features of natures. R. B. Cattell's *Source Trait C*, 'ego strength', is intended to be a concept used to attribute a permanent feature to a human being, central to his nature, in virtue of which that man manifests certain specific powers and liabilities.[8] Despite the dubious practice of interpreting factors as enduring, permanent dispositions,[9] it is sufficiently well known to serve us an illustrative example. It can be shown both that it is a generic power and can be related to a Freudian based psycho-physiological mix. If valid, Source Trait C would be a fine example of an N-term, fit to form the permanent generic power only one step from the psychophysical mix. As we shall see, it plays much the same role *vis-à-vis* a certain sort of cluster of powers and liabilities of human beings, as does electro-valency with respect to the powers and liabilities of the chemical elements. Or just as electro-valency is a fundamental power of the ionic components of sodium chloride, so ego strength is alleged to be a fundamental power of a human being.

First of all, Cattell offers a list or cluster of specific powers and liabilities which according to him, are characteristically manifested by people with high C. Such people are, he says, 'mature, steady, persistent, emotionally calm, realistic about problems, and do not suffer from neurotic fatigue'. Notice that these are O-terms, or neologisms conforming to the desiderata that define the O-system. Ego-strength is offered as a fundamental, generic power and comple-

T

mentary liability. 'The essence of the C factor', according to Cattell, 'appears to be an inability to control one's emotions and impulses, especially by finding for them some realistic expression.' In discussing low ego-strength or ego-weakness, Cattell connects this fundamental, generic power or liability with a variety of other terms, clearly and unequivocally of the group used to distinguish different human natures. 'Almost all forms of neurotics', he says, 'as well as alcoholics, narcotic addicts, and delinquents are abnormally low in this ego-strength factor.' Again notice that these conform to the O-desiderata for generic powers. Note the very interesting fact that each of these classificatory terms for people is clearly conditional, either ascribing generic liabilities, like 'alcoholic' or 'narcotic addict', or clusters of generic powers and liabilities like 'neurotic' and 'delinquent'. Each of these expressions ascribes a cluster of powers and is thus capable of being used as a term for a type of person. Ego-strength or weakness is a permanent power or liability of a human being in virtue of which he manifests that cluster of specific powers and liabilities that lead to such classifications as 'mature', 'delinquent' and the like. That Source Trait C is only one remove from N-concepts is shown by the fact that it is strongly connected with a psycho-physiological mix, a prominent feature of which is a psychoanalytic view of human nature, that is, the Freudian model. Cattell says 'Furthermore, there is evidence suggesting that ego-strength development is lower in clinical cases subjected to prolonged anxiety or given to excessive guilt proneness. This fits the psychoanalytic theory that excessive early demands by conscience can so add to the difficulties of finding suitable expression for emotional needs that the ego's capacity to handle impulses rationally is impaired.' One might add that it would not be surprising to hear of the discovery of some differences in the structure of the brain and in its system of chemical reactions among those who have been subjected to prolonged anxiety, from whatever cause. Indeed, if this anxiety was produced in a child by defective parental training which led to too demanding a conscience, then the damage might be permanent. Or, as in the use of MacLean's theory by A. Koestler,[10] where a feature of brain-structure is offered as the N-component for the explanation of a wide range of capacities, liabilities and tendencies. We do not have to accept the Freudian theory literally in order to account for the later or delayed effect of early experiences. The changes in a person's nature which account for them might be described adequately in physiological terms. Of course, we could only know that these physiological changes were relevant to human behaviour if we already took the general Freudian *standpoint* to the understanding of what people do and accepted the relevance of early experience to later character development. There need not be any particular theory of human nature and of its metaphysical status to make the Freudian standpoint viable. In our terms, all that Freud observed or conjectured about his patients' lives could be described in O-terms within the D-component. The N-component may be any sort of mix of the psychic and the physical.

Schematically Cattell says 'the nature of the underlying power in C can be seen dynamically as the self or ego, organized to give expression to the drives in a well-balanced way'. And here the power/nature sequence terminates in an organization or structure, the details of which are, of course, not known.

Finally, in the attempt to offer a hypothesis about the details of this structure, Cattell offers a striking example of the psycho-physical mix. In general 'a source trait as discovered by factor analysis is some kind of unitary influence in personality which affects a whole structure of responses'. But what of this unitary influence or fundamental generic power? In talking about Source Trait A, Cattell says 'but if we suppose that some constitutional, temperamental, physiological condition makes some people's drives naturally more persistent and unchanging, this might account simultaneously for the greater natural emotional steadiness of the sizothyme and also for his greater sense of frustration, hostility, and withdrawal (since to have greater perseverance is also to experience greater thwarting from an ordinary, unaccommodating environment'. The phrase 'constitutional, temperamental, physiological condition' is precisely the scheme of a psycho-physiological mix. Cattell's theory then, has the form of power/nature progression, and his genetic hypothesis as to the nature responsible for that power, though vague, at least has the form of a psycho-physiological mix.

We have also argued that it is very characteristic of human beings to manifest a changing flux of transitory powers and liabilities, which come and go under the agency of changes in intrinsic enabling conditions. Remember that these transitory features of a person's nature are contrasted with the more permanent features, which make up his essence, so to speak, and which are the product of the obtaining of some central core of intrinsic enabling conditions. The study of attitude change has been the occasion for the introduction of a philosophically interesting concept to which we have frequently referred and which we will use to illustrate the powers conceptual system at work in the case of transitory powers and liabilities. This is the concept of 'cognitive dissonance', first introduced by Leon Festinger.[11] 'Cognitive dissonance' was introduced as the name of a transitory state of mind which was supposed to be responsible for such phenomena as change of attitude or behaviour, and as time went by, a multitude of other phenomena were explained by it as well. The conditions for cognitive dissonance exist when there is an *inconsistency* of some sort between certain items, which might include attitudes, beliefs, pieces of knowledge, acts and actions, and so on. This is a somewhat broader notion than logical contradiction, which is supposed to hold between propositions or sentences. It can obtain between a belief and an action, or between a plan and an attitude, or between a judgment and a previous piece of behaviour, and so on. Almost any exercise of a human power can be inconsistent in this sense with an exercise of any other. It is not clear, even from the most recent literature, whether he who falls into a state of cognitive dissonance must be aware of the inconsistency which is held to be operative on the occasion. Indeed, in complex situations, items between which there are supposed to be inconsistencies may be very diverse, and it is not clear how one is to decide which is operative or whether, indeed, all possible inconsistencies somehow work within the person and, unknown to him, produce the dissonance.

Now the transitory state of mind, for which the term 'cognitive dissonance' was coined, can be interpreted as a feeling of discomfort, of greater or less intensity if inconsistency prevails. It is resolved into a comfortable feeling (or no feeling at all) when consistency prevails. Clearly, the notion is being introduced (à la Festinger) in conformity with the O-conceptual system. People were supposed to act, to think, to change their minds or their habits, and so on so as to reduce the disagreeable feeling of dissonance, as one might move away from a hot fire or stop thinking about an unpleasant encounter. This is an example of a transitory powers or liabilities theory, in which peoples' readiness to change their opinions or modify their actions is consequent upon the satisfaction of a fairly specific intrinsic enabling condition which has to do with a temporary psychic state. Inconsistency is not supposed to lead to large scale changes in personality, or the substitution of one social persona for another, but it is supposed to be the condition for a readiness to make small scale changes in belief, attitude and so on. The chain of effect is supposed to be that the existence of the inconsistency causes a bad feeling to exist, which renders the human being prone to, or ready to, take evasive or redirective action, etc., etc., when given the opportunity in order to remove the feeling. It would be agreeable to be able to report that 'cognitive dissonance' has now found a permanent place among the N-terms of our vocabulary, for those transitory states of a person in virtue of being which he or she is particularly prone to change their opinions. Unfortunately, serious objections, instructive for the philosophical issues, have been raised.

By tying the transitory state to a *feeling* through the particular part of the O-term conceptual system chosen to introduce the notion, Festinger laid himself open to the most powerful of all experimental tests. Do feelings of cognitive dissonance exist? Do people *feel* uncomfortable when acting, thinking, believing, and so on inconsistently? There is no evidence upon which to base such a supposition, rather the contrary.[12] If it is an inconsistency which makes one feel badly then the changes in attitude ought to lead to a more consistent and hence comfortable ensemble of actions, beliefs, etc. But alas, there is little evidence of consistency between attitude change and consequent behaviour.[13] Finally, many critics point out that there are many other explanations of attitude change possible in any given *particular* case.[14]

The first point of criticism would lead us to say that the cognitive dissonance theory was really an addition to the ensemble of models which we assemble to fill the gap produced by our ignorance of human nature, and the springs within it of human conduct. If we take this attitude then we evade the criticism that stems from the absence of the feeling of dissonance in so many cases. The second point of criticism, that in any case where an explanation in terms of cognitive dissonance seems to make good sense, another explanation in wholly different terms can be found, leads us into another issue altogether, namely, the relation between different accounts of some episode in which human beings took part. We have already dealt with the problems this raises in our discussion of accounts. This problem cannot be tackled in short compass, since it depends upon a prior analysis of the proper set of paradigms within which any episode involving human beings can be understood, and their actions accounted for. Whatever may be the ultimate fate of the theory of cognitive dissonance it is instructive as an example, since it is an attempt to provide an account of short-term powers and liabilities (readinesses) in exactly the way our theoretical analysis would recommend.

In developing the theory of powers we have made a general distinction between long-term powers, including competences, capabilities, capacities, liabilities and so on, and short-term powers and liabilities, which can be ascribed to people when we believe they are in certain states of readiness. The state of an entity in virtue of which it is ready to do something is transitory and may come and go, without affecting the identity of that individual. The very same individual is sometimes ready to do something and sometimes not. Long-term powers, on the other hand, are possessed in virtue of features of an entity which are logically related to its very existence as an individual and cannot be changed without that individual ceasing to be self-identical. The loss of certain human powers may be so drastic as to lead to a person being described as no longer a man but a mere vegetable. This kind of recategorization reflects the logical connection between certain states and conditions of an individual and his identity as a person. The distinction is ameliorated by the existence of intermediate medium-term powers, and we are often at a loss to say whether individuality changes with them or not. Before leaving the topic of states of readiness to subsequent generations of empirical ethogenists to explore in a study of actual episodes of human life, there is one further remark that should be made about the concept.

A state of readiness, is a state in virtue of which the person or animal is ready (prepared) to do an action or say a saying of a certain kind. A cat poised and about to spring, a speaker about to address his audience, and the like are individuals in the appropriate states of readiness. It should be clear that the concept 'state of readiness' is a *teleological* concept. By this we mean that the identification of a certain state of an animal or man by virtue of which it is ready to do something cannot be made without reference to what it is ready to do. Thus the concept is neither purely physiological, nor purely ethological. It is typical of a great many concepts with which we have had to deal in this study, having a foot in both worlds so to speak. There is, however, nothing mysterious about its teleological element, in that it is present as the result of previous investigations of the species, or previous experience of the life style of an organism. That is, the identification of a certain state of an organism as a state of readiness to pounce, say, depends inductively upon our having done some observing of cats and noticed that they adopt a certain manner when about to pounce. We may go so far as to study their physiological states and find out exactly what is their nervous and endocrine condition when ready to pounce. Though our knowledge of the connection of the state and the outcome or action is empirical in origin it is reflected in a conceptual connection in the internal structure of the concept 'ready to pounce', in that the concept 'ready to pounce' brings together the state, and the kind of outcome in a kind of semantic union. This conceptual connection is reflected in the fact that if the cat lets the passing mouse through we are much inclined to say 'Ah, see, the cat was not ready to pounce!' We believe that the substance of Taylor's account of action concepts is an attempt to study this and similar cases of an empirically based conceptual connection of a very similar kind. As our knowledge of the physiological basis of readinesses to act grows, so the conceptual connection must decline, while the generality of the empirical basis becomes stronger. We hope we have already made clear that extensions in physiological knowledge extend our grasp of the conditions for action, that is extend our understanding of the basis of readinesses and powers to act, and leave the origin and direction of action for the psychologist to explore, through his study of the rules, plans and so on that people follow and employ when they act, that is, when they monitor and control their performances.

In order to bring home this point with the kind of force which we feel should attach to it, we will look very briefly at the various routes that might be thought to exist to a knowledge of the natures of individuals in virtue of which they have or lack their powers, liabilities, capacities and so on.

THE PHYSIOLOGICAL ROUTE. In attempting to identify the conditions of readiness for action with physiological states of an organism there are formidable difficulties, of such practical intransigence, as to make this route of little use in the forseeable future for social science. We have already emphasized the importance of Schachter's discoveries of the paramount role that the giving of meaning plays in the way states of arousal operate in generating and effecting action. It seems that whatever similarities in state may be identified physiologically, the way the existence of that state affects the individual is determined by the meaning that he gives to it, and this is determined by such things as his beliefs about the situation and so on. We seem to pass from physiology into a wholly different realm.

A further point of considerable theoretical importance that has been stressed in the literature recently is the fact that the physiological study of people depends, for crucial steps in the very identification of the sites and states of relevant phenomena, upon the reports by people of their psychic states, or by descriptions of the behaviour of animals which are couched in terms of social meanings, rules and the like.[15] The discoveries of the seats of various higher mental capacities in people is an example of the first kind, and the search for physiological and genetic bases for threat displays in sticklebacks is an example of the latter. The taxonomy used by physiologists for their purposes is logically dependent upon a prior taxonomy from the realm of thoughts, meanings, intentions, rituals and the like.[16] There does not seem to be a useful and independent physiological route to those features of organisms in virtue of which they possess their powers, and are ready for this or that action.

THE ORDINARY ROUTE. The ordinary route and its extensions leads to the identification of specific human natures through the use of type-terms like 'coward', and of what we have called O-term neologisms like 'neurotic'. These are clearly type-terms and not just names for accidental clusters of dispositions, or alleged traits. This is clearly shown by the fact that they appear in explanations of the clustering of similarities in the readiness to behave of a person in some group of situations. We might, in ordinary discussion, explain the fact that a person was always ready to dispute with his boss, *and* a keen mountaineer, by explaining that he had these dispositions and interests because he was brave. However the explanatory force of such terms is largely illusory, and they are certainly, in our sense, enigmatic. Recently some attempt has been made to find a physio-logical ground for some type-terms, in particular neurotic,[17] but the success of this venture is controversial.

THE PSYCHOLOGICAL ROUTE. While less radical than the physiological route the psychological approach as we have sketched it, resolves the dilemma of the enigma of human nature, by offering an ensemble of models of this unknown. We have spoken of this ensemble loosely as a psycho-physiological mix. But this way of speaking glosses over what we believe to be a central problem in theoretical psychology, but for which, at this stage, we have no answer. The problem is this: in the natural sciences the assembly of an ensemble of models is not an uncommon occurrence, but the situation never rests there. Great efforts are made to organize the ensemble in accordance with prevailing ideas as to the true nature of reality, and to set up experiments which will reveal whether the ordering has been done aright. Thus the use of models for the crucial unknowns of natural science is under both a theoretical and an empirical constraint. At the deeper levels the theoretical con-straint is paramount, so that in assessing the viability of models in theoretical microphysics the empirical checking of their authenticity is not a serious feature of that science, since there are immense and perhaps insoluble technical difficulties in the way of doing it. What restrictions are there on the acceptability of models into the ensemble which is supposed to stand in for that central unknown, human nature? So far as we can see at this stage it is not possible to lay down, *a priori* any restrictions upon the development of such models, or upon their juxtaposition. We have ourselves pointed out how in such cases as the explanation of the effect of alcohol upon the powers and capacities of a person, it may be necessary to introduce both physiological and psychic considerations, and that the explanation would seem to be impoverished in the absence of either. We hope that further discussion of this topic, specifically in terms of the restraints upon possible psycho-physiological mixes, may lead to the development of some ground rules even if they are of only a very general kind.

Lastly we would like to draw attention once again to the vital and central part that the flux of the emotions, the meaningfully inter-preted arousal-structure of episodes, plays in the waxing and waning of powers and liabilities, and in the preparation that leads to a state of readiness or to its decline. We believe that the adoption of the ethogenic point of view leads to emphasis being placed upon two lines of research which from that point of view, would look promis-ing. The first is the further development of studies of the kind pioneered in recent times by Schachter, with a thoroughly ethogenic emphasis on the accounts of meanings and the like which are elicited from those who participate in such studies. It may be that certain forms of cognitive structure do begin to emerge from that kind of study. The other line involves a yet more vigorous pursuit of the linguistic and conceptual studies begun by Ryle,[18] Kenny[19] and Götlind.[20] In the field of emotion we have perhaps the most elaborate and sophisticated part of the common conceptual scheme. Ordinary language studies of this kind can be still further developed by relating them to studies in a similar vein from the clinical side, and to an investigation of the conditions and concepts at work in the understanding and genesis of the pathology of the emotions.

REFERENCES

1. S. Schachter, in *Advances in Experimental Social Psychology*, edited L. Berkowitz, Academic Press, New York, 1964, pp. 49–80.
2. H. S. Becker, *J. of Health and Soc. Behavior*, 8, 3, 67.
3. E. H. Erikson, 'Growth and Crises of the Healthy Personality', reprinted in *Personality*, edited R. S. Lazarus and E. M. Opton, Penguin Books, London, 1967, 167–213.
4. G. W. Allport, cf. Lazarus and Opton, *op. cit.*, Ch. 3.
5. P. S. Holzman and R. W. Gardner, 'Levelling and Repression', *J. abnorm. Soc. Psychol.*, 59, 151–5.
6. Such an expansion can be found in R. Harré, *The Principles of Scientific Thinking*, London and Chicago, 1970.
7. R. A. Gardner and B. T. Gardner, 'Teaching Sign Language to a Chimpanzee', University of Nevada Research Report, July, 1968.
8. R. B. Cattell, *The Scientific Analysis of Personality*, Penguin Books, London, 1965, Chapter III.
9. J. E. Overall, 'Note on the scientific status of factors', *Psychological Bulletin*, 61, 1964, 270–6.
10. A. Koestler, *Fourteenth Nobel Symposium*, 1969.
11. L. Festinger, *A Theory of Cognitive Dissonance*, Harper and Row, Evanston and New York, 1957, p. 3.
12. For instance, M. J. Rosenberg, 'Some Limits of Dissonance', in S. Feldman, *Cognitive Consistency*, New York and London, 1966, pp. 137–43.
13. cf. J. L. Freedman, 'Preference for dissonance information', *J. Person. Soc. Psychol.*, 66, 157–63; also, unpublished report of participant observation study of attitude change by B. E. and M. Wilson, University of Nevada.
14. cf. E. Aronson and J. Mills, *J. Abnorm. Soc. Psychol.*, 59, 177–81; and Wilson and Wilson, *op. cit.*
15. J. A. Fodor, *Psychological Explanation*, Random House, New York, 1968, pp. 107–11.
16. R. Harré, *op. cit.*
17. H. J. Eysenck and S. B. G. Eysenck, *Personality Structure and Measurement*, Routledge and Kegan Paul, London, 1969, Ch. 7.
18. G. Ryle, *The Concept of Mind*, Hutchinson, London, 1949, Ch. 4.

19. A. J. Kenny, *Act, Emotion, Will*, Routledge and Kegan Paul, London, 1963, Chs. 1, 2 and 3.

20. E. Götlind, *Three Theories of Emotion*, Munksgaard, Copenhagen, 1958.

CHAPTER FOURTEEN

Research Strategy in the Behavioural Sciences
Some New Methodological Directions

THE ARGUMENT

Preliminary

(i) The most serious defect of the old paradigm in behavioural studies is inadequate conceptual preparation for empirical research.

(ii) The traditional experiment takes no account of the meanings assigned to the experimental situation itself by participants. But this is crucial in determining how they respond to treatments.

Illustrations of New Methods

(1)   *Method*   Exploiting and Exploring Ordinary Language
      Example   Person Concepts
      (a) (i) Most studies have *provided* participants with a language and terminology.
         (ii) The 'experiments' have not usually involved real interaction with real people.
      (b) The analysis of free interview accounts of other people can be done, and has already produced very illuminating results.

(2)   *Method*   Extended Preliminary Conceptual Analysis and the Collection of Accounts.
      Example 1   The Concept of Involvement.
      (a) Actual studies can be shown to have involved not one concept, but a *range* of diverse concepts.

(b) Analysis yields a very complex conceptual field, which is

(c) further complicated by subtle modifications of the concept in different contexts.

(d) The collection and analysis of accounts is an essential preliminary to resolving the problem here.

Example 2 Attitudes.

(a) With only a few exceptions psychologists have been unduly simplistic in preparatory analyses.

(b) Philosophical analysis, in this area, has been profound. It yields the following schema:

(i) The objective features of a thing, action or situation, by which it is *identified* and in accordance with which,

(ii) it is *ranked*, i.e. place somewhere in an ordered sequence according to some scale.

(iii) If the ranking scale is attached to a preference scale, then the entity can be *evaluated*.

(iv) Attitude, for or against something, will be reflected at two different levels,

(a) with respect to choice of scale

(b) with respect to the preference order of the chosen scale.

(v) The justification of attitudes at either level may terminate directly in an expression of liking or disliking, or may involve intermediate steps in which factual beliefs may be addressed with respect to either (iv) (a) or (b).

(c) The study of attitudes is further complicated by the fact that each person usually displays a different attitude system in cool, verbal situations from the system displayed in tense, action situations.

(d) The only possible way to penetrate this immensely complex structure is by the analysis of accounts produced in a justificatory context.

(3) *Method* Developed Forms of Role-Enactment

Example The use of the Scenario method to study characters-in-situations.

(a) Previous attempts at using such methods have not allowed for the participants' construal of the situation.

(b) The fruitfulness of the method can be enormously expanded by exploiting this.

(c) From the actor's point of view *four* types of role playing possible.

(i) The individual as Everyman is asked to imagine the outcome of a situation. This exploits the imaginative rehearsal feature of human action, emphasized in clinical psychology.

(ii) The individual as Everyman is asked to enact a situation and report its ethogenic structure.

(iii) The individual is asked to imagine the outcome of a situation for a specific kind of person. This will involve imagining which persona to present.

(iv) The individual is asked to enact such a situation as in (iii), and report its ethogenic structure.

If, as we are inclined to believe, nearly everybody has nearly every possible human persona amongst their set of presentable selves, the total set of these developed forms should provide material for powerful explanatory theories of social actions.

Many psychologists and other behavioural scientists who have persevered in reading this book to the present point will have repeatedly asked the question, 'Well, if we accept the position outlined, how does it change the way in which we do research?' While this question certainly has merit, it cannot be answered directly and immediately. We have identified at length the assumptions and the model of man that have dominated psychology for decades, and have suggested how these background factors have influenced the way in which research is done. We have also suggested a model of man which is more in keeping with the true nature of science while also taking into account those aspects of man that require treatment distinct from that used in other sciences. But the next and final step, the development of research techniques and strategies especially suited to man is not the province of this book. This development is a time-consuming process requiring ingenuity and extensive effort on the part of many scientists. Current techniques and procedures must be modified and adapted, new ones developed, and all must be tried out and further modified.

Thus no *definitive* answers can be provided now, but in this final chapter we discuss the general direction that such strategies should take, as well as selected studies, some completed, and some only projected, that would be more in line with the ethogenic conception of behaviour than are more traditional approaches. Naturally none of these studies are definitive; not all of them were even conceived in terms of the position of this book. But they do often deal directly with at least a facet of the problems suggested by the ethogenic model of man. Studies discussed here include the following: the development of person concepts in children, which demonstrates the value of paying more attention to the ordinary language concepts actually used by people in contrast to limiting a respondent's conceptual possibilities, by confining him to the use trait words; an analysis of certain logical properties of the concept of attitude, with consequent revisions of the understanding of attitude statements, and some of the implications of these changes for the problem of determining the comparative strength of attitudes; a conceptual and empirical analysis of the concept of involvement and its effects on attitude measurement; a conceptualization of a method of research called the acting experiment or role-playing analysis, which is especially suited to research with the ethogenic model.

To begin with, we again call attention to the dangers of inadequate conceptual preparation in connection with empirical research. All too often investigators are content with representing the specific behaviour studied by experimental operations without thoroughly analysing this behaviour in contexts beyond the narrow confines of the particular laboratory situation and considering the logical structure of the language then employed to describe and explain it. This point has been well stated by Peter Ossorio:[1]

'Thus, it is customary for the psychological investigator to give a vague, nominal characterization of his subject matter (e.g., "complex behaviour", "symbolic processes", "problem solving", "verbal behaviour") and then move to an experimental paradigm as a way of "discovering what the central features of the phenomenon are". Almost inevitably, the experimental paradigm itself becomes the primary description of the phenomenon, and the major product of experimentation is the refinement of explanatory detail, leaving the original descriptive task unchanged. But we should have to question how one could discover empirically what the central features of a phenomenon were without knowing already what features *would* so qualify if they were ascertained. And if one knew that in advance, it would have to be possible to give, in advance, more than a nominal description of the subject matter under investigation.'

Thus, findings may too often be valid only for the narrow operations used in the experiment and not for the broader behaviour that the experimenter thinks is represented by them. Moreover, with inadequate conceptualization, the relation of the findings to closely related forms of behaviours remains unclear, and without some analysis of how that behaviour occurs in non-laboratory settings and how it is then described, it is difficult to generalize beyond the laboratory to naturally-occurring situations.

We have argued for a view of man as an active, self-directing, self-monitoring agent whose acts occur in a social framework constructed out of meanings. This contrasts with the behaviourist view, which stresses man as a passive 'subject' who is 'exposed to treatments' to which he reacts. Certain general research strategies follow immediately from the ethogenic model. Laboratory experimentation conducted in the usual manner is seen as, *in general*, inappropriate to the model though there are certain exceptions to this. The 'passive subject' is not really passive; he is apt to have ideas concerning the meaning of the experimenter's acts and the purpose of the experiment. If these are not taken into account, the results obtained are apt to be misleading at best and false at worst. But even more crucial is the inadvisability of designing an experiment as if persons were passive subjects responding in a mechanical fashion instead of as a thinking, self-directing agent, since the processes by which their behaviour is generated will, generally speaking, be thus automatically excluded from empirical investigation.

Recent years have seen some recognition of this problem, not only in research on the social psychology of the experiment, but also in an analysis of experimental findings which is combined with the designing of successive investigations to uncover what the person

U

might *in fact* have been doing in a particular experimental setting such as acting so as to create a favourable impression on the experimenter. But it seems that the implications of viewing man as a self-directing agent have not yet been exploited to the full. We see little direct, extensive questioning of persons serving in experiments to obtain *their* accounts of what they think they are doing, and of the plans, imaginative rehearsals and so on by which they prepared their actions. Perhaps too much continued reliance on methods which too greatly constrain the behaviour of the person inhibits the appearance of the natural methods of generating behaviour. A central problem in many experiments stems from the fact that a person knows he is serving in an experiment and thus is apt to behave in radically different ways from the way he acts in non-laboratory settings. Some small steps toward countering this problem have been taken; these need to be enlarged. Some attention has been given to developing unobtrusive measurements—quantitative observations of which the individual is totally unaware. More far-reaching is the movement toward non-laboratory experimentation.[2] Using considerable ingenuity, behavioural scientists have intervened in various life situations and made observations of the effects of their interventions without the people involved ever knowing that they had been the subject of study. This type of investigation has the considerable advantage of not contaminating the results through knowledge on the part of participants that they are serving as 'guinea pigs', although typically it has the disadvantage that no information is obtainable concerning their view of the situation and of their own actions. We turn now to briefly note a number of studies which, in lesser or greater degree, move toward a more adequate strategy which is appropriate to the ethogenic model we have fostered.

Illustration One: Person Concepts

Several times in our discussion we have emphasized the importance of making use of ordinary language concepts. Typically, the behavioural scientist has considered everyday language unsuited for use in behavioural science, and has favoured developing a language of his own, which, it was hoped, would have a superior precision. In fact, however, all that he has produced are a small number of theoretical and working concepts, far short of a complete language, and, ironically, not having the precision which has been shown to characterize the highly developed psychological and social terminologies of ordinary language, of the language of the law and so on. The aim, we think, is misguided. The very conception of human action is inherent in our language; indeed, most human social behaviour is linguistically mediated and is thus not directly observable in the sense that a physical movement might be. Thus, a person's use of ordinary language in describing his own and other's actions, in thinking about and preparing himself for action is vital to a proper behavioural science. We can illustrate one facet of this general observation by examining what has been done in the study of how persons are perceived or conceptualized by other individuals.

The overwhelming proportion of studies have not looked at how individuals describe other persons in their own words. Instead, most studies have prevented individuals from using ordinary language concepts. Typically, the investigator has provided participants with *his* own terms, usually trait-words, and moreover, has required participants to use a numerical scale to estimate how much of the trait the target person possessed. By imposing his own conceptual methodology on participants, the investigator has abrogated all possibility of learning how individuals in free situations conceive of other persons.

Recently, Peevers and Secord[3] have studied in a free interview situation the language that children of various ages use in thinking of persons. These data, in ordinary language terms, proved to be incredibly rich. Moreover, they were amenable to analysis by means of a coding system, and the coded materials could be treated with conventional statistics. The study yielded important new knowledge about how persons are conceived of in ordinary language terms. At the same time, it was possible to identify certain basic dimensions or categories that underlie ordinary language descriptions of persons. For example, with increasing age, children move from a highly egocentric description of other persons toward a more impersonal, other-oriented description. Children also increase their descriptive use of language as they grow older. The youngest children scarcely describe the other person as an individual at all—he is a person who lives across the street, who has a dog, or who goes bicycle riding with the describer. With age, the other person is increasingly seen and described as a unique individual with distinctive personal attributes. Age also brings the ability to conceptualize reasons for the other person's attributes or behaviours, and the ability to recognize that an attribute is conditional upon a particular situation or relationship.

As long as investigators constrained the participants in their studies to the use of quantitative trait ratings, this kind of information could not be discovered. Allowing the respondents to freely describe persons in their own terms has given us knowledge of the conceptual framework that persons use in knowing and evaluating others and forms the basis for a host of future studies relating such frameworks to a person's experience and personality.

Illustration Two: The Concept of Involvement

On several occasions we have noted the psychologist's resort to operations as a *substitute* for adequate conceptual treatment. Coke Brown has examined the concept of *involvement*, in social psychological theory and experiment, from this point of view.[4] Speaking generally, involvement means that 'an individual cares about or has an investment in something and that an involved individual will behave differently from one who is not involved'. While one might expect the concept to vary somewhat when used in different contexts, Brown has demonstrated that even when the concept is dealt with experimentally within the confines of a specific theory, Sherif and Hovland's judgmental theory of attitude change, problems arise because of the use of different operations in the different experiments and because of the failure to conduct a conceptual analysis of the concept. These procedures range from such operations as making judgments of the acceptability or unacceptability of attitude statements through direct ratings of one's own feeling of involvement, to creating high or low involvement through instructions to the persons in the experiment.

While it is in fact desirable to use a variety of operations, this is true only when such operations are carefully related to an overall theoretical analysis of the concept that is represented by the operations. Brown points out that a thorough conceptual analysis of involvement simply had not been done. He finds twelve different reasons for identifying an individual as involved:

'We are more likely to describe an individual as being involved and we are more likely to describe one individual as being more involved than another if that individual: (1) takes direct action in regard to the topic or object; (2) presently spends or devotes a large amount of time to the object or issue; (3) is knowledgeable concerning the topic; (4) has maintained an interest in the topic over a long span of time; (5) is not easily distracted from the topic when discussing it; (6) says that others should be interested in the topic and downgrades those who are not interested or who do not agree with his position; (7) expresses strong emotion or concern when discussing the topic; (8) reacts strongly or changes his behaviour dramatically at critical periods of success or failure (i.e. is despondent when his candidate loses); (9) maintains his position against strong opposition; (10) has a well-defined position on the topic; (11) is a member of one or more groups which are concerned with the issue; or (12) relates the topic or his position on the topic to a large portion of his life space.'

Differences between individuals in any or all of the respects listed above may lead to differences in prediction of behaviour or behaviour changes. Predictions may be further modified if the nature of the topic, the situation, and the individual's personality characteristics are taken into account, particularly if, as seems likely, those personality characteristics are themselves a function of the situation and how it is perceived. Some topics and situations are inherently more involving than others and may be more likely to elicit the kinds of behaviour listed above. Some individuals may display the above kinds of behaviour in ways which are related to the specific personality characteristics evoked by situations of challenge, e.g., a dogmatic person would maintain his position against strong opposition in a wide variety of contexts and this description may provide for greater understanding of his behaviour than a description of 'involved'. Of course it does not follow from this that the same individual would present an equally dogmatic appearance on other occasions and with respect to other topics.

Brown's own empirical work, like the previously discussed work on the description and evaluation of persons, stresses the importance of what a participant actually says about the matter, in an interview situation. The *content* of this material is coded and then processed statistically. Brown's analysis makes very clear that people, all of whom are clearly involved, can nevertheless behave very differently in ways that affect the outcomes of the research and its interpretation. Involvement, he notes, is not a single variable, but a rather complex state, which is best approached through a wide variety of factors, both behavioural and verbal rather than some single quantitative procedure.

Illustration Three: Attitudes

Another example of underconceptualization and the falsification which derives from focus upon too narrowly selected a set of operations can be found in most attitude research. Instead of thoroughly analysing the logical properties of the concept, investigators allow the attitude scale or questionnaire to 'represent' the concept. But the consequence of this neglect of conceptual analysis is that it is quite unclear what the attitude measurements mean, and how they are to be related to other phenomena. In the face of this self-generated problem, the psychologist resorts further to 'empirical' studies of the relation between attitude and behaviour. But these in turn are difficult to interpret, in the absence of the conceptual analysis.

This is not to say that the concept has received no theoretical attention. Among the important treatments of the concept by psychologists are those by Sherif and Cantril,[5] Krech and Crutchfield,[6] and Katz and Stotland.[7] More recently the concept has been discussed in connection with the various consistency theories of

Heider,[8] Festinger,[9] and Osgood and Tannenbaum.[10] But the earlier analyses have been largely ignored, and the measurement operations in terms of scales or questionnaires allowed to stand in their place. Moreover, the most popular form of consistency theory, the theory of cognitive dissonance, itself lacks adequate conceptual analysis.

One important feature of our recommendations is the priority we give to the preliminary analysis of the concepts to be employed in an empirical study, as these concepts are commonly used. Psychologists, we believe, should make allies of the linguistic philosophers, who have made very thorough and subtle analyses of a great number of psychologically interesting concepts. We can illustrate this point particularly strikingly in the field of attitude research. Attitude concepts are typically assessed by one of three procedures: A Thurstone—or Likert—type questionnaire consisting of a set of statements which the person endorses, a semantic differential scale, or in many specific experimental studies, simply a few statements which the person endorses. All of these approaches assume a simplistic treatment of evaluation which much reduces the value of the work done, and they overlook a vitally important feature of evaluative concepts which has been particularly clearly brought out by the linguistic analysts. To show this and bring out its importance we shall sketch the results of the conceptual analysis of those concepts which are ordinarily used for the expression of attitude. Attitude finds expression in action and in evaluation. To make this distinction, we could speak of attitudes and avowed attitudes, respectively. The use by psychologists of scales and interview techniques suggests that they have been primarily concerned with avowed attitudes, i.e., with attitudes expressed verbally in relatively quiet and low arousal situation where there is little demand for immediate action in accordance with the attitude expressed. Ethno-methodologists, such as Garfinkel, have been concerned more with the exploration of attitudes. Philosophers have paid a great deal of attention to the logic of evaluation in moral philosophy, and can provide psychologists with indispensable conceptual analyses to serve as the basis of more subtle empirical explorations.

Philosophers have been concerned with the analysis of such words as 'nice', 'awful', 'good', 'bad', 'clean', 'dirty', 'super', 'rotten' and the like, many of which figure in the word scales commonly used. One can, we think, extract a fairly sharply defined consensus from the most influential conceptual analysis. Evaluation is not a simple act, but involves several distinct logical moves: (a) the identification of the qualities associated with the attitude object, (b) placing the object on an ordered scale according to the qualities it possesses, and (c) expressing a liking or preference for the object. The last two of these are often confused; we will attempt to show that they must be sharply separated.

An evaluative expression is applied to an object, a situation, or an action, *on the basis* of certain qualities which that object, situation or action actually has. But the point of the evaluative statement is not to state that the object has these qualities but to locate it on an ordered scale, by virtue of its qualities. The attribution of the qualities is logically separate. Given the qualities, by reference to the scale, a thing is *ranked* or graded. The scale usually consists of a series of words having an underlying dimensional character. 'Super' puts it high, 'lousy' puts it low, for example. The ranking scales involved in the logic of evaluative words usually have a bipolar structure. In Urmson's classical paper 'On Grading', the principles of the logical construction of scales, and their relation to the evaluative words is clearly shown.[11] Thus, to evaluate an apple as 'Extra Fancy' is to state that, with respect to its various qualities, that apple falls high on an ordered scale, on the basis of the actual qualities that it has *independently* of whether anyone or everyone *likes* the properties at that end of the scale. There is no mention at this stage of the analysis of feelings, emotions, or affect. Logically speaking, we could introduce words into the language which would have an evaluative grammar, but which were to be used for qualities where there were no feelings or emotions engaged at all. For instance, a scale of qualities might be ordered by such relations as 'bigger than', 'hotter than' and so on. At this level of their grammar, evaluative words depend only on the possibility of some ordering relations existing among the qualities in virtue of which they are ascribed to things, situations and actions, and by which the things can be ranked. For instance, to describe someone as 'snappy' may depend only on the ordering relation 'quicker than' being applied to his and other people's actions, so that he comes at the quick end. We shall call this 'ranking'.

But evaluation plays a role in human life other than that of describing things in an ordered fashion. It is not just ranking. This other role is perhaps best expressed by saying that evaluation is generally used for commending things and courses of action to people, or for justifying the things one has chosen oneself, or the courses of action one has adopted. This commendation may be applied to some part of the ordered ranking scale we have just discussed. For example, a housewife may *prefer* not to buy 'extra fancy' apples, because their cost outweighs their enjoyment. Looked at another way, one might make the same point by noting that there may be any number of different kinds of explanation of the ranking of qualities in a scale of preference. A doctor recommending a diet may rank by the use of 'sweeter than' but may explain his high ranking of 'sweet' by reference to the dietary needs of a very thin patient, whereas a Viennese may give high ranking to 'sweet' in the context of *apfelstrudel*, evaluating simply on enjoyment. Evaluation seems now to be rather complex logically.

One of the few psychologists to make this point and to be aware of the conceptual complexity has been Fishbein, though he does not bring out clearly the importance of the distinction between ranking and preference that it implies.[12] He makes his point by distinguishing *attitude* and *belief* as two independent concepts, as follows: 'Two persons who are equally opposed to segregation may have quite different conceptions of its nature, causes and consequences, and may hold different views concerning the actions which should be taken to eliminate segregation. In the language of this paper these two persons are said to have the *same attitudes* towards segregation but to hold *different beliefs* about it.' Thus, one person may evaluate segregation negatively because he believes in equality of opportunity, while another may similarly evaluate it because it creates an impoverished group which is bad for the nation's economy. The evaluation comes out the same, but its conceptual structure is quite different in each case. Fishbein goes on to point out that 'many writers do not maintain this distinction . . . Both notions (i.e. "attitude" and "belief" are commonly subsumed under the single term "attitude", which is said to have affective (evaluative), cognitive, and conative (action) components).' He also seems to be aware that the same ranking may have preference attached to it in different ways, so that as he puts it 'affect, cognition and action are not always highly correlated'.

The complexity which the philosophers have uncovered in the analysis of evaluation can be mastered by a step by step decomposition of the language involved. The first step involves the separation of the objective qualities which are the basis of the attribution of the evaluation to particular objects. Some psychologists, notably Rokeach, have referred to this step as involving beliefs about the objects.[13] The second step involves the examination of the ranking scales for ordering these qualities in the attempt to discover their principles of order. This having been done, the last step involves the search for an explanation of the relation of the ranking order to the preference order, e.g., why a larger steak is rated high. This involves what Urmson calls the 'division of the criteria employed into criteria which we choose for themselves, and others which we choose for their consequences'.[14] The affect element appears in the explanation of the choice of criteria which we choose for themselves, that is, what one might call first order preference. Here explanations in terms of likings, enjoyments, feelings of disgust and so on are proper, and are complete, in the sense that, as Nowell-Smith has put it,[15] it would logically be odd to press explanatory questioning further. If someone explains his ranking of things which smell strongly of hydrogen sulphide low on a preference scale by saying that they disgust him, then to ask why things which disgust him should be ranked low is to ask a logically odd question, in that disgust is one of the standard reasons for putting things low on a preference scale. If one finds people sorting out a heap of objects, putting the most disgusting aside with laudatory and commendatory remarks as they do so, one must seek a special explanation, say, that they are getting ready for a political protest demonstration and are preparing their bag of missiles.

In some ranking scales, we find the order of preference to depend upon a further decomposition of the structure of the concepts involved. It may be that a certain quality is preferred or given low status because it is believed as a matter of fact to be related to some *other* quality the preference for which is explained directly. For instance, a person may endorse the attitude scale statement, 'Defensive wars are always justified' because he takes it for granted that self-preservation is always justifiable. What we are saying here is that both affect and logically adequate criteria for the preference for a certain ranking may emerge only after a second level of analysis.

We have thus to bear in mind the crucial distinction between mere ordering according to some ordering relation (ranking), and commending on the basis of a ranking matched to a degree of preference (evaluating). Attitude is a concept associated with the latter but not with the former. Though Thurstone must be regarded as the originator of the use of a single scale to measure a complex attitude concept, Osgood's cross-cultural studies, which use the idea of the semantic differential, have reinforced assumptions as to the utility of making measurements of complex concepts.[16] However, they do not clearly distinguish ranking in our sense from evaluating. It is quite clear from Osgood's studies that if people are given ordering concepts to play with, they will rank things in accordance with them. The discovery that this is so can hardly be regarded as more than underlining a tautology. The statistical discovery through factor analysis of an 'evaluation' component in semantic differential scales means little more than, given a heterogeneous set of scales containing qualities that have a dubious relation to the concepts being rated, persons can make ratings according to some very crude, global evaluation principle 'that is based on weak, tenuous relations between many bipolar pairs of adjectives and the concept being rated. Thus Osgood's cross-cultural studies show that evaluative words in different languages have the same grammar, not that these are intercultural evaluative systems.

The fact that these rankings exist in all cultures does not imply that they have attached to them the kind of preferences which we would expect from a contemplation of our own vocabulary, where ranking and preference, though logically distinct, are almost automatically associated.

All this shows up very sharply in the disparity between Osgood's view of Japanese attitudes toward battle and death, and Benedict's view of the complexity of these attitudes.[17] Evaluations of death in Japan depend upon context, and upon the particular *on* relation, that is, obligation relation, in which they stand with respect to someone, and which defines the situation in which an evaluation is made. 'Death' may evoke a favourable attitude when it is considered in the context of the resolution between *Gimu* and *Giri*, between obligations to the state and family, and obligations to one's personal honour, but may evoke a quite unfavourable attitude in other contexts. Again Osgood and Ruth Benedict find almost opposite attitudes toward guilt.

No doubt a place on a scale of pro and con attitudes can be found for a person, or, among the Japanese, for a person-in-a-context with respect to a given item. But the application of the philosophers' conceptual system gives us a further dimension for exploration. We can look into the structure of the attitude, and into the beliefs and further evaluations that lie behind the simple pro and con. It is our contention that little can be done with the simple index. We believe that in two important contexts it is almost useless. In social interaction it is, we believe, in the meshing and failing to mesh of background beliefs and preference structures that the explanation of certain features of interplay between people is to be found. The fact that two people are both pro capital punishment may have little effect upon their interaction, for instance, whether they will come to like each other, if the beliefs and preference structures behind their apparently identical evaluations are markedly different. This point has been made by several students of attitude, but not having the philosophers' conceptual analysis, they have lacked a theoretical background for developing an appropriate exploratory technique. We are also inclined to think that all single index measures of attitude are of little use to one who hopes to change attitudes, in that the items which must be changed to produce change in attitude may be extraordinarily various in logical status, ranging from immediate affect, for which desensitization as practised, for instance, by Gelder,[18] might be the appropriate technology, to systems of beliefs which can be changed only by reference to new facts, to logical consequences and the like. Rosenberg's studies of the effect of changing various cognitive ideas by hypnosis brings this out rather well.[19]

The belief and preference structure behind simple attitude avowals usually shows up only when the attitudes are challenged, thus producing what we shall call a 'context of justification'.

1. The first order response to challenge will be to instance the qualities that the evaluated item has which led one to value it highly. For example, if the endorsement of voluntary abortion is challenged, a person may rise to the challenge by noting that it may prevent stigmatized illegitimate births, avoid potential mental illness and delinquency resulting from bringing unwanted children into the world, etc. These can be used for a public evaluation on the assumption of a common scale of preference.

2. When the scale of preference is challenged with respect to the evaluation of the item on the basis of the qualities cited, then a second order response would involve justification of the quality as desirable. For instance, in evaluating child-rearing practices, one may defend certain anxiety producing actions on the grounds that a certain degree of neuroticism is a good thing in an adult, contrary to the idea that any degree of neuroticism is necessarily bad. These attempts may lead in any number of different directions. They may have reference to social, religious, legal or other considerations, or they may pass directly to affective evaluations, which, being logically simple, brings justification to an end, i.e., the reason for placing a quality high on a scale of preference may simply be that we like that quality.

It should be clear that the complexity of the structure of evaluative attitudes only shows up when they are challenged, and justifications have to be constructed for them. The complexity lies in the structure of the justification. Also we should expect considerable differences in the ways of changing attitudes which are fairly simply related to feelings compared with those which have very complex structures of belief and emotion. These differences should also show up in the ways that attitudes operate in the generation of actual behaviour.

Before we lay out a procedure for an empirical exploration of attitudes one further point needs to be made. Our earlier discussion of persons suggests that it is not possible to assume that any given person has one and only one attitude to any subject matter, persisting through very different episodes. This has a very important bearing upon empirical procedure. The questionnaire method, used by most students of attitude, assumes that what shows up in a participant's answers is *his attitude*, that is, something which is relatively situation-invariant, and which appears in genuine form in the questionnaire-answering situation. This assumption runs counter to two commonsense principles which we can see no reason to challenge.

1. There is a difference between attitudes which are avowed, say in a quiet discussion of some matter, and those which are acted out in a life situation.

2. There is a difference between attitudes which are manifested in 'hot' situations, in which the expression of an attitude leads to commitment to a future course of action on the part of he who expresses it, and attitudes which are manifested in less stringent conditions, where commitment may be theoretical only.

These principles are connected in that one would expect avowals to be associated with less strongly committing situations, and for attitudes to be evinced in action, where commitment is necessary. All these considerations will determine how we decide to carry out an empirical exploration of attitude.

It follows from all this that the empirical exploration of attitudes must begin with a situation in which each of the participants acts out or avows an attitude in a genuine context of commitment. This can either be engineered by the investigator, or identified in the course of field study. The above conceptual scheme must be applied immediately, in that subsequent exploration will depend upon whether the attitude is just an expression of feeling or genuinely evaluative. The empirical criterion for this will be whether the participant can or cannot produce reasons in justification of the attitude enacted or avowed. The investigator must take an *active* role at this point, whether the commitment has been engineered or has occurred in some natural situation, since the criterion for the partition of attitudes at this point depends upon the creation of a *justificatory context*, and this is achieved by the participant's attitude being challenged.

If the response to challenge is an account in justification of the attitude, this account must be collected and analysed. The accounts produced in response to challenge are the real material of the study. From a theoretical point of view it can be seen that an account will consist of two kinds of item; justifications of the attitude by reference to the qualities of the object of the attitude, and justifications of the choice of those qualities as preferable or desirable. The second stage may only be forthcoming to a further challenge. At both first and second stages some of the items will be factual beliefs, e.g. about the ways the objective qualities of the things evauated are related, some of which may be false. For example in the attitudes people have to various products, factual beliefs about reliability are usually involved, and in actual cases many such beliefs are false. The fact that a belief is objectively false is neither here nor there in this kind of study, if the participant thinks that it is true, though which beliefs are involved and which are objectively false may be of interest to someone who wants to change the attitude avowed or enacted. The items of the second stage which are not factual beliefs may be either logically simple avowals of affective attitudes, i.e., simple statements of feeling and emotion, or may be items whose justification calls on external criteria, such as legality.

The exploratory procedure might look something like this: a participant is manoeuvred into avowing an attitude to abortion, for example. Suppose the attitude is one of disapproval. A justificatory context is produced by a challenge from the investigator. Suppose a justification is forthcoming. It might consist of three propositions, that abortion is murder, that it encourages sexual promiscuity, and that it's disgusting anyway. Applying the partition between simple expressions of emotion and evaluative attitudes to these alleged qualities of abortion the first two seem to be logically complex evaluations and the third, being a simple expression of attitude related feeling, can be separated, and is not capable of further analysis or exploration at this level. Of course a Freudian account, for example, might be sought for the existence of such feelings. Challenge on the remaining logically complex evaluations will now yield the second stage. This might consist of the propositions that murder is illegal, and that sexual promiscuity is wrong. Only the second of these propositions is, for this person, the avowal of an evaluative attitude while the first is incapable of further justification.

The next step would be to try to uncover what features of sexual promiscuity were the basis of the evaluation, and to what rank and preference scales they were being related.

Further challenge may lead away from an empirical exploration of the structure of attitude, towards a procedure which is, in fact, changing the attitude. Notice that in the example cited the second stage contains the proposition that murder is illegal. Challenge at this point could perhaps take the form of suggesting that this proposition should be justified. It may be that it is playing the role of a tautology in the cognitive structure involved in this attitude, and cannot be justified, by that person without a change in cognitive structure, i.e. that 'being legal' is a simple good. The call for its justification could lead to a conceptual restructuring, in that a participant might respond by distinguishing between justified and unjustified homicide, a step which would leave him open to an attempt to reclassify abortion as justifiable homicide, or as the attempt to reclassify the aborted foetus as something pre-human and so on and so on. The investigator must stop short of the transition to attitude change.

The upshot of an exploration of attitudes to abortion would then be a set of accounts, falling into two stages; (a) the items which were partitioned between the logically simple in which simple emotional response is expressed, and (b) the logically complex, which are themselves open to further challenge. The skilled ethogenic investigator will break off the challenging at the point where further steps might be felt to be the opening moves of an attempt to change or modify the simple attitudes and basic beliefs. The final content analysis of accounts will yield internal structures of varying degrees of strength and connectedness. It is presumed that it may be possible to discern likenesses in structure, among accounts, as well as likenesses in content. By this procedure it may be possible to discover what are the possible cognitive structures associated with attitude.

Ideally, the authenticity of each account should be checked by testing for a disparity between avowed attitude and enacted attitude, based upon the commonsense assumption that if one is interested in attitudes as they are productive of action as well as of opinion, then the enacted attitude is the one that really matters, since it has shown itself to be productive of action. This test can be done in a variety of ways, one of which could be a second order garfinkel. One who has avowed an attitude is put into a situation in which action is called for. In our example, a person who has avowed an aversion to abortion may be confronted by a friend who is, in fact, a dedicated ethogenist, working as stooge for the investigator, who asks for financial help in arranging an abortion, or some other appropriate garfinkel. The action taken by the participant can then be used as a criterion of enacted belief, against which the avowed belief can be checked. We suspect that most people have widely different structures of avowal and enacted belief but this is a matter for empirical exploration.

Illustration Four: Behavioural Analysis: Man as Actor Instead of Subject

A proposed research strategy most directly relevant to the ethogenic model of man is found in a new type of role analysis. This has some relation to simulation studies, in which people are asked to imagine how participants in an experiment behaved, and also to the familiar role-playing experiment, in which persons are asked to take a particular position on an attitude topic, and perhaps to argue in favour of it, or to persuade another person to adopt it. The conceptual analysis of this strategy, as outlined by Don Mixon, however, is much more thorough, extended, and systematic than previous efforts, and our discussion is heavily based on his work.[20] This procedure has as its starting point a conception of man as actor. Thus in the situation under study, it is not the person himself who is the subject of analysis, but the character that he plays. If man is indeed a self-directing agent, as we have argued, it makes eminent sense for the behavioural scientist to treat him as such.

The simplest form of role-playing experiment proceeds by describing a situation to a person and asking him to imagine how he would behave if he were in that situation. This procedure has been used in an attempt to replicate the results of two well-known studies, one by Milgram and the other by Asch, with indifferent success. Bem, on the other hand, has had some success in replicating the results of dissonance experiments using this method. But the assumption that this procedure should produce results comparable to those of the actual experiment is unwarranted. First, any role replication of an experiment must reproduce the original experimental situation as seen by the original subjects, not as seen by the experimenter—a point clearly realized by Bem. This is especially important for deception experiments, since in them great pains are taken to insure that the participant thinks he is in a particular situation; successful simulation must duplicate that situation. Deception experiments are really two experiments, the one that the experimenter thinks the subject is in, and the one that the subject thinks he is in. But here, even if phenomenology is successfully reproduced, we still have a passive observer attempting to duplicate the outcome of an interaction for persons actively experiencing a situation. This relates to the crux of the argument between Bem and the dissonance theorists; the latter think that participants are affected by the experimental state called dissonance, while Bem does not.

This controversy and the experiments connected with it have, however, a limited usefulness for us. They are concerned only with attitude change as a dependent variable, but we are interested in a more general account. There are actually four distinct types of role playing that have hitherto not been clearly distinguished. In the first two, the individual is a kind of Everyman. In one of these, he is asked to imagine the outcome of a particular situation which is presented or described to him. In the other, he is put into the situation and asked to enact it. Two further types of role playing are possible. The investigator can specify a character with particular traits—here the actor is asked to imagine how that character would behave in the described situation, like the well-known 'Fenwick' study of Rosenberg and Abelson.[21] Finally, the actor may also be put into the situation and asked to perform as a delineated character.

In a sense, the role-playing experiment reverses the usual logic of the experiment. Ordinarily, the investigator works from a known set of treatments to an unknown outcome. Although he may have hypotheses about outcomes, he is basically interested in determining what outcomes are produced by the treatment. The role-playing experiment, in contrast, takes as its goal a particular outcome (e.g., getting participants to obey a distasteful instruction to a specified criterion) and sets about producing this desired result. An essential part of this strategy is to 'script' the behaviour of the participants in some fashion. While it is true that many experiments 'instruct' the participants, scripting in the acting experiments takes a more precise form in its best version. The participants may be given an explicit dialogue to carry out. They may also be instructed or trained in adopting the role of a particular character type. One advantage of this procedure is that it may be repeated as often as necessary, until the desired results are achieved. Once achieved, the experimenter has at hand information as to how to bring about specified actions.

It should be noted that these actions are not the actions of the participants as persons, but as actors or characters whose role is designated by the experimental procedures. The first reaction to the fact may be one of dismay, for it may seem that the 'findings' are not relevant to the behaviour of people being themselves, but only to people who are play-acting. But the whole argument of this book has been that the model of man as an actor putting on a performance is not only useful and viable as a model, but that it in fact represents what goes on in many life situations. From this it directly follows that at least one approach to studying man should involve the study of his performances in assigned roles and of the social context that produces performances of varying kinds. It could be further argued that what participants in the more traditional type of experiment are doing anyhow, is serving in the role of 'subject in a scientific experiment'. If they are acting anyhow, then it would seem desirable to exercise maximum control over what they are enacting and what roles they assume.

The role-playing experiment should not be thought of as a substitute for the more usual experiment. Each has different goals, and there is no reason to suppose that the results from each procedure should be congruent. The role-playing experiment may be especially useful for the study of topics that cannot be approached via the usual methodology; e.g., in one of its forms the person enacts the role only in imagination, not actually performing it. This permits the study of situations that would inflict pain or violate various other norms if actually enacted. In another sense the acting experiment is an alternative to the deception experiment, against which many ethical objections have been raised.

It would appear that the role-playing method has great generality, whereas traditional social psychological experiments are confined to situations which lend themselves to translation into experimental conditions in a laboratory. An unfortunate fact is that generalizing laboratory experiments to life situations requires that the degree of control in the life situation be comparable to that in the laboratory, (which is very great). Agricultural experiments are generalizable to the farm situation because the farmer can exercise control similar to that of the agricultural researcher. But usually the kind of control that the social psychologist exercises in the laboratory is not attainable (nor indeed desirable) outside of the laboratory. And so experimental social psychology is a kind of Utopian science: it tells what would happen if one could exercise very powerful controls in a precise way in life situations.

Most behavioural scientists are apt to feel very uneasy or downright scornful of methods which involve make-believe and theatrical procedures, and so are apt to be sceptical of the value of role-playing studies. But imagination is certainly a vital part of life. There is reason to think that rehearsal in the imagination may be the most central feature of all, when we ask how and why any particular piece of behaviour is manifested.[22] Should it not be studied? As Mixon suggests, rather than suppose that 'imaginings follow no law or a different law, why not assume the same kind of relationships that exist in any behaviour? And why not go a bit further and assume that lawful relationships exist between imaginings, role playing, and "actual" behaviour and that such relationships can be discovered and stated?' Without this type of empirical study and further conceptual work, it is not at all clear what the difference is between pretending and reality. When is a man pretending or playing a role, and when is he not? We used to think that through the use of deception, people in experiments were prevented from playing a role. But now it seems that possibly the result of our deceptions has been to prevent the experimenter from knowing *which* role the participant is playing.

A final perspective on role-playing analysis may be given in Mixon's words:

'One way of looking at a role-playing analysis is to see it as an attempt at a series of models ranging from a model representing the sparse and highly abstract game (or rule) framework of an episode to the complexity and richness of the actual episode. A perfect analysis would consist of a set of models with a rule-framework model at one end of a series and the real-life episodes at the other. A fact which may at first appear paradoxical is that rules and constraints are fewest at the abstract end and most plentiful at the real-life end of the series. The elaborate intricacies of the real-life episode are approached by adding rules and constraints to the rule-framework model'.[23]

REFERENCES

1. P. G. Ossorio, in *Contemporary Experimental Psychology*, Vol. III, edited by G. S. Reynolds, Scott, Fosesman, Chicago, 1970.
2. L. B. Bickman and T. P. Henchy. *Beyond the Laboratory: Field Research in Social Psychology*, New York, McGraw-Hill, 1972.
3. Barbara Hollands Peevers and P. F. Secord, 'The Development of Person Concepts in Children', MS. submitted for publication.
4. Coke Brown, 'Assessments and Manipulations of Involvement as a Variable in Attitude Research', Unpublished doctoral dissertation, University of Nevada, January, 1971.
5. M. Sherif and H. Cantril, 'The Psychology of Attitudes', *Psych. Rev.*, 52, (1945), 306–14.
6. D. Krech, R. S. Crutchfield, E. L. Ballachey, *Individual in Society*, McGraw-Hill, New York, 1962.

7. D. Katz and E. Stotland, in *Psychology: A Study of a Science*, **3**, edited by S. Koch, McGraw-Hill, New York, 1959, pp. 423-75.

8. F. Heider, *The Psychology of Interpersonal Relations*, Wiley, New York, 1958.

9. L. Festinger, *A Theory of Cognitive Dissonance*, Harper and Row, New York, 1957.

10. C. E. Osgood and P. H. Tannenbaum, in *Readings in Attitude Theory and Measurement*, edited by M. Fishbein, Wiley, New York, 1967, pp. 301-11.

11. J. O. Urmson, 'On Grading', *Mind*, 59, (1950), 145-69.

12. M. Fishbein, *Readings in Attitude Theory and Measurement*, Wiley, New York, 1967, pp. 257-66.

13. M. Rokeach, *International Encyclopedia of Social Science*, I (1968), pp. 449-58.

14. J. O. Urmson, *op. cit.*

15. P. H. Nowell-Smith, *Ethics*, Penguin Books, London, 1954.

16. C. E. Osgood, in *Reading in Attitude Theory and Measurement*, edited by M. Fishbein, Wiley, New York, 1967, pp. 108-16.

17. R. Benedict, *The Chrysanthemum and the Sword*, Routledge and Kegan Paul, London, 1967, pp. 156-7.

18. M. G. Gelder, I. M. Marsh and H. H. Wolff, 'Desensitization and psychotherapy in the treatment of phobic states', *Brit. J. Psychiat.* 113, 53-73.

19. M. J. Rosenberg, in *Current Studies in Social Psychology*, edited by I. D. Steiner and M. Fishbein, Holt, Rinehart and Wilson, New York, 1965, pp. 121-34.

20. D. Mixon, 'Behaviour Analysis treating subjects as Actors rather than Organisms', *J. Theory Soc. Behaviour*, 1, 1971, 19-31.

21. M. J. Rosenberg, R. P. Abelson, in *Attitude Organization and Change*, edited by M. J. Rosenberg and others, Yale University Press, New Haven, 1960.

22. I. M. Marks and M. G. Gelder, 'Transvestism and Fetishism', *Brit. J. Psychiat.* (1967), 113, 711-29.

23. D. Mixon, *op. cit.*

Index

'ABX' theory of attitudes, 16
access v. authority, 121
accessible v. quasi-accessible v. inaccessible mechanisms, 67, 72,
73, 74
accounts, 9, 10, 125, 126, 134, 141,
149, 159, 161, 166-7
and attitudes, 312-13
and natures, 244, 260
authenticity of, 163, 228, 232,
237-8, 313
of formal episodes, 231
standard form, 229
their role in science, 176, 181,
205
act-action sequences, 12
act-action structures, 13, 15, 128,
163-4, 167, 173
as homoeomorphic models, 180-1
as source of paramorphic models,
176-80
classification by dramaturgical
criteria, 212-13
actions, 10, 11, 14, 15, 29, 37, 128
and acts, 158, 164, 166, 167
v. movements, 39, 41
acts, 11, 15, 128
and actions, 158, 164, 166, 167,
230
advanced sciences, their methods, 5
agency, 142, 246
agent, 18, 28, 35, 37, 38, 39, 86, 148,
156
Allport, G. W., 276
alternative conceptual frameworks,
221-2

analogies for the subject, 91-2
analogy, 67, 68, 73
analogy with real science, methodological consequences, 125, 130-
131
animal behaviour, 34
Anscombe, G. E. M., 39, 161
anthropology, 42
anthropomorphic model of man, 6,
22-5, 84, 87, 93—4, 98-9
methodological consequences of,
126
summary of, 86-7
Argyle, M., 98, 132, 170
Aronson, E., 168
arousal structure, 150, 174, 222,
232
attitudes, 294, 302-13
and avowed attitudes, 303, 310
and beliefs, 305, 306
and desensitization, 308
empirical exploration of, 310,
311-12
justification of, 294, 309
audiences and the role of spectator,
230
Austin, J. L., 166, 185, 188, 189,
190, 191, 202
authenticity of accounts, 163
checking of, 227
lack of, 228, 229
of anthropomorphic models, preservation, 228, 233-5
of models, 227
of physical models, preservation,
228, 233-35